The Historical Series of the Reformed Church in America

No. 36

D0082578

Forerunner of the Great Awakening

Sermons by
Theodorus Jacobus Frelinghuysen
(1691-1747)

Joel R. Beeke, Editor

Wm. B. Eerdmans Publishing Co.
Grand Rapids, Michigan

The Historical Series of the Reformed Church in America

This series has been inaugurated by the General Synod of the Reformed Church in America, acting through its Commission on History, for the purpose of encouraging historical research and providing a medium wherein this knowledge may be shared with the academic community and with the members of the denomination in order that a knowledge of the past may contribute to right action in the present.

General Editor

The Reverend Donald J. Bruggink, Ph.D
Western Theological Seminary

Commission on History

Gerald F. De Jong, Ph.D., Orange City, Iowa

Sophie Mathonnet-Vander Well, M.Div., Pella, Iowa

Christopher Moore, New York, New York

Jennifer Reece, M.Div., Princeton, New Jersey

Jeffrey Tyler, Ph.D., Hope College, Holland, Michigan

© 2000 Wm. B. Eerdmans Publishing Co.

255 Jefferson Ave. S.E., Grand Rapids, MI 49503

All rights reserved

Printed in the United States of America

04 03 02 01 00   5 4 3 2 1

ISBN 0-8028-4899-0

CONTENTS

FOREWORD

This book contains a biographical introduction of Theodore Frelinghuysen (1691-1747), an updated translation of his sermons, and a bibliography of English sources.

Twenty-two of Frelinghuysen's sermons were printed in Dutch from 1721 to 1748. All of them were preached in North America, mostly in churches Frelinghuysen served in New Jersey. Several were preached on special occasions. Historically these sermons are significant because Frelinghuysen was one of the most important precursors of the Great Awakening.

Hendrik Visscher translated five of Frelinghuysen's sermons into English in 1731. William DeMarest translated 21 of Frelinghuysen's sermons in 1856. The Board of Publication of the Reformed Protestant Dutch Church only printed several hundred copies of DeMarest's translation.

In this book I have followed DeMarest's example of organizing Frelinghuysen's sermons into four collections, each of which begins with a preface by Frelinghuysen. The first collection includes five sermons preached by Frelinghuysen shortly after his arrival in America: *Drie Predicatien* (New York: William Bradford, 1721) and *Een Trouwhertig Vertoog van Een waare Rechtveerdige, in Tegenstellinge van een Godloose Sondaar* (New York: John Peter Zenger, 1729). These sermons reveal Frelinghuysen's earnest zeal for God's truth and glory as a young minister.

The second collection includes ten sermons from Frelinghuysen in his mature years of ministry. They were first issued in 1733. With the help of friends in the Netherlands, they were published as *Een Bundelken Leer-redenen* (Amsterdam, 1736). The collection includes a commendation from the theological faculty of the

University of Groningen, which referred to them as "noble fruit brought from the New World to our doors."

The third collection includes two sermons that Frelinghuysen preached in New Jersey shortly after an earthquake shook that area on December 7, 1737. The sermons were published at Utrecht. They are a powerful warning to people of what can occur if they do not heed God's Word.

The fourth collection includes four sermons that Frelinghuysen preached near the end of his life and published as *Versamelinge van Eenige Keur-Texten* (Philadelphia: W. Bradford, 1748). They reveal his mature insight into the Holy Scriptures and show how he rose above the opposition that he encountered for the greater part of his ministry. That is particularly true of "The Christian's Encouragement in Spiritual Conflict," based on Luke 22:31-32, which summarizes the gist of Frelinghuysen's mature ministry.

The final sermon on Proverbs 14:12, which is the only one not included in the DeMarest collection, is included in the Appendix. It was first translated by Visscher in 1730 and later published in James Tanis's *Dutch Calvinistic Pietism in the Middle Colonies*.

I have taken some liberty in updating DeMarest's mid-Victorian English without sacrificing content. I have shortened sentences, minimized repetition, added subheads, and updated spelling, word choices, and style.

I wish to thank several people for their input: Cornelis Pronk for assisting me on the biographical introduction, Phyllis Ten Elshof and Pauline Timmer for editorial assistance on the sermons, Lois Haley for typing, and Gary and Linda den Hollander for typesetting. I also thank Casey Keuning for sending me a copy of the scarce DeMarest translation.

May God graciously use this book of sermons both to foster greater awareness of Theodore Frelinghuysen's ministry and to encourage us in the spiritual conflicts we encounter daily in the third millennium.

Grand Rapids, Michigan   Joel R. Beeke

Biographical Introduction

Theodorus Jacobus Frelinghuysen (1691-1747), Precursor of the Great Awakening

Major historical movements, whether religious, political, or social, are the product of a period of fermentation. Spokesmen for these movements often seem to appear suddenly on the scene, but in most cases lesser-known individuals pave the way for great leaders. Thus Martin Luther and the Reformation cannot be understood apart from forerunners like John Wycliffe and Jan Hus. Similarly the Great Awakening, while associated with such great leaders as Jonathan Edwards and George Whitefield, had its precursors. One was Theodorus Jacobus Frelinghuysen, whom Whitefield referred to as "the beginner of the great work."

Who was this relatively unknown harbinger whose ministry made such an impact that many church historians trace the seeds of the revivals of the 1740s to him? Why did Frelinghuysen create so much controversy? What can we learn from him today?

Family and Educational Background

The Frelinghuysen family supported the Reformation from the sixteenth century. Theodorus's great-grandfather pioneered the Lutheran Reformation in the German village of Ergste. His grandfather introduced the family to the Reformed tradition in 1669; they joined a small Reformed church in nearby Schwerte. His father, Johan Henrich, became pastor of a newly established German Reformed church in 1683 at Hagen, Westphalia, an area adjacent to the eastern part of the Netherlands. Shortly after Johan was ordained, he married Anna Margaretha Bruggemann, daughter of a Reformed pastor. He baptized their fifth child, Theodorus Jacobus, on November 6, 1692.

God blessed the solid Reformed education Theodorus received at home and school and brought him to conversion. After Theodorus became a communicant member of his father's congregation at age seventeen, he attended the Reformed *gymnasium* at Hamm for two years to study philosophy and theology. The faculty at Hamm imbibed the teachings of Johannes Cocceius (1603-1669), a Bremen-born linguist and biblical theologian who taught at Franeker and Leiden, and whose covenant theology emphasized the historical and contextual character of specific ages. Upon completion of his pre-seminary education at Hamm, Theodorus enrolled at the University of Lingen for theological study. The faculty there adhered to the theology of Gisbertus Voetius (1589-1676), a professor at Utrecht who promoted a Reformed blend of knowledge and piety. Voetius represents the mature fruit of the so-called *Nadere Reformatie* (usually translated as the Dutch Second Reformation) — a primarily seventeenth- and early eighteenth-century movement that paralleled English Puritanism in time and substance. At Lingen, Theodorus became thoroughly committed to Reformed piety and the experimental divinity of the Voetian rather than Cocceian mode. There, too, he mastered the Dutch language and learned to preach in Dutch.

Ordination and Last Years in the Old World
After his classical examination, Frelinghuysen was or-

dained to the ministry in 1717 at Loegumer Voorwerk in East Friesland, near Emden. By that time the *Nadere Reformatie* had taken a firm hold on the Reformed community in East Friesland through the preaching and writing of Jacobus Koelman, Eduard Meiners, and Johan Verschuir. Those Reformed pietists emphasized the necessity of the new birth and holy living or the practice of piety as its inevitable fruit. That experiential theology had a profound, abiding impact on Frelinghuysen.

Frelinghuysen's pastorate in Loegumer Voorwerk lasted only fourteen months. A flood on Christmas Eve swept over the area and devastated much of East Friesland. It reduced his parishioners to such poverty that they no longer could support a minister. The young pastor accepted a position at Enkhuizen, North Holland, as co-regent of the Latin school. But only a few months after taking that position, he was approached by Classis Amsterdam of the Reformed Church and asked if he was willing to accept a pastorate in Rarethans. He responded affirmatively, but thought that Rarethans (Raritan) was in one of the adjoining Dutch provinces rather than in America! When he realized he was actually being called by four, small, Dutch Reformed congregations in New Jersey's Raritan Valley (Raritan, Six Mile Run, Three Mile Run, and North Branch), Frelinghuysen felt convicted by Psalm 15:4 to keep his word of acceptance: "[God] honoureth them that fear the LORD. He that sweareth to his own hurt, and changeth not." He was also influenced by what he felt was a providential meeting with Sicco Tjadde (1693-1736), a pietist minister who was searching for young ministers adhering to Reformed experimental theology to recommend for service in America. Being deeply impressed with Frelinghuysen's orthodoxy and godliness, Tjadde encouraged him to "give up the prospect of a successful career in the Old World in order to spread vital religion in the New." After bidding farewell to relatives and friends, Frelinghuysen sailed to New York and the New World in September 1719.

The Dutch Reformed Church in North America

Unlike the English Pilgrims and Puritans who came to the New World primarily for religious reasons, the Dutch who settled in North America were largely motivated by economic factors. Early in the seventeenth century, the Dutch West India Company had established trading posts on Manhattan Island and at other strategic locations near the Hudson and Delaware rivers. The population of the Dutch colony grew steadily, but little was done to promote its religious life. In 1623, when the settlement of Manhattan had grown to 200, two *ziekentroosters* (comforters of the sick) arrived, who undertook some pastoral duties. Two years later the colony received its own pastor, Jonas Michaelius, who organized the first Dutch-speaking Reformed church in the New World. In 1633 a second pastor, Everard Bogardus, arrived from Holland.

The chronic shortage of ministers posed a problem for the new Dutch churches in North America. The shortage reflected the short-sightedness of the mother church, which insisted that ministers for the New World be educated and ordained in the Netherlands under the auspices of Classis Amsterdam. Consequently, the spiritual life and moral tone of the colony was adversely affected.

Doctrinally these American churches were consistent with their mother church in the Netherlands. Their standards were the Three Forms of Unity adopted by the Synod of Dort: the Belgic Confession of Faith (1561), the Heidelberg Catechism (1563), and the Canons of Dort (1618-19). Practically, however, most members lived on a low spiritual plane. Dead orthodoxy had been a serious problem from the beginning and had only grown worse by the eighteenth century. Abraham Messler, who translated several of Frelinghuysen's sermons and eventually became one of his successors, noted: "The necessity of a new heart had almost entirely been lost sight of . . . formalism and self-righteousness almost universally prevailed. Christians were not ashamed to ridicule Christian experience, and many had become very resolute in opposing it."

The time was ripe for the waves of revival that would sweep over the Dutch and British colonies. And the minister who played a key role in initiating those revivals was Theodorus Frelinghuysen.

Arrival in New York

When the 28-year-old Dominie Frelinghuysen arrived in New York in January 1720, his honeymoon of adjustment in America was short-lived. He and a young helper, Jacobus Schureman, who had come to serve as schoolmaster and *voorlezer* (lay reader) in the church, were welcomed by two prominent ministers of the Dutch Reformed Church in New York City, Gualtherus DuBois (1671-1751) and Henricus Boel (1692-1754). They invited the new minister to conduct worship on the following Sunday. The reaction of the parishioners, who were accustomed to long, unemotional, and impersonal sermons, was discouraging. Many objected to Frelinghuysen's stress on regeneration, his experiential style of preaching, and what some called his "howling prayers." Moreover, when Boel asked Frelinghuysen why he omitted the Lord's Prayer in worship, Frelinghuysen replied that he was willing to follow the practice of the Reformed Church but he did not care for using form prayers in corporate worship. Right from the beginning of his ministry in the New World, Frelinghuysen's preaching style and his preference for free prayers over form prayers became sore points that would later develop into major issues.

Nor did Frelinghuysen endear himself to Dominie DuBois when he was invited to the senior pastor's home. Upon entering, Frelinghuysen asked his colleague why he had such a large wall mirror, and remarked that it was not justified "by the most far-stretched necessity." This ascetic tendency would also cause considerable friction between Frelinghuysen and others in the church.

Settlement in the Raritan Valley

The Raritan Valley area in New Jersey was settled mostly by Dutch Reformed farmers, who were attracted to its rich soil. Though most of them showed more interest in improving their economic condition than in pursuing spiritual growth, the farmers still looked forward to the arrival of their new dominie. But they soon perceived that they had received no ordinary Reformed preacher. Frelinghuysen preached his inaugural sermon on January 31, 1720, from 2 Corinthians 5:20: "Now then we are ambassadors for Christ, as though God did beseech you by us: we pray you in Christ's stead, be ye reconciled to God." The sermon caused quite a stir as the new minister made it abundantly clear that he intended to labor among them "in Christ's stead"— that is, with earnestness and personal examination as if Christ Himself stood among them.

If the Dutch Reformed parishioners of New Jersey's Raritan Valley were surprised by their minister's probing sermons and intense pastoral work, Frelinghuysen was no less surprised by his placid parishioners. Though he had anticipated their low level of spirituality because of the rumors he had heard in the Netherlands, he soon discovered that the situation was far worse than he had thought. Messler noted:

> He found that great laxity of manners prevailed
> throughout his charge . . . that while horse-racing,
> gambling, dissipation, and rudeness of various kinds
> were common, the [church] was attended at con-
> venience, and religion consisted of the mere formal
> pursuit of the routine of duty.

Bluntly put, Frelinghuysen realized that many of his parishioners showed no fruits of conversion. Practical
spirituality —"the life of God in the soul of man"— was
largely absent. General ignorance and blatant godless-
ness abounded. William Tennent Jr. later wrote of the sad
condition of the people at Raritan Valley during
Frelinghuysen's early years of ministry there:

> Family prayer was unpractis'd by all, a very few ex-
> cept'd; ignorance so overshadowed their minds, that
> the doctrine of the New Birth when clearly explained,
> and powerfully press'd upon them, as absolutely nec-
> essary to salvation, by that faithful preacher of God's
> Word, Mr. Theodorus Jacobus Frelinghousa. . . . [The
> new birth] was made a common game of; so that not
> only the preachers but professors of that truth were
> called in derision "new-born" and look'd upon as
> holders forth of some new and false doctrine. And
> indeed their practice was as bad as their principles,
> viz. loose and prophane.

Consequently, Frelinghuysen's preaching focused on
the conversion of sinners rather than on the nurture of
believers. He taught that an outward confession and upright life are not sufficient for salvation. The Holy Spirit
must reveal to a sinner his sinful state and lost condition
before God, which in turn drives the convicted sinner to
Christ for mercy and salvation. In a sermon on Isaiah
66:2, "The Poor and Contrite God's Temple," he said:

> In a contrite spirit are found: a deep sense and clear

perception of sin.... Heart-felt disquietude and sadness.... An open and free confession of sin.... Inward
dejection.... Cordial solicitude respecting a way of deliverance. Because of the greatness of his sins, the
sinner does not know where to look or turn. Nevertheless, he places his dependence upon the grace that
God can exercise through his Son. The contrite in
spirit thus flees from the curse of the law to the gospel.... Thus the sinner is driven out of himself to the
sovereign grace of God in Christ for reconciliation,
pardon, sanctification, and salvation.

Frelinghuysen taught that only those are truly saved
who have *experienced* conversion, which includes, according to the Heidelberg Catechism, not only the
knowledge of sin and misery, but also the experience of
deliverance in Christ, resulting in a lifestyle of gratitude
to God. In his sermon "The Way of God with His People
in the Sanctuary," Frelinghuysen invited sinners to come
to Christ as strongly as he warned them against sin: "If
you are weary of sin and sincerely desire to draw near to
God through Christ, then come." Later in the same sermon he presented God as running to meet those who
have repented, just as the father of the prodigal ran to
meet his returning son. In another sermon he said, "Jesus
still stands with extended arms to gather you." He urged
listeners "to be willing, and to arise and come to Jesus." He
said a true experience of joyous salvation in Christ, however, will necessarily reap a Christian life of gratitude, a life
of total submission to God's Word, "marked by a new and
hearty service." Progress in grateful sanctification is only
possible when the believer continually flees to Christ for
strength in his war against indwelling sin and in striving
to regulate his life by God's Word. The Voetian themes of
the narrow gate and the hard way, the life of precision and
the scarcity of salvation, the priority of internal motives
which effect external observance — all this and more con-

sistently reappear in Frelinghuysen's sermons as inevitable fruits of the life of Christian gratitude.

Though members in Frelinghuysen's church did not object to such scriptural and Reformed doctrines in themselves, many resented the forceful manner in which the pastor applied this experiential theology. Had he referred to people outside of the church as unregenerate, self-righteous hypocrites, church members might have concurred. But Frelinghuysen made it clear that he was speaking to his own parishioners. In one sermon, he applied the lesson of an earthquake in no uncertain terms:

> Come here, you careless ones at ease in sin; you carnal and earthly-minded ones; you unchaste whoremongers and adulterers; you proud, haughty men and women; you seekers after pleasure; you drunkards, gamblers, disobedient and wicked rejectors of the Gospel; you hypocrites and dissemblers. How do you think the Lord will deal with you? . . . Be filled with terror, you impure swine, adulterers, and whoremongers. Without true repentance, you will live with the impure devils. All who burn in their vile lusts will be cast into a fire that is hotter than that of Sodom and Gomorrah.

He addressed the wealthy with extra admonitions, based on James 5:1-6:

> You have lived in pleasure on the earth and been unduly lavish. You have nourished your hearts for the day of slaughter. You have condemned and killed the just, and he does not resist you. Know then, that you who are unrighteous, covetous, and idolaters, shall not inherit the kingdom of God.

Frelinghuysen clearly viewed most of his members as unregenerate and hell-bound. This was a bitter pill for them to swallow, especially when he warned against their casual attendance at the Lord's Supper. In his sermon, "The Acceptable Communicant," he said:

> Much loved hearers who have so often been at the Lord's Table, do you know that the unconverted may not approach? Have you then with the utmost care examined whether you have been born again?... Therefore reflect upon and bear in mind this truth. Remember, that though moral and outwardly religious, if you are still unregenerate and destitute of spiritual life, you have no warrant to approach the Table of grace.

For Frelinghuysen, the evidences of a true, personal conversion — which are repentance, faith, and holiness — are tests for admission to the Lord's Supper. Since, in his judgment, lack of the fruits of godliness revealed that most of his members were unregenerate, he felt obliged to warn them against coming to the communion table. In a few cases, he even forbade them to do so. For Frelinghuysen, this was in keeping with the calling of the minister and elders to faithfully and solemnly examine church members prior to each celebration of the Lord's Supper. If such members have departed from the faith or behaved unworthily, they "may be rebuked or admonished, and if necessary [be] suspended from the privilege of the Lord's Table" (*The Constitution of the Reformed Church in America*, section 70).

There were good reasons to maintain such examination, Frelinghuysen believed. Unworthy participants dishonored the Head of the church, profaned God's covenant, kindled God's wrath against the entire congregation, and rendered themselves liable to a severe doom. Consequently, during one communion service, when Frelinghuysen saw some approach the table whom he had admonished not to partake, he exclaimed, "See! See! even the people of the world and the impenitent are coming, that they may eat and drink judgment to themselves!" Several people who were approaching thought the minister meant them and returned to their seats.

Predictably, the disciplinary actions of Frelinghuysen and his consistory upset many in the congregation, particularly the wealthy. They complained to influential Reformed ministers in New York whose views differed from those of Frelinghuysen. Some of the ministers sided with the complainants — most notably, DuBois and Boel — who had had negative impressions of Frelinghuysen from the outset. They levied serious accusations at Frelinghuysen, who responded in kind. Matters became extremely tense when Frelinghuysen openly referred to colleagues who opposed him, including DuBois and Boel, as "unconverted ministers."

Supportive Colleagues and Family

Other pastors supported Frelinghuysen, although they cautioned him not to be too harsh in judging the spiritual lives of his people. Among those who supported Frelinghuysen was Guiliam Bartholf (1656-1726), an itinerant, pioneer pastor who was responsible for organizing all but two of the New Jersey churches north of the Raritan before 1702, including the four congregations to which Frelinghuysen was called. Bartholf had grown up in the Dutch village of Sluis, near Middelburg in the Province of Zeeland, and had been greatly influenced by his childhood minister, Jacobus Koelman (1632-1695), who is now considered by historians of the *Nadere Reformatie* to be one of the premier representatives of that movement. After Bartholf came to the New World, he so promoted his mentor's views that by the time Frelinghuysen arrived the roots of Dutch experiential Calvinism had been planted. As Frelinghuysen had also been influenced by Koelman's writings, the preparatory work done by Bartholf proved to be most helpful. Both men stood in the tradition of the *Nadere Reformatie* and shared its emphases, but Bartholf had a more irenic and tactful disposition than Frelinghuysen.

Two New York ministers who also held Reformed experiential views and would eventually publish booklets in Frelinghuysen's defense were Bernardus Freeman (1660-1743) of Long Island and Cornelius Van Santvoord (1687-1752) of Staten Island. Frelinghuysen developed a warm friendship with Freeman, a German pietist, who shared his evangelistic convictions and carried on an effective ministry among the Mohawk Indians while ministering to Dutch Reformed churches. Van Santvoord had been a favorite student of Johannes à Marck (1656-1731), an able Voetian theologian at Leiden, and remained friends with him in the New World.

Shortly after his arrival in the New World, Frelinghuysen married Eva Terhune. An orphan daughter of a well-to-do Long Island farmer, Eva had been cared for by Freeman after her parents' death. Their union was a happy one and was blessed with five sons and two daughters. All five sons became ministers, and both daughters married ministers.

The Opposition Grows

The majority of the Reformed pastors in the Middle Colonies held decidedly anti-pietist views. They viewed the members of their congregations as regenerate and rejected the experiential emphases of the Dutch Second Reformation as being too subjective and introspective.

By the end of the first spring, the situation in the Raritan Valley had become so tense that even Freeman, though basically supportive of Frelinghuysen, became alarmed and started to question his colleague's actions. When, for instance, Frelinghuysen turned the wife of a prominent member away from the Lord's Supper, Freeman became alarmed. He believed that she was a God-fearing member of the church. Soon other issues arose that confirmed Freeman and others in their opinions that Frelinghuysen was tactless and too unrealistic about his standards for admission to the Lord's Supper.

As attacks upon his ministry increased, Frelinghuysen took steps to defend himself. In a gesture of defiance, he had the following poem written on the back of his sleigh:

> *No one's tongue, and no one's pen*
> *Can make me other than I am.*
> *Speak slanderers! Speak without end;*
> *In vain you all your slanders send.*

He published three sermons that counteracted reports that he was "a maker of divisions and a teacher of false doctrines." In one sermon he wrote: "Men chatter a lot about my way of serving the Lord's Supper, but that I teach nothing different here than what has always been taught by the Reformed Church can easily be seen by any unprejudiced person." It is important to note that these sermons were published with the approval of Frelinghuysen's friends, Bartholf and Freeman, who considered them to be soul-searching sermons in full harmony with Scripture and the Heidelberg Catechism.

Frelinghuysen's sermons only intensified the conflict that swirled around his ministry. Boel and his supporters viewed the sermons as an attack rather than a defense and took sharp issue with Bartholf and Freeman for endorsing them.

Another source of contention was Frelinghuysen's use of the Frisian Catechism written by followers of Koelman as a supplement to the Heidelberg Catechism. Koelman had been deposed from his congregation at Sluis, partly for his opposition to Christian feast days and the use of prescribed liturgical forms, but also for his scathing criticism of colleagues whom he viewed as unconverted. Frelinghuysen's opponents, who suffered similar aspersions from the

Raritan Valley pastor, viewed Koelman as the real insti-
gator and referred to him as "the arch heretic."

What was there about this little book that so upset
Frelinghuysen's opponents? Basically, they took issue
with Frelinghuysen's emphasis on the need for vital
Christian experience. In their view, the Heidelberg Catechism addresses this need in a more balanced way. For
the composers of the Frisian catechism, however, personal experience of what was taught doctrinally was
critical, and any writing that enhanced this emphasis
was welcome. For Frelinghuysen and his supporters, opposition to the Frisian Catechism only augmented their
suspicions that most of their opponents had no vital
Christian experience.

The Battle Lines are Drawn

On March 12, 1723, several disgruntled members of
Frelinghuysen's congregation asked Freeman for support against their pastor. They charged Frelinghuysen
with preaching false doctrines. Freeman refused to take
their side. Although he agreed that Frelinghuysen had
his faults, this did not make him a preacher of false doctrines. After listening to their complaints, he responded,
"I perceive that you are all affected by the spirit of hatred and revenge. Because he sharply exposes sin, you
try to help the devil and to cause him to trample upon
the Church of Christ." He advised them to draw up a list
of complaints and present them to their consistory,
warning them that if they took their complaints elsewhere they would be regarded as schismatics.

The *Klagers* (Complainants), as they came to be called,
ignored Freeman's advice and turned to Dominie Boel
and his brother Tobias, an attorney, for aid and advice.
Instead of advising the *Klagers* to follow the principles of
Matthew 18:15-17 and the Church Order in dealing with

their grievances, the Boel brothers showed sympathy,
which evoked the anger of Frelinghuysen's consistories.
The consistories drew up a summons *(daagbrief)*, which
they sent to the *Klagers*. In this summons the *Dagers*
(Summoners), as they became known, listed the errors of
their opponents and warned that if they did not withdraw their accusations they would be excommunicated.
Later in the spring of 1723, Frelinghuysen's consistories issued two additional summons to the agitators. Each
summons threatened to excommunicate those who did
not repent and return to the church. When no replies
were received by September, the consistories controlled
by the *Dagers* unanimously excommunicated four ring-
leaders of the opposition: Peter DuMont, Simon Wyckoff,
Hendrick Vroom, and Daniel Sebring. This action sent
shock waves throughout the entire Dutch Reformed
community. Classis Amsterdam, which had to tread cau-
tiously as arbitrator, was thousands of miles away. Classis
forwarded a careful letter of caution to Frelinghuysen, to
which he responded in detail. Classis wrote back:

> We have already referred to the harsh expressions
> which you have used in your reply. . . . Also in your
> manner of exercising discipline, even excommunica-
> tion, on certain guilty persons, did you act as
> prudently as is becoming to a minister in such an
> important matter?. . . Would it not have been safer
> not to take such an important step without first con-
> sulting the Classis?

In 1725 the *Klagers* finally responded to the summons
in a *Klagte* (Complaint) — a document of 146 pages addressed to Classis Amsterdam. The *Klagte* was
presumably written by the Boel brothers and signed by
sixty-four heads of households, which represented close
to one quarter of Frelinghuysen's four congregations.
The *Klagte* details every conceivable criticism of
Frelinghuysen that might rouse the disaffection of classis

and lead to his dismissal. Many of the charges are petty or based on false rumor and reveal the bitter mindset of the *Klagers*. Frelinghuysen is presented as a tyrant with homosexual tendencies. The *Klagers* state that Frelinghuysen would not admit to the Lord's Supper those who could not give a satisfactory account of their conversion, that he insisted strenuously on a change of heart experienced as a result of conviction of sin, that he violated the Church Order by reserving the right of nominating elders and deacons to the consistory rather than to the congregation and by excommunicating members without the advice of classis, and that he preached pietistic doctrines that were contrary to the Three Forms of Unity. The *Klagte* charges Frelinghuysen with "straying from the pure doctrine and discipline, not wholly unlike those of Labadie, Koelman, and other Schismatics."

To add fuel to the fire, the *Klagers* decided to frustrate Frelinghuysen's efforts by locking him out of two churches. He responded by calling the *Klagers* "impious" and "the scum of these four congregations." He and his supporters maintained that they were only trying to keep the church pure by exercising the keys of discipline — both the key of preaching and the key of excommunication — as Lord's Day 31 of the Heidelberg Catechism directed them to do. They said that more than half of the signatories of the *Klagte* had never made a profession of faith and warned them, "the wrath of God and eternal damnation abide on them." Consequently, even though Article 76 of the Church Order states that "no one shall be excommunicated except with previous advice of Classis," Frelinghuysen defended his actions by appealing to Article 86, which declares that changes could be made in the Church Order if the well-being of the church required it.

The fierce opposition took its toll on Frelinghuysen's mental health. He suffered from what his major biographer, James Tanis, describes as "mild psychoses." In a sermon on Paul's "thorn in the flesh," Frelinghuysen suggested that the apostle's affliction may have been *morbus hypochondriacus*, a mental breakdown brought on by emotional stress, which Frelinghuysen felt had also afflicted him periodically for several years. The breakdowns, which occurred most frequently in the early 1730s, often left him incapacitated for several months.

Between breakdowns, Frelinghuysen continued to spread his experiential and controversial teachings by the printed and spoken word. One booklet that caused quite a stir was *Een Spiegel die niet vleyt* (A Mirror That Does Not Flatter), based on Proverbs 14:12: "There is a way which seemeth right unto a man, but the end thereof are the ways of death." Though no names were mentioned, the *Klagers* must have known that this sermon targeted them. Remarkably, Classis Amsterdam, which usually supported the *Klagers*, approved this pamphlet for publication. After carefully examining *Een Spiegel*, classis had found nothing in it that conflicted with God's Word and the Three Forms of Unity.

The controversy between the *Dagers* and the *Klagers* raged intermittently until, through the prodding of Classis Amsterdam, they reached a compromise. On November 18, 1733, the churches served by Frelinghuysen adopted eleven "Peace Articles," which were read from the pulpits on the first three Sundays of 1734, then forwarded to Amsterdam for final approval. The articles, to which the *Klagers* subscribed, stated that the consistories should forgive the shortcomings of the *Klagers* and rescind their excommunication, providing the *Klagers* accept Frelinghuysen as an orthodox Reformed minister and return to the church. Though Boel's opposition to Frelinghuysen and the revivals continued, DuBois inaugurated a movement to join the revival party in a petition for independence from Classis Amsterdam. Two parties emerged by mid-century, the *Coetus* and the *Conferentie*. The Coetus party was composed largely of ministers who represented Frelinghysen's pro-revivalist, progressive piety. The Conferentie party represented anti-revivalist, traditional orthodoxy and consisted of those who desired to remain "in conference" with Classis Amsterdam. For decades, the two parties exchanged a series of pamphlets. In the end, the goals of Frelinghuysen and the Coetus were reached: preaching in English was sanctioned, ministers were trained and ordained in America, and the American church was granted full autonomy.

Influence In and Beyond The Dutch Reformed Community

Despite relentless criticism, Frelinghuysen faithfully carried on his labors. While some people were offended by his searching preaching, others were convicted by it and came to a saving knowledge of Christ. Abraham Messler, one of Frelinghuysen's successors, wrote that his predecessor's banner years were 1726, 1729, 1734, 1739, and 1741, during which 16 to 122 persons made confessions of faith. It appears that more than 300 persons were converted under Frelinghuysen's ministry in New Jersey. That does not include the effect of Frelinghuysen's preaching beyond his own congregations. Those numbers become more significant when one considers that the total number of communicants in 1726 was approximately twenty. Messler exaggerated when he said that the numbers evidence "a great revival," though we may conclude that there were at least several mini-revivals under Frelinghuysen's ministry that paved the way for the Great Awakening.

Although Frelinghuysen remained firmly committed to the Dutch Reformed faith in which he had been nurtured, he ventured freely outside the confines of his

Dutch constituency. From the commencement of his ministry in North America, he sought contact with Christians from other backgrounds. Among his close associates were clergymen of Presbyterian, German Reformed, and Anglican persuasions. Due to these contacts, he was able to influence the English-speaking community in the Middle Colonies and thereby augment his contribution to the Great Awakening.

In 1726, one year after the publication of the *Klagte*, Gilbert Tennent, a young, Presbyterian minister, came to New Brunswick to labor among the English-speaking colonists. He had been trained for the ministry by his father, William Tennent, an Episcopalian turned Presbyterian. Convinced of the necessity of sound biblical and experimental preaching, William Tennent began a program for preparing godly young men for the ministry. A log house was built at Neshaminy, New Jersey, to accommodate the eager students, including three of Tennent's sons. This small, unpretentious theological institution, derisively referred to by its opponents as the "Log College," produced twenty preachers who played key roles in the Great Awakening.

William Tennent's oldest son, Gilbert, enthusiastically undertook his pastoral duties in New Brunswick. The young preacher soon won the admiration and friendship of his neighbor, Dominie Frelinghuysen. Tennent was impressed by the soundness of the numerous conversions that were taking place under his Dutch colleague's preaching and felt discouraged by his own, seemingly unfruitful labors. In his journal he wrote:

> When I came here I had the privilege of seeing much of the fruits of Frelinghuysen's ministry. . . . This, together with a kind letter which he sent me respecting the necessity of dividing the Word aright and giving to every man his portion in due season

through the divine blessing, excited me to great earnestness in ministerial labours.

Tennent's friendship with Frelinghuysen proved beneficial as a rebuke and as an inspiration. Tennent implemented his more experienced colleague's advice on how to preach and soon began to witness significant numbers of conversions. The revival begun under Frelinghuysen in the Dutch community now spread to the English-speaking settlers under Tennent's ministry.

What was it in Frelinghuysen's style of preaching that led, with the Spirit's blessing, to so many conversions? Hendrik Visscher, Frelinghuysen's friend and assistant, described it as "his exceeding talent of drawing one matter out of another, thereby discovering the state and condition of his auditors to themselves." Frelinghuysen, in other words, excelled in *discriminatory preaching*. As he stated in an ordination sermon of a colleague:

> Preaching must be structured to the differing conditions of our hearers. In the church there are godless and unconverted persons; civil, false, and pretending Christians. . . . There are also converted persons in the church, and little children and those more advanced. Each one . . . must be spoken to and handled according to his state and frame.

Tennent was a fast learner and soon excelled in discriminatory preaching. Emphasizing the necessity of regeneration, he challenged his hearers to examine whether they possessed the scriptural evidence of the new birth.

Tennent's ministry became increasingly bound up with Frelinghuysen's. On occasion they held combined worship services in the Dutch and English languages. The *Klagers* charged that by allowing "this English Dissenter" (i.e., Tennent) to preach and administer the sacraments in his church, Frelinghuysen was violating the

Dutch Church Order and liturgy, and thereby undermining the authority of Classis Amsterdam. Viewing themselves as the guardians of Dutch orthodoxy, they deplored his ecumenicity as inimical to the true, Dutch Reformed religion. As orthodox traditionalists they appealed to Classis Amsterdam, saying, "We must be careful to keep things in a Dutch way in our churches." Frelinghuysen's goal, on the other hand, was the conversion of sinners. Whoever shared this vision was his friend, regardless of denominational attachments, ethnic and linguistic backgrounds, parish boundaries, and social distinctions.

In June 1729, Classis Amsterdam charged Frelinghuysen with deepening the rift in the churches by moving beyond his denominational boundary and linguistic background:

> You did permit a dissenting candidate [Gilbert Tennent], in one of the churches where you preached, at the Communion, to offer a prayer in English before a Dutch congregation. . . . Also, you had no objection to letting him preach in our Dutch churches. . . . Is there to be no accounting for this before Divine and Ecclesiastical judgment seats?
>
> Then there is also that which was done against the order of the established Consistory of Navesink, and against the wish of Rev. Morgen their pastor. Did you not go there and preach in a barn? And did you not also go and preach at Joris Ryerson's in the Rev. Coen's congregation, where there is an established Consistory and pastor?

Critics and classis notwithstanding, Frelinghuysen continued to accept invitations to preach in barns and churches in New York, Staten Island, Long Island, and as far west as Neshaminy, Pennsylvania. He could not keep up with all the demands for his services, but responded as a man of vision. He published a number of his sermons in order to reach a wider audience. To foster the communion of saints and maintain a high level of spirituality, he held private devotional meetings of fellowship (conventicles or *gezelschappen*) for God's people. He transformed "helpers" (*voorlezers*) into lay preachers, several of whom he trained to assume the full duties of pastors, with the exception of administering the sacraments. During his absences to preach elsewhere, those lay preachers would lead services and preside over the *gezelschappen*. Most notable among them was the first translator of Frelinghuysen's sermons, Hendrik Visscher, whose sermons were published and cherished for years by Reformed pietists in Raritan Valley. Frelinghuysen also trained several men for ordained ministry (including Samuel Verbryck, John Goetachius, and Thomas Romeyn), advocated the establishment of a colonial theological seminary, and helped lay the groundwork that ultimately led to the ecclesiastical independence of the American churches from Classis Amsterdam.

The result of Frelinghuysen's preaching and contacts with ministers and lay people of kindred spirits, was that revivals gradually spread until much of New Jersey and New York was caught up in what was later called "the Great Awakening." When this revival was in full swing, George Whitefield came to preach in New Brunswick and met Frelinghuysen. Later he wrote in his *Journals*:

Among those who came to hear the Word were several ministers whom the Lord has been pleased to honour in making them instruments of bringing many sons to glory. One was a Dutch Calvinistic minister, named Freeling Housen, pastor of a congregation about four miles from New Brunswick. He is a worthy old soldier of Jesus Christ, and was the beginner of the great work which I trust the

Lord is carrying on in these parts. He has been strongly opposed by his carnal brethren, but God has always appeared for him in a surprising manner, and made him more than conqueror, through his love. He has long since learnt to fear him only who can destroy both body and soul in hell.

Whitefield not only acknowledged Frelinghuysen as God's instrument for the commencement of the revivals of the 1740s, but also was influenced by Frelinghuysen's method of preaching with which he became acquainted through Gilbert Tennent.

Frelinghuysen's Place in American Church History

Frelinghuysen has been called the father of American pietism, but this title needs further explanation. The words *pietist* and *pietism* mean different things to different people. For many, these terms are negative. In fact, they were originally used as derogatory terms, just as *puritan* originally downgraded those who desired to reform and "purify" the Church of England and were pastorally concerned about living a biblical, godly life within the scope of the Reformed doctrines of grace. All of these terms evoked images, real or imagined, of sanctimonious and hypocritical persons who went too far with their religious zeal. But people like Frelinghuysen used terms like piety to mean *vroomheid* or godliness.

Historically we have to distinguish between Lutheran, Reformed, Moravian, and other forms of pietism. All those forms of pietism emphasize personal, experiential religion. Pietism with a capital "P" arose in German Lutheran circles as a protest against the dead orthodoxy and formalism in the established church. Similar pietistic, protest movements (*Nadere Reformatie* and Puritanism) arose against the same abuses in the national churches of the Netherlands and England. Despite these similarities, there were important differences in these movements, especially with regard to the doctrines of grace. Frelinghuysen was a Calvinist; his pietism was of a distinctly Reformed variety. The Dutch Reformed pietism that he championed was more closely related to English Puritanism than to German Pietism. The Dutch learned much from the English in practical, daily sanctification. One of the first Puritan treatises translated into Dutch was Lewis Bayly's *The Practice of Piety*. But the Dutch pietists also contributed to the English Puritans and their successors, especially in their understanding of preaching. As we have shown, Frelinghuysen influenced Tennent's preaching, and Tennent's preaching impacted Whitefield's. Though Tennent and Whitefield were molded by generations of Puritan divines whose reputation was largely based on their pulpit work, they found in Frelinghuysen an ability to preach to different classes of hearers that went beyond most Puritans. This type of preaching has been designated by historians as "the classification method."

The Classification Method of Preaching

Frelinghuysen excelled in distinguishing between true and false religion. He developed this skill with the assistance of Dutch, pietistic mentors who divided a congregation into various states and conditions of soul and then made personal applications in preaching to each group. Pioneers of this classification method in Dutch pietism were Jean Taffin (1528-1602), Godefridus Udemans (1581-1649), and Willem Teellinck (1579-1629). This practice of classification expanded and developed under the Voetian circle of preachers, such as Jodocus VanLodenstein (1620-1677), Wilhelmus à Brakel (1635-1711), and Bernardus Smytegelt (1665-1739). Those *Nadere Reformatie* divines represented the cream of Dutch pietism. Frelinghuysen's foremost mentor, Johannes Verschuir

(1680-1737), belonged to this Voetian circle of preachers. Verschuir was born and raised in Groningen and spent his entire ministry in that northern province. Verschuir is known mainly for his *Waarheit in het Binnenste, of Bevindelyke Godtgeleertheit* (Truth in the Inward Parts, or Experimental Divinity). In that treatise, Verschuir argued that true Christianity is a rare thing; many who think they are believers are deceiving themselves. Since ministers must be able to distinguish between what is true and false in religion, Verschuir wrote especially for young pastors to help them deal with souls entrusted to their care. Verschuir distinguished between several categories of churchgoers, all of whom need to be addressed by the preacher: (1) the strong Christian (*sterk Christen*) who is converted and has reached a degree of maturity in spiritual life; (2) the concerned Christian (*bekommerde Christen*) who is also converted but struggles with many doubts and lacks assurance of faith; (3) the "letter-learned" (*letterwyse*) who are unconverted but instructed and conversant in truth though not knowing its experience or power; (4) the ignorant (*onkunde*) who are unconverted and unlearned but who may still be persuaded to learn because they have native intelligence. Further distinctions are made among the various types of the wicked.

Frelinghuysen's sermons show that he usually followed Verschuir's method of classification. More preaching is devoted to counselling the concerned Christian than the strong Christian. By the time he spent on encouraging this class of hearers, we may conclude that Frelinghuysen believed that most of the true believers in his congregation belonged to this category. Most of his warnings are directed to the "letter-learned." They are viewed as being in great danger because they are "almost Christians," not far from the kingdom of God. They walk with Christians and talk like Christians, but they do not possesses the new birth. Despite their outward morality and profession of truth, they will perish if death over-takes them.

Frelinghuysen's conviction that the one thing needful is regeneration constitutes the heart of his theology and that of the *Nadere Reformatie*. In a typical sermon, he exhorts his hearers to examine whether they possess the evidences of the new birth. Closely related to this is the call to *conversion*, by which Frelinghuysen usually does not mean the daily conversion of the believer but the initial conversion of the unsaved. He used conversion in that sense interchangeably with regeneration or the new birth.

Frelinghuysen preached that the new birth must be experimental. That is to say, a convert had to know how he had passed from death to life and was expected to be able to relate what God had done for his soul. Particularly these two things — a heavy emphasis on the necessity of the new birth and on classifying churchgoers into various categories — impressed Tennent, Whitefield, and other revival preachers.

All of this is consistent with Frelinghuysen's philosophy of preaching. In the application to a sermon, "Duties of Watchmen on the Walls of Zion," he reflects upon his duty as a preacher:

> Though I would not prescribe a method of preaching to anyone, yet I believe that the application should be discriminating, adapted to the various conditions of the hearers (Jude 20-21; Jer. 15). The church includes all kinds of people: wicked and unconverted persons, moral persons, and Christians in appearance and profession. This last group is the largest, for "many are called, but few are chosen."
>
> There are also converted people in the church. These include babes in grace as well as those who are more advanced. Each has desires and needs. Each must therefore be preached to and dealt with according to his condition, as Jeremiah 15:19 says.

Many zealous divines have shown how dangerous
general applications can be (Ezek. 13:19-20).

According to Teunis Brienen, who wrote his doctoral
dissertation on the subject of the classification method
used by preachers of the *Nadere Reformatie (The prediking
van de Nadere Reformatie)*, this approach varies from the
method of Calvin and other early Reformers who simply
divided church members into two categories, believers
and unbelievers. Not that Calvin was unaware of differences between strong and weak believers and that there
are various kinds and degrees of unbelief, but he did not
draw such detailed distinctions as did the later representatives of the *Nadere Reformatie*. The difference between
early Reformers like Calvin and and post-Reformation
divines like Frelinghuysen are due in part to the different
settings in which they preached. The Reformers
preached, as John Macleod pointed out, to "a generation
of believers on which the Gospel of the free grace of God
in Justification burst in all its wonder as something altogether new." Post-Reformers like Frelinghuysen preached
in a setting in which mere assent to the given truths of
Scripture without a believing response from the soul was
regarded as sufficient for salvation. Against this background, it became essential to distinguish clearly between
saving faith and historical faith by placing a heavier emphasis on self-examination, the marks of grace, and the
classification of hearers into various groups.

Brienen said that the English Puritans did not go as
far as their Dutch counterparts in making distinctions
among various hearers. That explains why Tennent and
Whitefield were impressed by Frelinghuysen's preaching. His method of classifying hearers and his
soul-searching applications went beyond what they had
been accustomed to hearing. Tanis concluded:

Tennent's preaching was Frelinghuysen's method

perfected. . . . Whitefield's own method of preaching was greatly affected by this instruction, and so
the torch which Frelinghuysen bore from East Friesland passed to Tennent, on to Whitefield.

Was Frelinghuysen's classification method of preaching
biblical in every respect? Brienen goes too far in rejecting
the classification method, but is he not correct in pointing
out the danger of its going beyond Scripture? The Bible
generally draws only one distinction between hearers; it
says people respond in either faith or unbelief. While the
Scriptures do recognize different stages in the life of faith,
as well as varying degrees of unbelief, they do not support a detailed system by which everyone is *habitually*
placed in a separate category. On the other hand, we
should not forget that the positive, scriptural purposes of
categorizing were to focus on the necessity of the new
birth; to foster growth in grace through specific instruction, encouragement, and warning; and to point out the
danger of deceiving oneself for eternity. The classification
method has its place, providing it is not overdone by forc-
ing itself out of the text being expounded. If the preacher
is controlled by his text, the classification method yields
specificity and a rich harvest of diverse applications.
When applications in preaching are not controlled by the
text, the classification method tends to produce repetition
or, even worse, promotes the preacher's criteria for self-
examination rather than the criteria of Scripture.

Calvin and Frelinghuysen on the New Birth
and the Covenant of Grace

The classification method of preaching brings to light
another difference in emphasis between Frelinghuysen
and Calvin: the *manner* in which they preached about
the new birth. Both agreed that regeneration was essential to salvation. But while Frelinghuysen stressed the
necessity of looking for evidences of the new birth

through Word-centered and Spirit-directed self-examination, Calvin emphasized faith in the promises of the gospel. He said such promises addressed the whole congregation or covenant community.

Calvin viewed the covenant of grace as established by God with believers and their children. He taught that all are under the promise of salvation. Though he distinguished two kinds of covenant children — those who were savingly united to Christ by faith and those who were only outwardly connected to Him — both are in covenant with God, the Isaacs as well as the Ishmaels.

Frelinghuysen's view of the covenant had a somewhat different focus. For him and for most of the *Nadere Reformatie* theologians, the covenant of grace was established only with the elect, and therefore the promises of the covenant were meant only for them. For such theologians the emphasis on marks of grace as evidences of the new birth and election played a larger role than for Calvin. Frelinghuysen said a person could appropriate the promises of the gospel and entertain hope that he was in the state of grace only when he, by the light of the Spirit, was able to conclude from these marks that he belonged to God's elect.

Frelinghuysen's view of the covenant naturally had consequences for his view of the church and the sacraments. Frelinghuysen believed that the church was essentially a congregation of believers to which only those should be admitted who could give an account of their conversion. This was the view of Jean de Labadie for whom Frelinghuysen had some sympathy, though he realized that a perfect church cannot be expected in an imperfect world. But if a pure church could not be attained, at least a pure communion table must be sought. That is why Frelinghuysen set high standards for admission to the Lord's Supper.

We can appreciate Frelinghuysen's concern for the

sanctity of the sacrament. In an environment in which many church members lived immoral lives, he had to apply strict rules. The problem is that he also may have kept from the Lord's Supper some whose lives were exemplary but who, in his estimation, did not possess the marks of grace. Here he went too far because he assumed the right to judge the heart, and that is God's exclusive prerogative. That increased tension in the congregations he served.

Concluding Observations

The Great Awakening and similar revival movements have been used mightily by God to bring sinners to Christ and into His kingdom. But they have their downside as well, due to the sinful tendencies of human nature. In some instances they have led to rampant individualism and have contributed to divisions in congregations and denominations. It is not difficult to see why this was so. The revivalists' emphasis on new birth and sudden conversion caused some who experienced such radical change to think of themselves as the true church. This led to the desire to organize into exclusive fellowships of visible saints, fostering conventicles (*gezelschappen*). While these conventicles helped believers edify each other and experience the communion of saints, they also tended, if not carefully monitored, to split congregations into various factions or "churches within the church" (*ecclesiolae in ecclesia*). Frelinghuysen realized this danger of exclusivity in his latter years, and in 1745 took the radical step of opening his conventicles to anyone who desired to attend.

Despite his weaknesses and shortcomings, Frelinghuysen was used powerfully by the Lord in building His church in America. Heinrich Melchoir Mühlenberg, a Lutheran pietist who toured the Middle Colonies in 1759, referred to Frelinghuysen as "a converted Dutch preacher who was the first in these parts to insist upon true repentance, living faith, and sanctification, and who had much success." God is sovereign and accomplishes His purposes through a great variety of instruments. Though Frelinghuysen did not have an irenic character, he was a man of profound spiritual conviction and of tremendous courage. He personified the concluding words of the preface to a collection of his sermons, *"Laudem non quæro; culpam non tiemo"* (I seek not praise; I fear not blame). When matters concerned the truth, he would not waver: "I would sooner die a thousand deaths," he declared to his flock, "than not preach the truth." He was an eloquent speaker, a vigorous writer, an able theologian, and a zealous, experiential preacher. "By the fervor of his preaching," Leonard Bacon wrote, "he was to win the signal glory of bringing in the Great Awakening." Jonathan Edwards regarded him to be one of the greatest divines of the American church and, under God, attributed the success of the revival in New Jersey to his instrumentality. Throughout his long tenure in New Jersey, he served as God's man of the hour to herald a number of bountiful harvests which promoted Reformed, spiritual piety. Tanis concluded: "His influence in the developing structures of American theology was enormous. His role was that of a transmitter between the Old World and the New; his great contribution was his infusing into the Middle Colonies that Dutch evangelical pietism which he carried within himself."

Age often mellows, matures, and sanctifies people. In his later years Frelinghuysen became more aware of his character flaws. He became less judgmental of others and realized that he had at times made life unnecessarily difficult for himself and others. It troubled him increasingly that he had treated some of his colleagues with disdain, and he apologized for calling some of them unconverted. Reconciliation efforts between Frelinghuysen and DuBois were successful; at a revival meeting in 1741 at which Whitefield preached, both dominies sat together on the platform. May we experience in our divisive day more spiritual unity with all who love the Lord Jesus Christ in sincerity and who long for revivals like those given by God in the days of Frelinghuysen, Tennent, and Whitefield.

Few could remain neutral to Frelinghuysen; his searching theology of regeneration, his demand that the converted live in a holy and precise manner, and his zeal to keep the church pure produced many friends and many foes. In the end, however, Frelinghuysen's indefatigable work, zeal, and piety won the day; even many of his former enemies came to accept him, for they could not deny the fruits of his ministry. His ministry underscores for us the importance of enduring hardship as good soldiers of Jesus Christ and of keeping our hand on the plow in kingdom work.

— Joel R. Beeke and Cornelis Pronk

INTRODUCTORY NOTICE

It is a gratifying circumstance that so large a number of the sermons of the elder Domine Frelinghuysen, published during the first half of the last century in the Low-Dutch language, have been recovered, and that now they are translated into the English language, and published by our Board of Publication. The disuse of the Dutch language, some time ago, had concealed these sermons from our ministers and churches. A few years ago, I met with a volume containing ten of his sermons, all of which are included in this book. I handed the volume to the Rev. DeMarest, the present translator, and cherished the hope that a translation might be made which would prove an acceptable service to the churches, which was afterwards urged by Dr. Messler upon him. By diligent inquiry in that part of New Jersey which was the extended field of Rev. Frelinghuysen's labors, Rev. DeMarest succeeded in discovering and obtaining the remaining portions. It is believed that this collection of his sermons contains all that he ever published (with the exception of a sermon on Proverbs 14:12 which is added in this volume as an appendix).

The character and ministry of Rev. Frelinghuysen have been transmitted through succeeding generations, as comprising fervent piety, bold, discriminating evangelical preaching, and great success in the conversion of souls as well as the promotion of vital piety amid strong and violent opposition. His ministry extended from 1719 to about 1747. Very soon after the commencement of his ministry, a powerful influence accompanied it, and a re-

vival took place in a period of formality and slumber
which took root amid the opposition that was excited,
and which was tested by its abiding fruits. The section of
the church in which he labored has proved, until now,
one of the fairest and most fruitful within the bounds of
the Dutch Reformed churches. May this not be properly
connected with the precious seed sown and the purify-
ing salt spread by this ministry which remain to the
present time, not having been eradicated or evaporated?
The revival under Frelinghuysen preceded by many
years the *great revival* under the labors of Whitefield, the
Tennents, and others, about the middle of the last century. At his first visit to America in 1741, Whitefield refers
in his journal to the revival then existing under the ministry of Frelinghuysen, and makes affectionate mention of
his character and successful labors. Gilbert Tennent and
Jonathan Edwards make an equally distinct and decided
reference to his ministry as soundly evangelical, most discriminating and pungent, and largely blessed.

It will therefore be a matter of interest not only to
members of our own churches, but those of other evangelical denominations, to have access to these sermons,
in order to discover in them those characteristics which
qualified them to make the living impression induced by
their delivery. A careful perusal of them will enable us
easily to discern these characteristics. They are *clearly and
thoroughly evangelical* everywhere, emphasizing the great
truths of the gospel in their harmony, fullness, and right
adaptation. The sinner convinced of guilt and depravity,
the Savior exalted in His finished work and all His offices, and holiness commended and enforced, are the
topics which pervade them all.

The sermons are *richly scriptural.* We find frequent
quotations from Scripture shining forth on almost every
page, illustrating and enforcing the sentiments expressed with a "Thus saith the Lord." "I love," said a
pious person, "those volumes and sermons, which
abound in quotations from Scripture." In sermons of

more recent days these are more rarely and sparsely introduced. Is it not to be feared that there has been a corresponding loss of evangelical unction and savor? These sermons are *discriminating*, "commending the truth to every man's conscience in the sight of God." Preaching should not only be in its aim directly personal, but it should be so faithful in the statement of divine truth in the variety of its application to the conscience and the heart of the sinner, as to individualize itself in the audience and reception of it. The preacher should aim to apply the Word of God to his hearers as "quick and powerful," "a discerner of the thoughts and intents of the heart." The reader of these sermons will rise from their perusal with the conviction that such was the prayerful aim in their preparation, and such their proper tendency under divine blessing. These sermons are distinguished for their *delineation of Christian experience in its various phases*, and well adapted for the cure of a wounded conscience, and the comfort of a troubled and grieved heart. The very list of texts selected shows how readily this field opened to him. In one or two sermons, there is a reference to seasons of his deep gloom and inward spiritual conflict amid outward trials, so that, like his divine Master, having been "tempted himself, he was also able to succour them who are tempted."

The selection of Rev. Frelinghuysen to be commissioned by the Classis of Amsterdam to proceed to America to take charge of the newly formed churches in Somerset county, New Jersey, is an interesting one. Some years ago, I found in the hands of a pious Hollander a volume containing the *Life of Sicco Tjadde*, a pious minister in North Holland, who died in the prime of life. Connected with the life are a large number of his letters. These letters are exceedingly rich in the delineation of Christian experience, and reminded me of the letters of Samuel Rutherford and John Newton. In one of these letters he states that while solicitously engaged in searching for a minister of fervid and devoted piety, as well as other requisite qualifications for the churches in New Jersey, his attention was directed by one of his elders to Rev. Frelinghuysen, who had stayed with him on his way to Embden, and had left a deep impression of his piety. Tjadde immediately sought the acquaintance of Rev. Frelinghuysen, became strongly attached to him in the affinity of common faith and ardent piety, and procured his appointment by the Classis of Amsterdam. In the letter now referred to, he warmly breathes his affection towards him, and anticipates that if his life should be spared, he would prove a great blessing to the church in America. In another letter he makes a similar allusion to Rev. Frelinghuysen. I consider this testimony of Sicco Tjadde a strong tribute to the character of Rev. Frelinghuysen, as formed and developed in early life, and afterwards exhibited in his ministry. I afterwards greatly regretted that I did not procure and retain the volume in which these letters are found.

Reference must be made to the bitter opposition raised against Rev. Frelinghuysen and his ministry, and the controversy connected with it, which is also alluded to in the sermons. There were controversial pamphlets published at the time. I have seen one of considerable size, published by his opponents, detailing their grievances and charges. Upon perusing it, I was strongly persuaded by its internal evidence that while the wisdom of the "serpent and the harmlessness of the dove" were not on all occasions exercised by Rev. Frelinghuysen and his friends, yet the evidence is plain that the opposition mainly arose from the searching and pungent character of his evangelical preaching, and his efforts to enforce the purity of God's house.

Rev. Frelinghuysen was favored, in the blessing which rested upon his descendants, with the faithfulness of the promise of the covenant, "I will be a God unto thee, and to thy seed after thee." His name is now borne by one whose name is embedded in the affections of the Christian and American community, and who now presides over our Rutgers College at New Brunswick.

The general character of these sermons reminds me of the sermons and writings of the divines of Holland in the sixteenth and seventeenth centuries, which were popular in the pious families of our Dutch ancestors, such as Wilhelmus à Brakel, Jodocus Lodenstein, Abraham Hellenbroek, and others.

— Thomas De Witt

FIRST COLLECTION

THREE SERMONS

The First, on Isaiah 66:2

The Second, in relation to those who are entitled
to the Holy Supper, on the 30th Lord's Day
of the *Heidelberg Catechism*.

The Third, on the use of the keys of the kingdom
of heaven, founded on the 31st Lord's Day
of the *Heidelberg Catechism*.

Preached By

THEODORUS JACOBUS FRELINGHUYSEN
MINISTER OF THE REFORMED DUTCH CHURCH
ON THE RARITAN

PUBLISHED BY SOME OF HIS FRIENDS

PRINTED AT NEW YORK BY WILLIAM BRADFORD
IN THE YEAR 1721

TO THESE ARE ADDED

Two sermons on 1 Peter 4:18, "*And if the righteous scarcely
be saved, where shall the ungodly and the sinner appear?*"

PRINTED IN NEW YORK IN THE YEAR 1729

RECOMMENDATION

We the undersigned, ministers of the Word of God, by virtue of the commission received from our respective Classes, and to prove ourselves faithful to the trust committed to us by our superiors; namely, that in accordance with our office and bounden duty, we faithfully labor to promote the orthodox and scriptural doctrines of our church, and oppose those which are contrary in their nature — we have by request attentively read, and with the utmost care examined, three learned, well-digested, and moving sermons, previously preached, and now being published for sufficient reasons, by the Reverend and learned Theodorus Jacobus Frelinghuysen, our brother in the ministry of the gospel, faithful minister of the gospel in the Church of Jesus Christ at Raritan.

The first sermon is upon Isaiah 66:2.

The second sermon is upon the words of Paul, 1 Corinthians 11:29, and the 30th Lord's Day, Questions 81 and 82 of our *Heidelberg Catechism*.

The third sermon is upon the words of Christ, Matthew 16:19, and the 31st Lord's Day, Questions 83-85.

We have also found the contents of these sermons very sound and scriptural, agreeing in every detail not only with the written Word of God, but also with the teachings of our *Heidelberg Catechism*, adopted as a rule of doctrine, as well as with the forms employed in our Dutch churches. We cannot therefore doubt that all who hold the Reformed faith in its purity — all the pious and lovers of the truth as it is in Christ — will acquiesce in and readily accept our recommendation. We also sincerely wish that the principles set forth in these sermons might be put in practice consistently by ourselves and all our ministers for the peace and welfare of our churches.

Your servants in Christ,

Guiliam Bartholf
Bernardus Freeman

AUTHOR'S PREFACE

Impartial and truth-loving reader:

You may possibly inquire why in an age so learned and abounding in illustrious works, issued by learned and renowned men on the very subjects here treated of, I should give to the public the following discourses. Be pleased to know that I have been influenced by the following considerations.

In the first place, I have for some time been solicited to publish these sermons by several of my friends. I know not, however, whether this would have been a sufficient inducement, since I make no pretensions to superior skill in composition.

The second and principal reason is that necessity has compelled me. For if you are not a stranger in our New Netherlands Jerusalem, you are aware that I have been slanderously charged as a schismatic and a teacher of false doctrines. That I am thus accused is too manifest to require proof. You will allow that it is the duty of those who thus accuse me to establish what they say, either by word of mouth or by pen; but since this has not been done thus far, let no one imagine that it is here my intention to vindicate myself. The trifling stories and the notorious falsehoods that are circulated concerning me, and are by some so greedily received, are not deserving of mention, much less of refutation.

It is true, there is much said of my manner of handling the Lord's Supper, but that I teach nothing else concerning this ordinance than what has in every age been taught by the Reformed Church can, in the following discourses, be readily discerned by any impartial person. The charges made against me are serious in nature and affect not my person but my office. That I may give no one reason to entertain suspicion in relation to the doctrines which I teach, I cheerfully permit these sermons to be published and don't hesitate to acknowledge them as mine, being assured that I have written nothing that is inconsistent with the rule of faith and the genuine doctrines of the Reformed church. I have followed the steps of numerous orthodox, faithful, and godly men, whose writings I have also employed since I felt unable to make any improvement upon them.

If you be sanctified through the truth, and understand the truth as it is in Christ, you will also know His voice and follow Him, and maintain the truth in love. My desire and prayer is that the Lord Jesus will come and cleanse and purify His church, do good unto Zion, and build the walls of Jerusalem.

I am and remain your devoted servant in Christ,

Theodorus Jacobus Frelinghuysen

New York, June 15, 1721

— 1 —

The Poor and Contrite God's Temple

*"But to this man will I look, even to him that is poor
and of a contrite spirit, and trembleth at my word."*
— Isaiah 66:2

Long ago, when the prophet and judge Samuel was about
to anoint one of the sons of Jesse king of Israel in place of
Saul, Samuel received from the Lord this salutary instruction: "Man looketh on the outward appearance, but the
LORD looketh on the heart" (1 Sam. 16:7). As the prophet
stood ready to pour forth the holy oil, the oldest son, Eliab,
first presented himself. Eliab was a young man of such
good proportions, full stature, and agreeable countenance
that Samuel was prompted to say: "This is he whom the
Lord hath chosen as ruler of his people." But the Lord said,
"Look not on his countenance, or on the height of his stature; because I have refused him." That is, God did not
choose Eliab as king but passed by him, giving the reason,
"Man looketh on the outward appearance, but the LORD
looketh on the heart." God reproved in Samuel that human
frailty by which we are apt to be inordinately affected by
the external appearance. God declared His infallible judgment, which is regulated not by the outward and visible
appearance but by the frame of our hearts; by our courage,
skill, zeal, patience, diligence, and fear of God, which in a
special manner have their abode in the heart. The Lord
looks upon the heart rather than on the outward appear-

ance, especially in regard to religion and the practice of true godliness, in which He delights. Of those who draw near to Him with the mouth and honor Him with the lips while their hearts are far from Him, God says: "In vain they do worship me" (Matt. 15:8-9). The nominal and formal Christian, however diligent his religious observances, is content with external performances. But God regards him as an idolater; for the end of all His commandments is love, "out of a pure heart, and of a good conscience, and of faith unfeigned" (1 Tim. 1:5). Without these, however precise a practicer of the outward forms of godliness may be, he is an abomination to the Lord. If prayer is to be acceptable to God, it must be offered "in spirit and in truth" (John 4:24). If attendance at the Lord's Table is to be pleasing to God and profitable to man, the attender must be adorned with the wedding garments of repentance, faith, and love; for the Lord looks upon the heart. God hates the outward performance of religious duties without a suitable frame of mind. But He looks favorably upon the poor and contrite in spirit and those who tremble at His Word, as is said in the words of our text.

In verse 1, the Lord reproves the Jews for their idolatrous attachment to the visible temple. "The heaven is my throne, and the earth is my footstool: where is the house that ye build unto me? and where is the place of my rest?" God asks, thereby saying that in the New Testament He would no longer have a fixed throne or footstool, as when He showed Himself between the cherubim above the ark as if upon a throne, and made the temple upon Mount Zion at Jerusalem in the land of Canaan His footstool. Now forsaking the earthly sanctuary, He would have no throne but heaven and no footstool but the whole earth. It would then be impossible to select a place in which to build Him a house as the place of His rest, as under the Old Testament. The Lord gives the reason, "For all those things hath mine hand made, and all those have been" (v. 2). God then shows who are His acceptable worshipers. It is as if He says, "But wilt thou know to whom I will look and in whom I will dwell as in a spiritual temple? It is to such as are spiritually poor and contrite and who tremble at My Word."

The people to whom we would draw your attention have three characteristics: They are (1) poor; (2) of a contrite spirit; and (3) they tremble at His Word. We will also examine the promise made to them: "To these will I look."

The People in Whom God Dwells

People who are poor, according to the meaning of the original word, *hani*, are humble, distressed, and meek. The word is derived from a root word which, among other things, means to be humbled and oppressed. Hence it is not wrongly used to describe that dejected and sorrowful state of mind that frequently marks the Lord's people because of either temporal afflictions or a sense of sin and divine judgments. Poor corresponds with the word *meek*. Similarly, we find the poor associated with the meek in Isaiah 11:4: "But with righteousness shall he judge the poor, and reprove with equity for the meek of the earth." This epithet is eminently appropriate to the people of God. For believers are poor, inasmuch as they are humble, not puffed up, but little and insignificant in their own estimation, humble in countenance, carriage, attire, words, disposition, and in their outward walk. But, above all, like David, they are humble in the frame of their souls. 2 Samuel 6:22 says: "And I will be yet more vile than thus, and will be base in mine own sight." Psalm 131:1 adds: "LORD, my heart is not haughty, nor mine eyes lofty: neither do I exercise myself in great matters, or in things too high for me." Do they direct their attention to God? They are led to exclaim with Job, "Behold, I am vile; what shall I answer thee? I will lay mine hand upon my mouth." Do they turn their attention to themselves? A sense of their spiritual helplessness and need causes them to cease glorying in themselves and in their emptiness as they betake themselves to the fullness of Jesus. But the people of the Lord are also meek because of that humble and gentle frame of soul which is to be found in believers. It is a fruit of the Spirit of God, for the fruit of the Spirit is also "meekness" (Gal. 5:23). They exhibit this meekness in discourse with their fellow men, not yielding to anger and revenge, but rather, in a teachable and obedient temper in relation to the commandments of the Lord and in patient endurance of reproach and injuries, of adversities and afflictions.

For this reason the word *poor* is used synonymously with the word *meek*, for what is deemed poor or lowly in Zechariah 9:9 is called meek in Matthew 21:5.

Believers are called poor because they are afflicted and must struggle with numerous troubles and calamities. Sometimes these afflictions relate to the mind, which inwardly distresses them and makes them exceedingly poor in spirit. Sometimes they relate to the body and affect them outwardly. The persecution and malice of enemies are especially difficult. Hence it is said in Zephaniah 3:12, "I will also leave in the midst of thee an afflicted and poor people." Those Jews who would believe in Christ are called "the poor of the flock" (Zech. 11:11). The afflictions and poverty of believers are spoken of in Revelation 2:9. According to John 16:33 and Acts 14:22, this condition was to be expected. Certainly that was clearly seen in the early ages of Christianity. Into what depths of poverty and affliction were believers plunged by numerous persecutions!

This, then, describes one who is really poor. Poverty in general is a lack of those things that are needed by man for his subsistence; so the poor are those who lack the necessities of life, such as food, meat, drink, and clothing. Sometimes, with anguish, distress, and concern, the poor are compelled to seek their livelihood at others' doors. This is a sad condition, which David referred to when he prayed that the children of his enemies who rendered him evil for good might be "continually vagabonds, and beg: let them seek their bread also out of their desolate places."

Poverty is twofold: physical and spiritual. The former is not excluded here, since the two are frequently associated. Believers are often materially poor; they do not always have many worldly possessions because there are other and better treasures in reserve for them. Poverty and need are frequently their portion. Riches are frequently a hindrance in following Jesus, not only because the heart is usually too much set upon them and cleaves so tenaciously to them, but because they have such great reluctance when it is necessary, like Moses, to prefer the reproach of Christ to the treasures of Egypt. Many who are called to count these things loss for the excellency of Christ, such as the rich young ruler, go away sorrowful. For this reason Jesus uttered the hard saying that is recorded in Matthew 19:23-24: "Verily I say unto you, That a rich man shall hardly enter into the kingdom of heaven. And again I say unto you, It is easier for a camel to go through the eye of a needle, than for a rich man to enter into the kingdom of God."

We see, therefore, that many who have embraced the gospel of Jesus are poor. This is taught also in James 2:5: "Hath not God chosen the poor of this world rich in faith, and heirs of the kingdom which he hath promised to them that love him?" The people of Christ are frequently obscure and lowly in their worldly condition. It was therefore foretold that Christ would turn His hands upon the little ones (Zech. 13:7). Paul declares the same thing in 1 Corinthians 1:26-28. Fishermen and, for the most part, obscure persons were the first people who were converted to Christ. The multitude and common people were the ones who adhered to Him (John 7:40-41). Subsequently it was mostly poor and obscure persons from among Jews and Gentiles who could readily leave their worldly possessions and stations who became the followers of Jesus in the gospel. Hence we find that the heathen upbraided the early Christians with their poverty and obscurity; as for example, Caecilius, who calls them the dregs and refuse of the people, the most and best of whom were a poor, beggarly, and starving race, having neither riches nor reputation to secure for themselves a standing in society. Herein, however, he exceeds the limits of truth, for when the boundaries of Christianity were somewhat enlarged and its professors increased in number, there were many of the great and rich to be found among them. There is, nevertheless, much truth in it; and believers are for the most part poor and obscure as to this world, though not to the dishonor of the gospel.

But since worldly poverty is not here the principal subject of discourse, we shall not further enlarge upon it, but pass to the consideration of spiritual poverty. Indeed, all believers are truly poor in spirit, and must be such in order to be the objects of divine favor. Thus the Savior characterizes them in Matthew 5:3, "Blessed are the poor in spirit: for theirs is the kingdom of heaven." The spiritually poor are then not only such as are destitute of all spiritual blessings; all men are by nature spiritually destitute. It is true, God created man good and upright, after His own image, so that he was rich in God, in knowledge, love, and glory, and abounded in spiritual blessings. But this state did not last long. Man sinned and thus lost that divine image — that costly pearl — those great treasures. He was divested of his spiritual garments; he was deprived of his inestimable riches. Hence we are all poor and destitute of spiritual blessings and without hope of eternal life. For we "all have sinned, and come short of the glory of God" (Rom. 3:23), are darkened in understanding, "alienated from the life of God" (Eph. 4:18). By sin all men have been plunged into an abyss of misery — into a state of fearful and overwhelming destitution. But although all men are thus poor, yet all are not poor in spirit; for the greater part (like drunkards) imagine themselves rich, and increased with goods, and in need of nothing. The poor now under consideration, therefore, are such as have a knowledge of their spiritual need. They see it and are sensible of it. They are:

1. Such as have a lively, convincing apprehension of their spiritual need, sinfulness, ill-desert, and impotence. They are thus made sensible of their lost, damnable state and of their inability to achieve their own deliverance, so that with David they can say, "Behold, I was shapen in iniquity; and in sin did my mother conceive me" (Ps. 51:5).

2. They are such as are, hence, also lowly and humble in their disposition and conduct, having low thoughts of themselves (as those who are really poor always have); not regarding themselves as anything, but as destitute of all that is good, like the publican (Luke 18).

3. They are such as (by these means driven out of themselves) become humble suppliants at the throne of grace — full of desire to be filled out of the fullness of Jesus, as that poor one by the wayside who exclaimed, "Lord Jesus, have mercy on me." Are they poor as to the body? They bear their poverty with patience and cheerfulness and esteem it more highly than the treasures of this world. They are content with what they have; and the rest they humbly expect from God, who is the Father of lights, from whom all good and all perfect gifts come (James 1:17). Do they have an abundance of earthly blessings (which may be found associated with spiritual poverty)? They trust not in uncertain riches; to do good and communicate they forget not. It is for these reasons that the people of Jesus — the objects of divine favor, are called poor. These are the poor to whom Jesus referred in His message to John the Baptist: "The poor have the gospel preached to them" (Matt. 11:5). These He specified as the object of His evangelical commission, saying, "He hath anointed me to preach the gospel to the poor" (Luke 4:18).

Those who are thus poor and destitute must also necessarily be concerned regarding their poverty, having a painful sense of it. Therefore the prophet adds, "of a contrite spirit." By the spirit we must understand the rational, immortal soul of man in its operations and inward state, by which he understands, wills, and judges. Or it is one's habit and frame and those exercises — those affections and motions which have their seat in the soul, also called the mind. The original word translated contrite, signifies to strike, beat, crush, and is equivalent in meaning to that translated as bruise (Isa. 53:10), and as to be broken, or ground and reduced to powder (Isa. 19:10). So it appears that it is here to be taken in a figurative sense; for the soul, being spiritual, cannot literally be smitten and broken. The mode of expression is derived from hard substances that must be struck with force in order to be broken. This, applied to the soul, conveys the idea that previously they were elated, proud, hard, and inflexible as adamant; as is also said in Zechariah 7:12. The contrite in spirit, then, are those who lay aside all pride, haughtiness, and ideas of inherent worthiness, and humble themselves deeply before the Lord. They confess and acknowledge themselves to be dust and ashes, unworthy of the least favor, expressing heartfelt sorrow for their sins and desires after mercy. In a contrite spirit are found the following qualities:

1. A deep sense and clear perception of sin that convince the sinner of his miserable and condemned state, his unworthiness, his many sins, and his helplessness. His sins are a heavy burden that weigh him down. Thus his heart becomes sensitive, tender, and dejected in view of the curse of the law and the wrath of God against sin. The hammer of God's law smites the soul, and the Word of God becomes like a fire and a hammer by which the stony heart is broken in pieces (Jer. 23:29). A sense of sin arises as a heavy burden too heavy to be borne, so that with David the sinner is compelled to say, "O LORD, rebuke me not in thy wrath: neither chasten me in thy hot displeasure. For thine arrows stick fast in me, and thy hand presseth me sore" (Ps. 38:1-2).

2. Heartfelt disquietude and sadness on account of the sins that have been committed, together with regret, not so much of the punishment as of the hatefulness of sin as sin. That sin is what has displeased so gracious a God and dishonored One who is so good and holy. That sin is what has filled the sinner, like Ezra, with shame (Ezra 9:6). Like the publican, the sinner dares not lift his eyes unto heaven (Luke 18:13). Tears run down from his eyes and saturate, as it were, his heart. It is the godly sorrow of which Paul speaks in 2 Corinthians 7:10, which proceeds from hatred of sin and love of God and virtue. This sorrow works a repentance unto salvation that is not to be repented of. Thus said the church, "Mine eyes do fail with tears, my bowels are troubled" (Lam. 2:11).

3. An open and free confession of sin in all its circumstances and aggravations, along with accusation, condemnation, and abhorrence of self. As Job expressed it: "Wherefore I abhor myself, and repent in dust and ashes" (Job 42:6). David also offered such a confession of a contrite heart (Ps. 51; 32:5). So did the prodigal son (Luke 15:18-19).

4. Inward dejection, through which the sinner is rendered entirely hopeless and at a loss in himself, seeing nothing but guilt and helplessness, hence unavoidable destruction. Like the prodigal son, he cries, "I perish with hunger" (Luke 15:17). Those penitent Jews who were likewise affected asked, "Men and brethren, what shall we do?"(Acts 2:37).

5. Cordial solicitude respecting a way of deliverance. Because of the greatness of his sins, the sinner does not know where to look or turn. Nevertheless, he places his dependence upon the grace that God can exercise through His Son. The contrite in spirit thus flees from the curse of the law to the gospel. He pants and longs after grace and forgiveness, saying, "How shall I receive pardon and reconciliation? How shall I obtain deliverance? Oh that I were possessed of spiritual life!" He hungers, thirsts, and

pants after the refreshing water brooks. The soul thirsts after the righteousness of Christ as a thirsty land in the heat
of summer (Ps. 143:6). Thus the sinner is driven out of himself to the sovereign grace of God in Christ for
reconciliation, pardon, sanctification, and salvation. How
graphically and concisely this is seen in the penitent publican (Luke 18:13), who was indeed sorry and ashamed on
account of his sins as well as contrite in spirit, for he stood
afar off and would not even lift up his eyes unto heaven
but smote upon his breast. Nevertheless he cried to God,
"Be merciful to me a sinner," which is to say, "Be reconciled
to me through the sacrifice of Thy Son." Another example
of a contrite spirit is the woman described in Luke 7:37-38.

Since contrition of spirit also reveals a heart broken, pli-
able, tender, sensitive, lowly, humble, and affected by deep
reverence for the high and everywhere present majesty of
God, those who are contrite in spirit also tremble at the
Word of God. "And trembleth at my word." There is a sinful, slavish fear and trembling that's found in the ungodly,
who, hearing of the curses and punishment to which they
are exposed, are filled with exceeding great terror and fear
of hell. That may produce in them for a time a feigned repentance. Such was the effect upon Saul (1 Sam. 26:21),
and upon King Belshazzar when he saw the hand recording his doom upon the wall (Dan. 5:6). Likewise, when
Felix heard Paul reason of the judgment, he trembled (Acts
24:25). Such trembling, however, is not meant here. True
trembling at the Word of God is found in those of a contrite
spirit who are affected with holy and reverent emotions in
response to the majesty and supremacy of God. They have
an earnest desire not to displease Him, so they fear and
tremble at His commandments, receiving them and sub-
mitting themselves to them with filial fear. This trembling
is therefore a humble estimation of self associated with
profound reverence for the high majesty of God, as ex-

pressed by Job in chapter 37:1. To tremble at the Word of God is then:

- To entertain lively esteem and profound reverence for the Word of God as being the Word of the living God and a Word that is quick and powerful (Heb. 4:12); to fill the mind with deep impressions of the promises, threats, and commandments of the gospel; to be much occupied with the Word and to highly value it.

- To take pleasure and satisfaction in the Word of God and to glory in it, like David, as a word worthy of all acceptation (Ps 19:10; 139:17).

- To hear the Word with delight; to not be slow but swift and ready to hear (Ps. 119:14; James 1:19).

- To live in meditation upon the Word (Ps. 1:2); to read, to search, to attentively consider it, to earnestly labor to penetrate its true meaning (John 5:39), and, like the Bereans, to search for that meaning as for hidden treasures (Acts 17:11).

- To cherish the Word and so imprint it upon the heart that it cannot be effaced, to be continually engaged with it, and, like Mary, to keep all the words of the Lord in the heart. As David says in Psalm 119:11, "Thy word have I hid in my heart."

- To not only know and understand the truths revealed in the Word but to receive them with love, humility, and renunciation of our own wisdom; to repose in the infallible testimony of God and thus to obey from the heart that form of doctrine into which we have been delivered (Rom. 6:17).

- To experience a heartfelt solicitude and care not to sin against the Word, whether by failing to unreservedly and universally confess its truths or by deviating from the path of righteousness that the Word of God prescribes. As David said, "I have not departed from thy judgments: for thou hast taught me" (Ps. 119:102).

• To fear the commandments of God and to keep them, comparing one's walk and conversation with them and regulating one's actions by them (Gal. 6:16), thus working out one's salvation with fear and trembling (Phil. 2:12). For this trembling is associated with diligence and care to do what is acceptable to God, which cannot be done except by keeping His commandments (Eccl. 12:13). This was David's prayer in Psalm 119:135.

• To tremble at the threats, punishments, and judgments recorded in the Word, and, in proportion to the knowledge of one's ill desert, to fear the chastising hand of God. As David wrote in Psalm 119:120: "My flesh trembleth for fear of thee; and I am afraid of thy judgments." This is the proper effect of the dreadfulness of divine wrath (Ps. 2:11-12). It is also the frame of the people of the Lord. To such people comes the illustrious promise that the Lord will "look to" them.

The Promise Made

Our text says, "But to this man will I look." The Lord God is a Spirit without bodily members, so looking here is ascribed to Him in a figurative sense. To the poor who are contrite in spirit and who tremble at God's Word, the Lord will look upon in these ways:

1. He will be gracious and favorable to them. Since they are poor, destitute of all things, and of a contrite spirit, they are proper objects of God's favor. Their frame of mind is acceptable to Him (Ps. 51:19).

2. By his gracious omniscience, He knows them by name in a special manner (2 Tim. 2:19). He has known them from eternity according to the purpose of His grace, and now He knows them as the objects of His favor. He is intimately acquainted with what they do and what they leave undone. He knows their uprightness, their secret devotion, their prayers, supplications, and wrestlings; their sighing and crying, their reading and meditating upon the Word of God

— in a word, their godly walk. He sees and knows their striving against sin, their sadness and sorrow on account of sin, their missing God and other troubles of soul (Ps. 88:10). He knows their bodily wants, adversities, trials, and afflictions.

3. He provides for them and sustains them with all they need in spiritual and corporal blessings. They will lack nothing necessary for life or godliness. This care extends to them in body and soul, both in prosperity and adversity. Those who are poor and of a contrite spirit are graven on the palms of God's hands (Isa. 49:16).

4. He loves them with sympathy; for as a father pitieth his children, so He pities them that fear Him (Ps. 103:13). They are His special property. He will therefore spare them, "as a man spareth his...son that serveth him" (Mal. 3:17).

5. He grants them a sensible experience of His lovingkindness so that they taste that the Lord is good. They know this when He speaks peace to them and powerfully impresses upon their minds such words as: "Thou art mine" (Isa. 43:1); "I have loved thee with an everlasting love: therefore with lovingkindness have I drawn thee" (Jer. 31:3); "I know thee by name, and thou hast also found grace in my sight" (Ex. 33:12); "Thy sins be forgiven thee" (Mark 2:5); or "Thou art an heir of eternal life." Such words fill their souls with light and strength. They experience such sweet composure, delightful satisfaction, and quickening joy that they become intoxicated with love and feel in themselves the beginnings of eternal life. The love of God is shed abroad in their hearts, assuring them that their hope shall not make them ashamed (Rom. 5:5). This was the desire David asked for in Psalm 35:3 and confirmed that he had received when he said, "Thou hast put gladness in my heart, more than in the time that their corn and their wine increased" (Ps. 4:7). Such assurance causes the poor and contrite in spirit to exclaim with Isaiah, "I will greatly rejoice in the LORD, my soul shall be joyful in my

God; for he hath clothed me with the garments of salvation, he hath covered me with the robe of righteousness" (Isa. 61:10). This inward witness of the Spirit of God is how assurance is imparted to the people of God. As Romans 8:16 says: "The Spirit itself beareth witness with our spirit, that we are the children of God."

6. Finally, He will dwell in them as in a spiritual temple and be present with them in a peculiar manner. For they are united with Him; there is a mutual familiarity between God and them. They walk with God and God with them. He dwells in them by the gracious and powerful operations of His Spirit, for the Spirit dwells in them (John 14:17). They are led, comforted, and strengthened when He dwells in them as temples of God, according to His promise. This gracious presence of God, so quickening to their souls, is delightful beyond expression. It was what David so greatly desired (Ps. 63:2)

The testimony throughout the Word of God is that the Lord will be gracious and favorable to the poor, the broken in heart, and contrite in spirit. And no wonder, for such a spiritual frame is highly acceptable to Him (Ps. 51:19). This is seen in the account of the sinful woman (Luke 7), the prodigal son (Luke 15), and the publican (Luke 18:13). God demands and loves such a frame (Joel 2:12-13). God is the author and efficient cause of a contrite spirit (Ezek. 36:26). A contrite spirit forsakes and denies itself for the glory of God. For this purpose the Savior came into the world (Isa. 61:1-2; Matt. 11:28). God therefore pronounces them blessed (Matt. 5).

So we see, dear readers, that those who are in covenant with God — the people of Christ, believers, heirs of salvation — have an altogether different spiritual condition from what is generally supposed. The promises of God's favor and grace are made to those who have a low, humble, and despicable state in the world and who possess very little to attract notice. For they are spiritually poor and contrite in spirit. They tremble at the Word of God; are humble, bruised, and broken in heart (Isa. 57:15); are mourners with a sad spirit (61:1-3); and are poor and needy. As Isaiah 41:17 says: "The poor and needy seek water (i.e. the water of life), and there is none" (for they cannot find it in themselves or others); their souls "faileth for thirst." Those who cannot keep their own soul alive (Ps. 22:29) are destitute, but, according to Psalm 102:17, "He will regard the prayer of the destitute, and not despise their prayer." Isaiah 40:1 says, "Comfort ye, comfort ye my people," which presupposes sorrow, inward conflict, and temptation. Such people are compared to a bruised reed that is bowed down, broken, and crushed to pieces; and as a smoking wick in a state of darkness, without much light of joy and gladness. They are "afflicted, tossed with tempest, and not comforted" (Isa. 54:11). Yet they are the very ones who are in covenant with God. They are the people of Christ and heirs of salvation whom Christ declares blessed (Matt. 5).

Only people of such condition are free to appear at the Table of the Lord. This the Lord's Supper Form teaches, for after it says that people of ungodly and scandalous conduct should abstain from the Table, the form adds, "but this is not designed to deject the contrite hearts of the faithful." It is the poor and contrite in spirit who tremble at the Word and to whom the Lord looks who may partake of the sacred meal. Each will now be compelled to admit that those who do not bear this character, who are not poor and contrite in spirit, and who do not tremble at the Word of God, are not in covenant with God and therefore may not appear at the Table of the Lord, lest they bring down judgment on themselves. It is therefore necessary that we examine ourselves to see whether we have this frame. That is especially the duty of those who propose to observe the ordinance of the Lord's Supper. This is the express command of God (1 Cor. 11:28).

What do you think, readers? Are you poor and contrite in spirit? Do you tremble at the Word of God? If you have given earnest attention to my words, you have learned where you stand in this respect. Calmly ask yourselves in the presence of the all-seeing God the following questions:

1. Am I spiritually poor? Have I sensible knowledge of my sad, condemned state? Do I feel that in myself I am so guilty, impure, and evil; so alienated from God and the life of God; so wretched, poor, miserable, blind, naked, and unable to do anything toward my deliverance that I must perish if I remain in this condition?

2. Have I, through a sense of my spiritual need and desperate state, become distressed, concerned, and totally lost? Do I accuse, condemn, and loathe myself? Am I anxious to know how I may be delivered from so sad a condition? Is my spiritual need and misery the chief cause of my lamentation and grief? And does my soul cry, "What shall become of me? Ah, miserable creature! How poor, blind, unbelieving; how destitute of sensibility and affection! Truly, unless God has mercy on me, unless I obtain part of the atonement of Jesus and become truly sanctified, I will be eternally miserable." It is proper for the poor to complain, or, in the language of Solomon, to use such "entreaties" (Prov. 18:23). The heart of one who is poor and needy is wounded within him (Ps. 109:22).

3. Am I contrite in spirit due to this painful sense of sin? Do my sins oppress me? Are they burdensome? Do I experience in my inmost soul such sorrow for sin that proceeds out of the love of God and true excellence as well as from hatred and aversion to sin in its shamefulness, loathsomeness, and deformity? Am I sorry for my sins because they are committed against so holy, good, and righteous a God? Do I have the purpose of heart henceforth to live according to the will of God? Oh, how distressed, straitened in spirit, and dejected are those who possess a proper sight and sense of their sins, multiplied transgressions, and spiritual need!

4. The poor in spirit naturally try to seek fulfillment of their wants and the means to that end. You should therefore ask whether you know and feel such need that you only desire the holy Jesus; that you crave and long for nothing but to be enriched through Jesus Christ with spiritual blessings such as knowledge, faith, love, and holiness, so that you may live to the glory of God. You should ask whether the chief things you look for, long for, and most labor for, are the blissful fullness and riches that are in Jesus, and whether you use the means of grace, such as prayer and the hearing and reading of the Word of God, to that end so that in them and through them your spiritual needs may be supplied and that you may become truly sanctified.

5. You should also ask, "Do I tremble inside at the Word of God? Do I have high reverence for it? Do I take delight in searching it and meditating upon it? Am I anxious not to sin against it, and do I desire to regulate my life in accordance with it?" If, after asking these questions, you realize that you have not experienced the conviction that you are poor and contrite in spirit, that you do not tremble at the Word of God, and that you are not deeply and painfully affected by your sins, condemned state, and helplessness, then judge, I pray you, whether you can rightfully conclude that you are in covenant with God. Most certainly you are not. Do not let Satan and your own deceitful heart persuade you that you may approach the Lord's Table.

Will the Lord look to those who are poor, contrite in spirit, and who tremble at His Word? Then He will not look to those or be favorable to those who are not. If you are not poor or contrite in spirit, you are not in covenant with God. You go your way of ease without concern for the state of your soul, with ignorance regarding the mysteries of the gospel and the institution and import of the Lord's Supper. You are not heartily humbled by your sins but live content without seeking reconciliation through Christ. You have no desire for a sense of pardoned sin, sanctification, and assurance of salvation. Neither do you have a right to the sacrament of the Lord's Supper. Like the people of Laodicea described in Revelation 3:17, you are spiritually rich in your own eyes and imagine that you need nothing. You have no clear, lively sense of being dejected and despondent on account of your sins and helplessness and have never felt lost on account of them. You are strangers to the exercise and acts of faith. You have not chosen Christ as your surety, and you do not look for Him, long after Him, and pursue Him with prayers and supplications, receiving Him for justification and sanctification. You who do not have profound reverence for the Word of God and do not tremble at it are not in covenant with God. You are not converted. Therefore, we most solemnly warn you not to appear at the Table of the Lord. For you have no part in Christ and His benefits; the Lord's Supper is not for you. If you still approach the Table, you will incur heavy judgment and make yourselves guilty of desecrating the body of the Lord, which is the most dreadful sin that can be imagined.

You may be unwilling to believe that you have no right to come to the Lord's Table, even if you clearly perceive that you are not truly poor, contrite in spirit, and do not tremble at the Word of God. But whether you choose to believe it or not, the Word of God says you have no right, and if you come to the Table anyway, you will seal your condemnation. Oh how necessary it is to realize that no one can find favor with God unless he be poor and contrite in spirit! Seek, then, after the following:

• To be fully convinced that the soul's only riches are found in communion with God and the Lord Jesus so that you may become increasingly small and empty in yourself.

• To have a humble opinion of all that is your own without esteeming your own righteousness and capacity for that which is good and without aggravating your sins and helplessness in your own estimation. Seek after knowledge of your spiritual need.

- To see yourself in light of the holy majesty of God, which will cause you, like Job (42:5-6) and Isaiah (6:5), to become poor, contrite, and trembling.
- To acquire deep reverence for the Word of God.

Those, however, who are poor, contrite in spirit, and who tremble at the Word of God may approach the Holy Table. They realize they are wholly lost, feel the burden of their sins, and are filled with sorrow, shame, and regret on account of them. They desire an interest in Christ, through whom they may obtain forgiveness and sanctification and may live in holiness and without blame before Him. In addition, they:

- Realize their great misery and need, and seek refuge in Jesus. They look for, long after, and call upon Him, yielding themselves to Him and receiving Him to be justified by His blood and sanctified by His Spirit.
- Have great hatred and aversion to sin and suffer great sorrow when they sin. They constantly rise from such falls, seeking the blood of Jesus for reconciliation. They desire and delight to live in a manner well-pleasing to the Lord and according to His commandments. Those who truly experience these things, and only those, may — yes, must — partake of the Lord's Supper.

To appear profitably at the Lord's Table, we should carefully prepare for it. For each person who appears will be inspected to see whether he is wearing a wedding garment, meaning he has put on a suitable frame of mind. This frame of mind is extremely important. It is also solemnly commanded. Preparing for the Lord's Supper requires an adorning, much like we would carefully adorn ourselves before going to a wedding. We must be even more circumspect about getting ready for the Lord's Table.

Matthew tells us that a guest without a wedding garment was readily detected and cast out of the feast (22:11).

To be properly adorned, we must be suitable objects of sovereign grace and divine favor. We must view our nothingness and sinfulness so that we may be rendered small in our own esteem. We must meditate upon and be sensible of our unworthiness, saying in our hearts, "Who am I, unworthy one, that the Lord should think upon me? I am nothing. In me is nothing but sin. I am by nature destitute of the image of God and a child of wrath. What abominations proceed from my evil heart! What sins have I committed in thought, word, and deed! How heartless am I in the service of God! Truly, I am not worthy that God should look upon me or show me the least favor." We should pause until we acquire the necessary frame of mind, which consists of a low esteem of ourselves (Gen. 32:10), heartfelt shame (Ezra 9:6), sincere penitence and sorrow for sin, humiliation and self-loathing (2 Sam. 24:10), fear of the chastising hand of God (Ps. 6:2), sincere and full confession of sin with acknowledgement of its hatefulness and consequences (Ps. 32:5), hearty prayer for reconciliation and peace (Ps. 51:3-4), and elevation of heart by faith in the promise made to those who confess their sins (1 John 1:9). A true adorning includes a desire after Christ and a firm purpose to lead a holy life (Ps. 119:5) as well as a going forth in love to all the children of God and all mankind (2 Pet. 1:7).

Happy are those who are poor, contrite in spirit, and tremble at the Word of God. To such God displays His sovereign grace, beginning in this life, and continuing hereafter in the perfection of glory. Amen.

— 2 —

The Acceptable Communicant

"For he that eateth and drinketh unworthily, eateth and drinketh damnation to himself, not discerning the Lord's body."

— 1 Corinthians 11:29

The Heidelberg Catechism — Lord's Day 30

Question 81: For whom is the Lord's Supper instituted?
Answer: For those who are truly sorrowful for their sins, and yet trust that these are forgiven them for the sake of Christ; and that their remaining infirmities are covered by His passion and death; and who also earnestly desire to have their faith more and more strengthened, and their lives more holy; but hypocrites, and such as turn not to God with sincere hearts, eat and drink judgment to themselves.

Question 82: Are they also to be admitted to this supper, who, by confession and life, declare themselves unbelieving and ungodly?
Answer: No; for by this, the covenant of God would be profaned and His wrath kindled against the whole congregation; therefore it is the duty of the Christian church, according to the appointment of Christ and His apostles, to exclude such persons by the keys of the kingdom of heaven till they show amendment of life.

Under the Old Testament, a law was given by God by which strangers, the uncircumcised, and the unclean were forbidden to approach the sanctuary and the sacred things (Ex. 12:34-35; Lev. 22:3).

The children of Israel were not to allow anything that was unclean to approach the sacred things, and they were also required not to allow it in their midst. They were strictly commanded to remove all that was unclean from the camp. The reason the Lord gave for this was that nothing should defile their camps (Num. 5:2-3; 19:13, 20). So extensive was this command that when the children of Israel allowed only one unclean person in their midst and had fellowship with him, although they themselves were free from guilt and even unaware that such a person was among them, punishment came upon all of Israel, as we see in the case of Achan in Joshua 6:17-18 and 7:12. Furthermore, God the Lord instantly departed from the whole congregation when only one unclean person was found in its midst. The Lord warned, "Neither will I be with you any more, except ye destroy the accursed (the guilty Achan) from among you" (Josh. 7:12). "These things were our examples" (1 Cor. 10:6).

We also have a sanctuary in the Lord's Supper of the New Testament, which has come in place of the Passover. It is explicitly and solemnly declared that none of the unconverted, who are still in their natural and unclean state and unsanctified by the Holy Ghost, should approach this Table. For the Lord has pronounced a severe punishment upon all who unworthily approach this sanctuary and partake of these holy things. He has at the same time impressed upon the overseers of the church that they exclude strangers and the ungodly, lest the covenant of God be profaned, His wrath be stirred up against the whole congregation, and the blessings of His Spirit and grace be removed from His church. This is what is taught in this Lord's Day.

Two grand subjects are here suggested for our consideration:

I. *Who may and who may not approach the Lord's Table.*

II. *The exclusion by the church of those who lead offensive and wicked lives.*

I. In relation to the first point, the instructor asks: "For whom is the Lord's Supper instituted?" It is not instituted for the dead, for they already are in the place where they shall remain forever. It must not be administered to the dying, either, for they are not in a state to receive it; nor to children, because they are unable to examine themselves. It is to be administered to living adults, yet not to all who are partakers of corporal life. It is rather instituted only for the regenerated who possess spiritual life. For it is spiritual food that only spiritual people can partake of as refreshment. It is a sign and seal of the covenant of God, so it naturally follows that all truly in covenant with God are entitled to it. "Christ hath ordained this meat only for His faithful followers," says the Lord's Supper Form. He thus kept it only with His disciples, who were renewed persons. This is the general understanding within the Reformed Church, which appears not only from what is stated here by our instructor but also from the *Belgic Confession of Faith* of the Reformed Churches. That confession states: "We believe and confess that our Savior Jesus Christ did ordain and institute the sacrament of the Holy Supper to nourish and support those whom He hath already regenerated and incorporated into His family, which is His church" (Art. 35). So that no others may approach, the instructor presents some characteristics of those who *may* and those who *may not* come to the table of the Lord.

1. The catechism states that "Those who are...sorrowful for their sins"— who are convinced of, and suitably impressed with them — who discern their grievous ill-desert, their criminal, condemned, and miserable state, may approach the table. They are affected with grief, concern, shame, self-condemnation, and loathing, and thus mourn over their wickedness, saying, "What have I done?" (Jer. 8:6). We see this in Ephraim (Jer. 31:19). This sorrow is the hearty penitence by which a believing sinner is truly humbled because of his sins and bitterly laments and mourns

over them out of love to God and hatred of sin. For such
the Lord's Supper is instituted. For these by virtue of God's
covenant of grace think on their evil ways and their doings
that are not good and loathe themselves on account of their
iniquities and abominations, according to the Lord's promise (Ezek. 36:31). Such are proper objects of the grace that is
sealed in this sacrament, for the poor in spirit and those that
mourn are pronounced blessed (Matt. 5:3-4). The Lord
promises to look with favor upon such people (Isa. 5:7, 15,
18; 66:2). Mere sorrow is not sufficient; for Cain, Esau, Saul,
and Judas also experienced conviction and sorrow for sin.

2. Sorrow must be united with trust that our sins are forgiven for Christ's sake and that our remaining infirmity is
covered by His passion and death. This trust is no self-
created impression. It is that act of faith by which the soul
regards with contentment the divine plan of reconciling
and saving sinners through Jesus Christ as Surety, and
with entire satisfaction acquiesces in that plan, esteeming
and approving of it as good, wise, and holy. One with such
trust desires to be sanctified and saved in that way and in
none other; and thereupon, through a painful sight and
sense of his sins, turns to that Surety and Mediator, desiring to be found in Him only.

Therefore, abandoning everything in self, such trust
looks for and longs after Christ with restless desire, seeking
all its salvation in Him. Such trust desires nothing besides
Christ, discerning in Him a suitableness and sufficiency capable of satisfying all its need. The soul then goes forth in
active desire after Him, choosing Him alone as its portion.
It engages in inward dealings with Him and resigns itself
wholly and unreservedly to Him on the ground of His gracious invitation and offer. The soul entrusts itself and its
salvation into Christ's hands, reposing with entire confidence in Him. It thus receives the testimony of God and
establishes its seal that God is true (John 3:33). Such are entitled to the Lord's Supper, for the hungry and thirsty are

invited and promised that they shall be filled (Isa. 55:1; Matt. 5:6). "He that believeth on the Son hath everlasting life" (John 3:36). So we see here in grace, which is spiritual life, the commencement of life eternal.

3. To this is to be added that "they desire to have their faith more and more strengthened," the instructor says. It is the nature of spiritual life to desire progress. The cry of the weak believer is, "Lord, I believe; help thou mine unbelief" (Mark 9:24), or "Increase our faith" (Luke 17:5). Hence it appears that this meat is also intended for the weak in faith, for the instructor does not demand the highest degree of faith, or full assurance. However, he who is favored with full assurance of faith is prepared to partake of the Supper with much profit. He is freely able to approach the table as an accepted guest, to discern the Lord's body, and to receive the emblems as a seal of the forgiveness of his sins.

4. That it may be manifest that this trust is not a mere delusive impression, the catechism also states as a prerequisite, a desire to live a more holy life. Believers regard their constant wanderings with sorrow and regret. They heartily hate sin and strive against it. They are therefore exceedingly desirous of growing in holiness, indeed even of attaining to perfection. They know that they cannot fully attain perfection in this life, but they are aware that they can more nearly approach it. Therefore they follow after it and reach toward it so they may more fully apprehend it (Phil. 3:12, 14). Sincere desire after holiness is necessary for those who approach the Table of the Lord, for here all is holy. By the use of this seal of the covenant, we declare not only that the Lord is our God but also that we are His people and will keep all His commandments. The sacraments are also means of sanctification. They are tokens that obligate us to show forth the Lord's death (1 Cor. 11:26), which cannot be done except by holiness of life.

It is only for partakers of these things that the Lord's Supper is instituted. It is for those who have these evidences of the indwelling of the Holy Ghost, namely, a godly sorrow for sin, a living faith in Christ as the only author of life, an unfeigned love for God and one's neighbor, and a firm resolve to lead a holy life, to glorify God in all things, and to live according to His commandments. Hence it plainly follows that those who do not possess these things have no right to partake. This the instructor shows when he names those for whom the Lord's Supper is not instituted. They are:

1. Hypocrites, dissemblers, and deceivers who, professing a form of godliness and an outwardly unblamable walk, seem to be something. By their gestures, sighs, and other assumed ways, they seek to impress those around them, especially accommodating themselves to the ideas of pious ministers. But their behavior is not consistent; they act one way now and another way later, as can be perceived from their conversation and deportment. Most of their behavior is so gross that whoever examines them soon becomes aware that they are not acquainted with, much less partakers of, the power of godliness. Rather, their object is only to secure the name of good Christians.

These may not approach the Table because their hearts are not right with God. They are not really possessors of grace. They are still enemies and haters of God, upon whom Christ so frequently pronounced His woes. These are required to abstain.

2. "All such as turn not to God with sincere hearts." The instructor says that the unconverted, or those who do not turn to God, have no right to come to the Table of the Lord. To the question, Who are the unconverted? comes the answer: All natural men who are still alienated from life with God, such as:

a. All ignorant persons who are unacquainted with the fundamental truths of religion, such as the mediatorial office of Christ and the nature of regeneration and faith, and who do not know how to be incorporated by faith into

Christ. They have no knowledge of the justice of God and the ill-desert of the sinner and do not understand the nature of the Lord's Supper. They cannot associate the sign with the thing signified and are ignorant of it as a seal.

b. All who are not truly humbled on account of their sins but live in unconcerned ease respecting the state of their souls.

c. Those who are strangers to the exercise of faith and are not engaged in choosing Christ as Surety or longing after and looking to Him. Those who do not follow after Him with prayers and supplications or receive Him for justification and sanctification, and who do not surrender themselves to Him to live in union with Him.

d. Those who are earthly minded; whose delight, longing, seeking, concern, love, satisfaction, and fear are fixed on the things of the world — the lust of the flesh, the lust of the eye, and the pride of life. In short, the unconverted willfully and wittingly cleave to any sin without striving against it, and content themselves with external propriety and an outwardly religious character. They have never realized their lost state apart from Christ and have not become inwardly changed and sanctified. In addition, they are not leading a holy and self-denying life through union with Christ. Such are the unconverted. The Reformed Church, in accordance with God's Word, teaches that such people may not approach the Lord's Table. This is proper for these reasons:

- An uncircumcised stranger and unclean person had no right to eat the Passover. So today the unconverted who are uncircumcised in heart and not washed in the blood of Christ are not sanctified by His Spirit, and those who lie in their natural uncleanness may not eat of this bread nor drink of this cup.

- An unconverted person has no title to the promises or to the sealing of them. An unconverted person does not have the Spirit of Christ and therefore is not of Christ.

Hence the Spirit will not seal in him an interest in Jesus and His benefits (Rom. 8:9).

• Unconverted persons are destitute of spiritual life. They are dead in trespasses and sins. Those who are spiritually dead cannot partake of spiritual food.

• Unconverted persons are destitute of faith, which is the mouth of the soul. Therefore they cannot benefit by eating that bread which is prepared only for believers.

• Unconverted persons are servants of sin, members and bondslaves of Satan. How dreadful that such unholy ones should be members of Christ, who is so holy (2 Cor. 6:14-15)! However, if such unholy ones approach the Table, as they often try to do, they must be informed that they will eat and drink judgment to themselves. This the instructor observes through the words of Paul in 1 Corinthians 11:29. They aggravate their condemnation, the instructor says, for judgment is a sentence of condemnation that implies punishment, which must be understood as everlasting punishment. The hypocritical and unconverted thus eat to their condemnation. This is not strange, for when they partake unworthily, they make themselves guilty of the body and blood of the Lord (1 Cor. 11:27). Like the Jews, they mock and crucify Christ anew (Heb. 6:6). They profane the sacrament, which is a token of the body and blood of Christ, and thus become charged with such great sin against Christ that they are liable to both temporal and eternal punishment. Such hypocrites are not much better than Judas who betrayed Christ, and the Jews and Romans who crucified Him and shed His blood. "Whosoever shall receive this sacrament unworthily is as guilty as if he had slain the Lord Himself and shed the blood of Christ. Oh horrible wickedness!" says Theophylact.

If the hypocrite and unconverted may not go to the Lord's Table, why then was Judas allowed to partake? Although we admit that Judas might have eaten of the Lord's

Supper, it would not follow that he was entitled to the privilege. Likewise, today many unconverted persons are permitted to partake who really are not authorized to do so, as we have already shown.

But we also maintain, with many distinguished divines, that Judas did not partake of the Lord's Supper. This may be inferred from John 13:26-27, 30, which expressly says that as soon as Judas received the sop, was exposed, and had the devil enter into him, he immediately went away. "He then having received the sop went immediately out," says verse 30. This took place previous to the Supper. Christ would have spoken a lie had He given Judas the Supper and said, "This is my body broken for you; this is my blood which is shed for you." That could not even for a moment be entertained as true. Therefore, it remains true that the unconverted may not approach the Table and that the rulers of the church should also bar and prevent them from approaching.

II. The instructor therefore asks in *Question 82:* "Are they also to be admitted to this Supper, who, by confession," etc.? His answer is no. All those who by confession and life declare themselves unbelieving and ungodly must be barred. Those who have erroneous conceptions of the truths of the gospel, those without correct knowledge of themselves or of Christ or of the import of the Lord's Supper must be barred. For they are unbelievers, since without knowledge there can be no faith (Rom. 10:14). They are not capable of discerning the Lord's body. Solomon says, "That the soul be without knowledge, it is not good" (Prov. 19:2).

Those who lead scandalous and offensive lives, such as drunkards, profane swearers, whoremongers, and contentious persons — all who live in open sins, of which the Lord's Supper Form presents a list — must also be barred. For if such people are permitted to come, the Catechism says, "the covenant of God is profaned." The seals of the covenant, and thus the covenant itself, are dishonored, and "the wrath of God is stirred up against the whole congregation." For

God is displeased with and will punish the desecration of His covenant, not only because of those who are guilty of it but also because of those who do not seek to prevent it. God says to the wicked: "What hast thou to do to declare my statutes, or that thou shouldest take my covenant in thy mouth?" (Ps. 50:16). Such was the case with the Corinthians, who were careless with respect to the Lord's Supper. Many of them were punished with weakness, with sickness, and with the sleep of death (1 Cor. 11:17-34).

By whom must these be barred? "By the church of Christ," says the instructor. Church leaders are under obligation to do so, according to the command of Christ (Matt. 7:6) and of the apostles (1 Cor. 5:2, 11; 2 Thes. 3:6). These are bound to "exclude the unworthy by the keys of the kingdom of heaven," which is Christian discipline, "until they show amendment of life." On this we must dwell the following Lord's day.

This then is the doctrine of the Reformed Church regarding those who are entitled to the Lord's Supper and those who are not entitled. Throughout the ages, this doctrine has been the practice of those who have sought faithfully to discharge their duty in the administration of the Lord's Supper. The godly in times past showed great care and discrimination in whom they admitted to the Holy Supper. Calvin, that distinguished man of God, offers clear proof of this when he says:

> And here also we must preserve the order of the Lord's Supper, that it may not be profaned by being administered indiscriminately. For it is very true that he to whom its distribution has been committed, if he knowingly and willingly admits an unworthy person whom he could rightfully turn away, is as guilty of sacrilege as if he had cast the Lord's body to dogs. On this account, Chrysostom gravely inveighs against priests who, fearing the power of great men, dare exclude no one. "Blood," he says, "will be required at your hands

(Ezek. 3:18; 33:8). If you fear a man, he will laugh at you; but if you fear God, you will be revered also among men. Let us not dread the fasces, the purple, the crowns; here we have a greater power. I truly would rather give my body to death, and let my blood be poured out, than participate in that pollution" (Calvin's *Institutes*, Book 4, Chapter 12, Section 5).

The writers of our own time insist the same. That illustrious and learned man, J. d'Outrein, thus writes in a small book titled, *The Proper Use of the Keys of the Kingdom of Heaven, in Relation to the Sick*:

It is truly no small thing to open to one the door of the kingdom of God; to declare him a child of God, a member of Christ, a partaker of His merits and benefits, and to admit him to the reception of the seals and pledges of communion with the crucified Redeemer — to which no one is properly entitled who is a stranger to faith and regeneration. This is an acknowledged truth, and one which must be admitted by all the Reformed; for when in the eighty-first question of the Heidelberg Catechism it is asked, "For whom is the Lord's Supper instituted?" it is replied, "only for those who are sorrowful for their sins," etc.; whence it appears that only penitent, believing, upright, and converted persons should be admitted to that holy seal of the covenant (p. 108).

Who then will think ill of a minister of the gospel who endeavors to preserve this sacred ordinance from profanation? None but the formal, blind, nominal Christian, who desires to be dealt with not according to the Word of God but according to his own distorted conceptions. When we consider how awful the sin of partaking unworthily is, what minister who fears God and loves his neighbor would not carefully watch that God's sanctuary should not be profaned and that none of his hearers should approach unworthily to eat to their death and destruction? I pray you, decide. Should not one who is zealous for the honor of Christ and the welfare of his neighbor prefer to lose his life rather than allow himself to be charged with so great a sin? Such was the example of Chrysostom, that pious doctor of the ancient Christian church.

But alas, how far have we departed from the purity of the early churches! How far do we yet depart in the present day! For this sentiment of the early Reformers is still the confession of our church today. But where is the faithfulness that is required in a steward of the mysteries of God (1 Cor. 4:2)? Truly, we are aware that the Lord's Supper is frequently desecrated today. For not only do some unworthily approach the Table, but how many of those who receive the sacred elements are ignorant or ungodly; are drunkards, slanderers, backbiters, profaners of God's Name and day, vain and worldly-minded, or merely moral persons who do not possess but rather hate true godliness! It is undoubtedly true, as the Rev. d'Outrein declared in the work just quoted, that

> When we attentively consider the mode of procedure in our churches, we are compelled to acknowledge that this weighty business is not correctly viewed by many, much less properly attended to. Members are admitted to the Table who do not possess a definite knowledge of the truth which is according to godliness; who have an incorrect idea of the design of the Lord's Supper; who are not aware of the duty to be performed there; and who do not know of the things signified and sealed by outward circumstances. When things are conducted in the best manner, the members who present themselves for admittance are examined about their knowledge of fundamental truths and their external deportment to some degree, but by many scarcely an inquiry is made in regard to true repentance, faith, and holiness of life, not to mention that none but those in whom these things are at least hopefully found should be allowed to participate in this holy meat and

drink, which, to employ the language of the Form, "Christ hath ordained only for the faithful."

The doctrine of the Reformed Church says that no unconverted persons may approach the Table and that the ungodly must be repelled. Why then is this sacrament so easily extended to all who ask for it and call themselves church members, even though they're often as ignorant as the heathen, openly living in gross sins and not marked by the least morality, not to speak of true godliness? With reason may we exclaim with the holy Polycarp: "Oh good God! To what evil times hast Thou preserved me!" For it has now come to this, that many may be found who bear the name of Reformed and yet are ignorant of Reformed doctrines. Some even oppose, calumniate, and practically deny them. I have three times (it is now the fourth time) administered the Lord's Supper and stressed that the unconverted may not approach and that the wicked must, according to our doctrine, be barred. What murmuring has this excited! How many tongues, set on fire of hell, have uttered their slanders! I would ask you who have been and perhaps still are so greatly displeased on this account: Is not this the doctrine of the Reformed Church? I imagine that no one will deny it, for whoever has not willfully closed his ears must have sufficiently heard it. Why, then, do you disobey the truth? Why make yourselves guilty of such slanders and backbitings? Do you say that I speak too sharply? Must I not speak in accordance with the Word of God?

Does not the Spirit of God say through Paul in 1 Corinthians 11:29, "He that eateth and drinketh unworthily, eateth and drinketh damnation to himself"? Can a more awful denunciation be conceived of? Does not our Catechism declare that if we grant access to the ungodly, the covenant of God is profaned and His wrath kindled against the whole congregation? Could anything harder be said? Truly, you cannot do otherwise than condemn yourselves. If your consciences were not insensible, and if you but saw and knew what you have done, you would tremble in view of God's wrath! But upon this I may no longer dwell. As far as I am concerned, I care little about what is said behind my back by ignorant, carnal men who desire to substitute their own perverted ideas for God's truth. They are greatly deceived if they imagine that they will thus put me to silence, for I would sooner die a thousand deaths than not preach the truth.

Much loved hearers who have so often been at the Lord's Table, do you know that the unconverted may not approach? Have you then with the utmost care examined whether you have been born again? Were you aware of what is required in acceptable observance, when you so calmly approached the Table? Or did you go blindly forward, not only without a wedding garment but also without concern? Did you not examine yourself to see whether you were among those who were invited? Were you not aware that so much is required? You should have known it; you should at least have been acquainted with your Catechism. It is so dangerous to unworthily partake of the sacred Supper, since by so doing so such great guilt is contracted and such fearful judgment incurred. How then is it possible that Satan should so blind men and cause them so lightly to esteem it, so little to fear God's judgments, and so thoughtlessly to lay hold upon that food which, instead of eternal life, may seal to them eternal death? How is it possible that in a matter of so great importance men should act in so inconsiderate and trifling a manner?

My hearers, I beseech you, be no longer ignorant about this truth, but lay it to heart: For if there is anything about which we should be discriminating, it is this. Let us then be careful here if we would be careful anywhere. He who loves danger deserves to fall into it. Nowhere is danger so great as here! Here, by a morsel and a swallow, can the covenant of God be desecrated, His wrath brought upon the whole congregation, and ourselves made liable to temporal and eternal punishment. Therefore reflect upon and bear in mind this truth. Remember, that though moral and outwardly religious, if you are still unregenerate and destitute of spiritual life, you have no warrant to approach the Table of grace. You who are ignorant, worldly minded, ungodly, and live in your sins, know that we dare not grant you access but are under obligation to bar you, not to your destruction, but for your good, that you may thus amend your lives and turn to the Lord. If you give evidence of real amendment, we will admit you with good conscience and the utmost cheerfulness.

Remember also, that each member is bound to subject himself to the examination of the minister of Christ and thus be able to give a reason of the faith and hope that is in him, but with meekness and fear. This is God's command (1 Pet. 3:15; Heb. 13:17). Who dares to resist the command of God? Although the knowledge and persuasion of one's conversion is not the ground upon which he is to be admitted (as the Labadists erroneously maintain), yet it is the duty of a minister to examine members. For the ministers of Jesus are the spiritual fishermen described in the parable of Matthew 13:48, who sit down on the shore to sort out the fish drawn up by the net of the gospel. They put the good fish into vessels and cast away the bad. The Lord declares this act to exemplify how he distinguishes between the evil and the just. Figuratively speaking, there are angels in the gates of the new Jerusalem who determine who may enter into the city (Rev. 21:27). This duty is described most suitably by d'Outrein in the work previously mentioned. D'Outrein observes that ministers who receive members must not only instruct them beforehand with the utmost care in the principles of the doctrine of Christ; or, if they have been already instructed, test their ability to make confession of the truth. But the ministers must also examine whether these members exhibit true repentance, sincere saving faith, and heart-renewing conversion. The ministers must earnestly impress upon their minds the necessity of these things to examine whether they possess them, and to caution them against self-deception (p. 109). For if the ministers admit any to the Table without carefully examining them and faithfully warning them, thus affording them occasion to eat and drink judgment to themselves, is it not possible that the guilt should to some extent rest upon themselves (Ezek. 33:7-8)?

Therefore, if an overseer is to receive or admit one with good conscience, he must see to it that the person makes a good confession of the truth, of his sins, of his faith in Christ, and of his purpose to lead a holy life, and that his walk is consistent with his confession. Such is the requirement of the Church Order, Article 61: "No one shall be admitted to the Lord's Supper except those who, according to the usage of the church to which they unite themselves, have made confession of religion, besides being reputed to be of a godly conversation, without which also those who come from other churches shall not be admitted." But this is not sufficient for the communicant himself, who must be a true believer and be sorrowful on account of his sins, and who seeks salvation and forgiveness in Christ, and aims to lead a holy life, in order to properly and profitably observe the ordinance.

Therefore examine whether you have a right to the Lord's Supper and whether these things be found in you. "Prove your own selves," says Paul in 2 Corinthians 13:5; for it is an undoubted truth, shown in the clearest manner, that none other may approach. But he who really possesses these properties of the divine life not only *may* but *must* approach. He should remember that anyone who proposes to go to the Lord's Table engages in an important undertaking and should accordingly make personal and particular preparation, upon which we shall not now enlarge, but conclude with the words of the psalmist: "Whoso is wise, and will observe these things, even they shall understand the lovingkindness of the LORD" (Ps. 107:43). Amen.

— 3 —

The Church's Duty to Her Members

*"And I will give unto thee the keys
of the kingdom of heaven."*
— Matthew 16:19

The Heidelberg Catechism — Lord's Day 31
Question 83: What are the keys of the kingdom of heaven?
Answer: The preaching of the holy gospel, and Christian discipline, or excommunication out of the Christian church; by these two, the kingdom of heaven is opened to believers and shut against unbelievers.

Question 84: How is the kingdom of heaven opened and shut by the preaching of the holy gospel?
Answer: Thus: when according to the command of Christ it is declared and publicly testified to all and every believer, that, whenever they receive the promise of the gospel by a true faith, all their sins are really forgiven them of God for the sake of Christ's merits; and on the contrary, when it is declared and testified to all unbelievers, and such as do not sincerely repent, that they stand exposed to the wrath of God and eternal condemnation, so long as they are unconverted; according to which testimony of the gospel, God will judge them both in this and in the life to come.

Question 85: How is the kingdom of heaven shut and opened by Christian discipline?

Answer: Thus: when according to the command of Christ, those, who under the name of Christians maintain doctrines or practices inconsistent therewith, and will not, after having been often brotherly admonished, renounce their errors and wicked course of life, are complained of to the church or to those who are thereunto appointed by the church; and if they despise their admonition, are by them forbidden the use of the sacraments; whereby they are excluded from the Christian church and by God Himself from the kingdom of Christ; and when they promise and show real amendment, are again received as members of Christ and His church.

In extolling the beauty and endowments of His spouse, the Lord Jesus says, "A garden enclosed is my sister, my spouse; a spring shut up, a fountain sealed" (Song of Sol. 4:12). The sister and spouse of Christ here must be understood as the true church, consisting of elect and called saints as His body and congregation. They are thus named because they are united to Him in the most intimate manner by a spiritual espousal, are loved by Him, and enjoy His love. In addition, He dwells in them, rules over them, and is in return loved by them. They are also called a spring shut up, or a fountain sealed, with respect to the administration of the gospel, which God has committed to the church. From this gospel, as from a spring and fountain, the living waters of consolation flow forth, quickening and refreshing the sorrowing in heart (Ps. 33:2). These waters are shut up and sealed off from the unbelieving and unconverted, who have neither part nor lot in this matter (Acts 8:21), for the water of grace is the property only of the penitent and believing.

The church is also called an enclosed garden because the Lord preserves it from its foes. Not only is it pure and chaste as a virgin (2 Cor. 11:2), but also by ecclesiastical discipline it excludes the ungodly as filthy and impure. This is according to the command and authority given to it by the

Lord Jesus. The church uses the key of God's Word to open the kingdom of heaven to believers and to shut it against the unbelieving and impenitent. By means of Christian discipline, it also casts out those members who lead grossly offensive lives. This article of faith is our subject here, in the order prescribed by our Christian instructor.

This Lord's Day is connected with the one preceding in which the instructor teaches that the penitent and believing are entitled to the Lord's Supper and that those who exhibit themselves in doctrine and life as unbelieving and ungodly must be barred by the keys of the kingdom of heaven. In this Lord's Day, the instructor declares what these keys are and how they must be used.

Three points require our attention:

I. What are the keys of the kingdom of heaven
   (Question 83).
II. How the first key, the preaching of the gospel,
   should be used *(Question 84).*
III. How the next key, Christian discipline, is to
   be used *(Question 85).*

I. In the first point, the instructor asks: "What are the keys of the kingdom of heaven?"

The kingdom of heaven is frequently understood as the kingdom of grace, that is, the church of the New Testament (Matt. 13:11). In this kingdom, all is heavenly. This kingdom is ruled by a heavenly King, the Lord Jesus, over heavenly subjects, the elect, also called saints. The kingdom includes heavenly blessings, such as "righteousness, and peace, and joy in the Holy Ghost" (Rom. 14:17); heavenly laws, which subjects must obey to serve their King; and heavenly power, by which God admits or excludes people from this kingdom.

The heavenly kingdom is closed to the sinner. Through his father Adam, man was sent forth from Paradise. But in establishing the kingdom of His Son upon earth, the Lord

God granted entrance into it. He said His Son could have the heathen for His inheritance and the uttermost parts of the earth for His possession (Ps. 2). For this purpose, God has committed to His servants in the church the keys of that kingdom. This term is a metaphor; the keys are not literal but figurative. They represent the ecclesiastical and spiritual authority, upon the command and in the name of the Lord Jesus, that is used to administer the affairs of the church, to open it to the penitent and to close it to the impenitent. Thus, says the Savior in Matthew 16:19, "I will give unto thee the keys of the kingdom of heaven," that is, the power to admit and to exclude. Similarly, in our daily affairs, when committing to another the care of a house, we give him keys so that he can admit the members of the household and allow them the comforts of the house, and exclude strangers, placing its contents beyond their reach. Civil authority is also represented by keys (Isa. 22:21-22).

The keys of the kingdom of heaven, then, represent the power of church government. This includes the supreme, absolute jurisdiction that belongs to Jesus only as Lord and King (Rev. 3:7; 1:18); and the subordinate, or ministerial authority, that Christ has conferred upon His servants.

There are two keys: the preaching of the Word and Christian discipline. The Lord has committed the first key, the preaching of the Word, to His church. The Word is to be proclaimed by Christ's servants in His name. As Christ Himself said, "He that heareth you, heareth me; and he that despiseth you, despiseth me." With this authority, Christ's servants proclaim to the penitent and believing the forgiveness of sin and eternal life. With the same authority, they shut the kingdom of heaven against the unbelieving and unconverted, as long as such sinners remain in their unbelieving and impenitent state.

The second key, Christian discipline, is the ministerial power committed to the church to exclude the disorderly and ungodly from the kingdom of heaven. It also includes the power to open the kingdom to sinners who repent of their sin and promise to amend their life and to show evidences of that.

Here the question arises, Does the church possess such jurisdiction? The Remonstrants deny that. Perceiving that they could obtain no indulgence for their doctrines in the church, these Remonstrants sought the assistance of the magistrate to whom they had conceded power over the church to secure his favor. They said that the authority possessed by the church is dependent upon that of the magistrate who exercises it through the overseers of the church as its servants and deputies.

We, on the contrary, maintain that the Lord has committed such power to His church and that it is entirely distinct from that of magistrates and independent of them. It is to be exercised in the name of Christ, not in theirs. We maintain that on the basis of the following:

1. Our text, Matthew 16:19, in which Christ confers the power of the keys, not upon magistrates, but upon His apostles (cf. Matt. 18:17-18).

2. The Old Testament, in which ecclesiastical power was distinct from civil power. God commanded His people to cast offenders out of fellowship and to cut off their souls from among their people, that is, to erase their names from the genealogical register of the children of Israel (the Old Testament Church) and not to reckon them among the seed of Abraham but count them as heathen and publicans.

3. Paul's teaching in 2 Corinthians 10:8 about the existence of such a power: "For though I should boast somewhat more of our authority, which the Lord hath given us." The church possesses power derived not from the magistrate but from the Lord, which, according to Paul, can be used with sharpness (2 Cor. 13:10).

4. The Lord Himself has appointed certain offices in His church that include the authority to govern the church, such as ministers and stewards (2 Cor. 4:1; Titus 1:7), gov-

ernments (1 Cor. 12:28), rulers (Heb. 13:17; 1 Tim. 5:17), those who are over others (1 Thes. 5:12), ambassadors (2 Cor. 5:20), and overseers whose business is to rule (Acts 20:28). All such offices have authority to do certain things. Power is thus vested in the church and is exercised by its overseers as ministers of Christ.

5. The very nature of the case. The power of a magistrate barely extends over the kingdom of nature, whereas the power of the church extends over the kingdom of grace. The power of the magistrate relates only to the temporal state of man, whereas the power of the church extends to the spiritual state of its members. The power of the magistrate is absolute; the church's is ministerial, not under the magistrate but under Christ (1 Cor. 4:6). This has been the practice of the church in all ages, and the unwavering confession and practice of the Reformed church from the time of the Reformation, as appears from the Form of Ordination of the Ministers of God's Word.

6. Finally, the duty of the ministers of the Word to keep the church of God in good discipline and to govern it according to the Form of Ordination of Elders and our Heidelberg Catechism.

Have magistrates no power whatsoever over the church? They have no power in the church but in relation to the church. Church members are citizens subject to a magistrate. They may be punished for any civil crime, such as Abiathar, who was thrust out by Solomon for his conspiracy with Adonijah (1 Kings 2:27). Magistrates may also inquire whether the truth is preached in a church. They may eradicate errors and preserve the church from molestation within and without. They also have power over the external circumstances of public worship as well as a compulsory power regarding ecclesiastical subjects to cause ministers, elders, deacons, and others to carefully perform their duty. But to whom is this power committed? Surely not to the pope of Rome, who is not the head of the church, nor to each member of the church, which would create great confusion. It is the will of the Lord that all things in the church should be done decently and in order (1 Cor. 14:40). Much less is this power committed to women, as some enthusiasts maintain, for women are forbidden to speak in the church (1 Cor. 14:34-35; 1 Tim. 2:12). Rather, this power is committed to the rulers of the church who are extraordinary as apostles and evangelists, who were called by the Lord Himself in an unusual manner, and who were endowed with the gift of preaching the gospel in all languages and to all people, confirming it with miracles (Matt. 10). It is also committed to ordinary men, common to all ages of the church, called elders. There are elders who teach and who rule (1 Tim. 5:17). Those who only rule are called governments (1 Cor. 12:28). Taken together, they are called the presbytery (1 Tim. 4:14). To these have been committed the power of the keys by the Lord Jesus as King of His church, which Matthew 18:17 says gives them the power of casting out the incorrigible. These rulers assemble together in consistories, classes, and synods to preserve good order that divine worship may be performed in a proper manner and without distraction, that offenses may be prevented, and that the keys of the kingdom of heaven, such as Christian discipline, are exercised towards the offending. Thus the authority to preach the gospel and exercise Christian discipline are two keys by which the kingdom of heaven is opened to believers and shut to unbelievers.

II. The first key, authority to preach the gospel, is committed to those lawfully called and sent by God to do so (Rom. 10:15; 2 Cor. 5:19-20; Heb. 5:4-6). Sin bars the sinner from access to the kingdom of heaven and all its privileges. He is held captive in the snare of the devil (2 Tim. 2:26). He is shut up under the law (Gal. 3:23). The power of depravity and the weakness of faith cuts him off from God's face. Even believers experience this when doubt of their interest in the blessings of the kingdom fills them with darkness and fear (Job 19:6-8; Ps. 31:22; Lam. 3:7).

The preaching of the gospel opens the kingdom of heaven, not by declaring that Christ died for all men and that everyone has but to imagine that Christ is his Savior. Arminians maintain that in direct opposition to the Word of God, as is shown in the seventh Lord's Day. But the gospel we preach declares that God has sent forth His Son as a propitiation for sin through faith in His blood; that upon His invitation and call the sinner may be turned to Him, receive Him as Mediator, surrender himself to Him, go to the Father through Him, and be admitted into His kingdom. That is how Paul opened the kingdom of heaven when he preached the gospel (2 Cor. 5:19-20).

The kingdom of heaven is opened to the penitent and believing who mourn over and strive against sin and who cling to the promise proclaimed that all their sins are truly forgiven for the sake of Christ's merits. This duty given to ministers of the gospel includes preaching the remitting of sins (John 20:23) as well as the forgiveness of sins in Christ's name (Luke 24:47; Acts 10:43, etc).

To perform this duty well, ministers must not merely state the promises in general. They should propose the kind of evidence that shows who are and who are not entitled to those promises. That was frequently done by the apostles, as recorded in Romans 8:13-19; James 2:14-26; and 1 John 3:14; 4:13. It is done either in public assemblies where the gospel is preached (Acts 13:38-39) or in private when a minister personally addresses a concerned believer, applying the promises of the gospel to him, offering him words of encouragement, and removing his occasions of concern. This should be done when a believer apprehends the promises of the gospel with true faith and gives evidence of his faith and repentance, as was done by David to Nathan or the man sick of palsy to Jesus. As Matthew 9:2

says, "Jesus seeing their faith said to the sick of the palsy; Son, be of good cheer; thy sins be forgiven thee." When forgiveness of sins is proclaimed to such a one, the kingdom of heaven is opened to him and he is assured that he is made to sit with Christ in heavenly places (Eph. 2:6).

In addition to telling the righteous that it shall be well with them, ministers of the Word are also called to pronounce a woe upon the ungodly (Isa. 8:9-10). As the instructor says, this key, the preaching of the gospel, declares and testifies to all unbelievers, and those who do not heartily turn to the Lord, that the wrath of God and eternal condemnation will abide upon them as long as they remain in their unconverted state. The kingdom of heaven is shut against unbelievers. As Mark 16:16 says, "He that believeth not shall be damned," or John 3:36, "He that believeth not the Son shall not see life." Luke 13:3 warns the unconverted and Matthew 23:13-29 proclaims, "Woe unto you...hypocrites!"

To shut the kingdom of heaven against such is to declare that they have no part in the kingdom of grace or of glory; that they cannot enter heaven but are bound under their sins and the wrath of God. Thus they retain their sins, according to John 20:23, and treasure up to themselves "wrath against the day of wrath" (Rom. 2:5). Ministers are to declare this in a way that seeks to penetrate the hearts of unbelievers. Peter used this key against Simon the sorcerer (Acts 8:21-23), and Paul used it in relation to Elymas, associating it with a denunciation of the divine curse upon the sinner (1 Cor. 16:22).

It is true that anyone who possesses the requisite knowledge can make these declarations respectively to believers and unbelievers according to the Word of God; but not as ambassadors in Christ's name and as ministers of the gospel can, and are bound to do (2 Cor. 5:19-20). There is a great difference between a private person or a minister of Christ saying these things. If a minister of Christ in Christ's name declares: "Thou believing, seeking soul! Thou art an heir of eternal life! Thy sins are forgiven thee!"; or on the other hand: "Thou ungodly! I declare to thee, that the wrath of God abideth on thee! and thou shalt be damned, if thou dost not repent!"; this should in both cases so impress the mind and excite such emotions in the one of comfort and in the other of conviction and terror, as if uttered by the Lord Jesus Himself. He sadly mistakes who regards this opening and shutting of the kingdom of heaven by the preachers of the gospel, as vain and without force, since it is to be recognized as the voice of God, and not merely of man. For "according to which testimony," says the instructor, "God will judge them both in this and in the life to come." God himself says, He "confirmeth the word of his servant, and performeth the counsel of his messengers" (Isa. 44:26); "and whatsoever thou shalt bind on earth shall be bound in heaven: and whatsoever thou shalt loose on earth shall be loosed in heaven" (Matt. 16:19; John 20:23). Likewise an apostle speaks of "the day when God shall judge the secrets of men by Jesus Christ according to my gospel" (Rom 2:16).

III. The second key is the Christian ban, or ecclesiastical discipline. This is a ministerial power committed to the church to exclude the scandalous and ungodly from Christian communication and to readmit them after repentance and the promise and manifestation of amendment of life. This key is to be used, not with people outside the church, but with those within (1 Cor. 5:11-13). Those who have united themselves to the church by a profession of faith are subject to Christian discipline if they are unchristian in doctrine or life, and though admonished, persist in the same. "An heretic... reject," says Paul (Titus 3:10; 2 John 1:10-11). We may not keep company with a brother that lives ungodly (1 Cor. 5:11; 2 Thes. 3:14). The Christian ban excludes such people and no longer acknowledges them as members of the church. It also bars them from the table of the Lord. Paul calls this a delivering to Satan (1 Cor. 5:5).

He thus delivered Hymenaeus and Alexander to Satan, not giving them over bodily for Satan to possess and torment, but rather ejecting them from the church. As Paul said in 1 Corinthians 5:13: "Put away from among yourselves that wicked person."

Satan reigns outside the church, therefore, he that is cast out of the church is delivered to Satan and shut out of the kingdom of heaven. The sacraments are forbidden and denied to such a person, and he is delivered to his sins and destruction. This key is administered by various steps; for while the overseers of the church should not be slow to perform their duty in this respect, neither should they be too hasty. They should proceed with all equity, without respect of persons, with great prudence and meekness, with great gravity, and with all humility. Their demeanor should show that they are doing this not to gratify a lust for power but with sorrow and compassion and because it is required for everyone's good. The instructor says this must be done when, after having received frequent brotherly admonition, wicked persons "will not renounce their errors and wicked course of life" but rather despise the admonition of the church.

· This work of exclusion includes four steps:

1. Admonishing, warning, or reproving, done in private. If this goes unregarded, it is to be done in the presence of the consistory.

2. Forbidding the privilege of coming to the table of the Lord.

3. Bringing the matter to the congregation so that it may be known that the keys of the kingdom of heaven are being used and that the errant one must be prayed for and made ashamed so that he is persuaded to turn to the Lord. This must be done first by withholding the name. Upon continuance in obstinacy, the name must be announced so that a deeper impression may be made, both upon the offender and the congregation. If this proves ineffectual, we are led to the fourth and last step.

4. The cutting off of the offender. He or she is forbidden all fellowship with the church and is no longer recognized as a brother or sister but as a heathen and publican. This is the apostle's command: "Put away from among yourselves that wicked person" (1 Cor. 5:13).

These four steps are included in the command of Jesus, which requires that I first declare to an offending brother his fault in private. If he disregards my word, then I seek to restore him in the presence of one or more additional believers. If he remains unreformed, then I complain of him to the rulers of the church. If he yet remains obstinate, I must count him as a heathen and publican (Matt. 18:17).

This corresponds with the requirement of Church Order, which teaches that we first admonish, then withhold the Lord's Table, then bring the matter to the congregation, without and then with his name, that each one may exhort him to repentance and pray for him. If all this is of no avail, then he is to be completely and publicly cut off, that he may be ashamed and repent. The purpose of this ban is:

1. To cause shame and encourage reflection (2 Thes. 3:14).

2. To regard this exercise of authority as an indication of the displeasure of the Lord Jesus, so that the offender may turn from his evil ways (1 Cor. 5:5).

3. To cause others to fear divine inflictions.

4. To remove offenders from the church, for the sake of those who are within as well as without who might otherwise take occasion to blaspheme God and His worship (Rom. 2:24).

5. To preserve the whole church from judgments; for when the wicked are admitted to the Lord's Table, the covenant of God is profaned and His wrath excited against the whole congregation (Jer. 5:25-26). "If we would judge ourselves, we should not be judged" (1 Cor. 11:31).

If a sinner who has been excluded repents, he may be received back into fellowship and permitted to approach the Table of the Lord. His offense must be forgiven and he should be comforted, lest he be "swallowed up with overmuch sorrow" (2 Cor. 2:6-7). Haste in this matter is to be avoided, however, for he should first give satisfactory evidence of repentance. The incestuous person whom Paul referred to in 1 Corinthians 5 was not received until he had become affected with vehement grief and stood in absolute need of consolation. The instructor says that the excluded are to be again received "when they promise and show real amendment."

The first Christian church was exceedingly faithful and strict in the discharge of church discipline. When a member stayed away from the public assembly without sufficient reason, he was sharply rebuked. When someone who lived in a city was absent from church for three Lord's Days, he was temporarily suspended from the Lord's Supper to show that notice was taken of his fault. Christian discipline was exercised for all offenses against the divine law as well as for every departure from good morals which was either manifest of itself or made known and confessed to the church. The Christians of that time were extremely zealous for the honor of their religion and hence sought to suppress all sins at the first appearance. For this reason they kept a watchful eye upon each other, pointing out to each other in private their faults and errors. When this wasn't effective, they presented the matter to church leaders for investigation. No offense was overlooked.

They were equally careful in readmitting a person into the church. They did not receive those who had departed from the path of duty into the church until they had given evidence of repentance. They divided penitents into four classes:

- Those who stood at the door of the church clothed in sordid and negligent garments and who, with sad countenance and tears, bewailed their transgressions and besought the prayers of those who entered the church. It was customary at this time to also make public confession of sin.

- Those, called hearers, who were permitted to listen at the entrance of the church with the catechism students to the reading and exposition of the Word of the Lord but were dismissed before the administration of the Lord's Supper.

- Those who humbly prostrated themselves upon the floor of the church and confessed their sins before the whole assembly. After being kindly raised up by the overseers, they were placed near the desk at which the Word was read. These, too, were dismissed with the catechism students before the administration of the Lord's Supper.

- Those who did not withdraw with the students but continued standing with the assembly to hear the Word and to engage in prayer and singing. They were permitted to witness the administration of the Lord's Supper but not yet invited to partake, although they were soon allowed this privilege.

Everyone, whether high or low, was required to make severe amends. Even Emperor Theodosius the Great was not excepted. For his bloody and cruel slaughter of the Thessalonians, he was forbidden the Lord's Table by Ambrosius, Bishop of Milan. The emperor was required to openly confess his sins and to make satisfaction for them for eight months. He accepted the punishment, readily and willingly rendering the requirements. Counting himself unworthy to stand or kneel before God, he habitually prostrated himself, exclaiming in the words of David, "My soul cleaveth unto the dust: quicken thou me according to thy Word" (Ps. 119:125). Having many times plucked off his hair, smitten his countenance, deluged his face with tears, and humbly cried for peace and forgiveness, the emperor was finally absolved and restored to communion with the church (Cave's *Early Christianity*).

Here we see, beloved, the true doctrine of the Reformed Church concerning the power conferred upon its rulers with respect to the preaching of the gospel and the exercise of authority. With what fidelity and strictness were those things practiced in the early church. Its rulers were faithful and the pious zealous for the honor of God and the well-being and salvation of those committed to their care.

In light of the present state of the church, no one can deny that the church has become exceedingly corrupt and has greatly departed from its pristine purity of former years. Indeed, everyone must see that there is too much slackness at present in relation to the great duties that have been considered. For how many ignorant members are found in the church who are unable to discern the Lord's body! How many people who set no example of the image of Christ by neither knowing nor following after holiness! Understand me well, and let no one twist and misunderstand my words. I speak now of the church in general, and not of this or that church in particular. The Lord says in Jeremiah 5:26, "Among my people are found wicked men." So it is today also. Oh, how many ungodly are to be discerned in the church of God! But what is done to correct it? Where is Christian discipline exercised to exclude them? And where do we find people who have been disciplined?

The forms generally are used, but the form relating to the exercise of discipline is treated as if it did not exist. Who will seek to faithfully discharge this duty? Those who would, many times are not encouraged. Instead, they are vigorously slandered by many and meet with much opposition, as if the Lord had not committed these keys to the rulers of the church, or as if they were not under obligation to be faithful, to cry aloud, and to lift up their voices like a trumpet to love their neighbor and seek his conversion and salvation. The key of Christian discipline is so little used that it appears to be lost. This confirms the ungodly, saddens the pious, withholds the blessing of God from the church, and excites His wrath. But it is still more lamentable when offenses are left undisturbed and the authority of the church is unlawfully directed against the pious. This is what Wilhelmus à Brakel alludes to in *The Christian's Reasonable Service*, when he says: "Is a church so degenerate, and its rulers so wicked, that they suffer offenses to go unpunished, and assail those who are distinguished for soundness of doctrine and excellence of life? Their acts are not to be regarded, either by those who are thus unjustly censured, or by other godly persons; for they are not in accordance with, but contrary to, the ordinance of Christ. 'The curse causeless shall not come' (Prov. 26:2), but redound upon their own heads, who with lies have made the heart of the righteous sad, and strengthened the hands of the wicked."

We have good reason to shed a flood of tears over the sad state of the church and to say with Jeremiah, "Oh that my head were waters, and mine eyes a fountain of tears, that I might weep day and night for the slain of the daughter of my people!" (Jer. 9:1). But to indulge in mourning without putting our hands to work will be of little avail. It is therefore necessary that I endeavor to stir up myself, the elders, and everyone, without exception, to the proper use of these keys.

The duty of magistrates and others who are in positions of authority is to humbly submit themselves to the supreme authority of the King of kings and Lord of lords. To these the Lord says: "Be wise now therefore, O ye kings: be instructed, ye judges of the earth. Serve the LORD with fear, and rejoice with trembling. Kiss the Son," etc. (Ps. 2:10-12).

It is their duty to use their authority and influence for the good of the church by cherishing it, maintaining its rights, protecting its ministers, defending its truths, restraining its enemies, and with force and authority rectifying the corrupt manners of society. Magistrates do well when they enact laws against profaning the Sabbath, cursing, swearing, drunkenness, and other sensual and similar excesses.

The duty of ministers is exceedingly weighty, as I shall briefly show. Why shall I show this? Because it flows from my subject; I am to rouse myself to faithfulness so that no one might take offense when I discharge my duty with divine assistance, and that each one may be led in accordance with his duty to pray for his minister. Should anyone misinterpret my meaning, let him bear the responsibility.

If we would not be blind watchmen, dumb dogs, slumbering and carnal men, we must apply the keys of the kingdom within ourselves. As Romans 2:21 says, "Thou therefore which teachest another, teachest thou not thyself?" We are required to teach people to examine themselves (2 Cor. 13:5), so should we then fail to perform this duty towards ourselves? Or should we entertain the vulgar conceit that all ministers are believing and pious because they are able to preach and pray? We know this is not the case from Judas, Demas, and the false teachers who preached Christ out of envy, of whom Paul so frequently complains. Ministers, as well as others, must be regenerated and converted. Neither a complete education nor an elevated calling imparts grace. Having no further qualifications, how dreadful will be our fall from the pulpit into perdition!

We must judge ourselves and flee for refuge to the Savior, that we may save ourselves and others. We, whose office it is to call others to repentance and to the enjoyment of God's favor, are also called by God to be reconciled to Him. Each minister may with propriety ask himself the following questions, stated by a pious writer:

What is the character of my teaching and life? Do I, through my manner of preaching and life, sadden the hearts of the righteous and strengthen the hands of the wicked? Have I ever seriously considered what it means to watch for souls? What it means to deliver someone out of the snare of the devil? Have I so studied the devices of Satan and the artifices of the human heart that I might, by cunning and craft, delude Satan and the hearts of men and thus catch men with guile (2 Cor. 12:16)? Have I seriously weighed the awful doom that will be mine if I am a dumb dog that cannot bark (Isa. 56:10)? Have I considered the doom due to me if I fail to warn sinners and they sink into hell, calling for vengeance upon me? Have I sought to take the precious from the vile, that I might be the mouth not of the devil, but of God (Jer. 15:19)? Have I been particularly careful to comfort the mourners and to speak a word in season to the weary (Isa. 50:4)? Have I, as a faithful physician, sought to understand spiritual diseases that I might better heal them? What if the wretched sigh and cry to God, the heavenly Physician, against me, saying, "O God, our teacher does not take our misery to heart! He wounds our souls instead of healing them! He is much more occupied with preaching what gratifies the fancy, what lets the carnally secure continue in their security and the sorrowful in their sadness than in trying to bring men to themselves or in strengthening the weak. He is anxious to learn whether his preaching is gratifying but never inquires whether souls are converted. Nor does he try to show in all his conduct his pursuit of a holy life."

Let these inquiries be proposed, and let those who do not approve of such self-scrutiny and who live at ease in its neglect be assured that a time of reckoning will come when the condition of many will be found opposite to their present imagination. Oh how wretched shall those be who will then be cast out as slothful and unfaithful servants (Matt. 25:26)! However, happy are they who by careful investigation discover that they are conscious of the leadings of the Spirit of God in their hearts. For they can apply to themselves all of God's promises and be assured that the Lord will be with them, as Paul writes (1 Tim. 1:13,16; 2 Tim. 1:12).

Precious, immortal souls committed to our care should weigh heavily upon our hearts. Therefore we should be diligent to know the state of our flocks and look well to our herds (Prov. 27:23). When we direct our attention to an assembled audience, we should remember that each listener has an immortal spirit and that by nature each pursues the broad road that leads to destruction. If allowed to continue in that course, each shall be lost forever. Whose soul should not be inflamed with desire to help? When a person falls into the water or into the fire, everyone cries out in alarm, and each does what he can to help. Shouldn't we then be alarmed about the eternal destruction of men, which involves both soul and body? Shouldn't we who are called by God to do so expend all our energies for their rescue by instructing, exhorting, and reproving them? Shouldn't all of our powers be called into service to pluck sinners out of everlasting fire, to deliver their souls from the mouth of hell, and to place them at the feet of Jesus? Sad will it be for us if through our negligence a sinner is lost! The Lord will require blood at the hand of the watchman (Ezek. 3:18, 20).

We cannot be indifferent about how the keys of the kingdom are employed. This duty must be discharged with discretion. We may not open what the Lord shuts nor may we shut what the Lord opens. What minister that fears God and loves his neighbor dares to make sad the heart of the righteous and strengthen the hands of the wicked (Ezek. 13:22), that he should not return from his wicked way? If a minister would proceed wisely and according to the Word of God, he must, as Jude directs in verses 22 and 23, "Of some have compassion, making a difference: and others save with fear, pulling them out of the fire." To be the mouth of God, a minister must, like Jeremiah, take the precious from the vile, rightly divide the Word of truth (2 Tim. 2:15), and give everyone his portion in due season (Luke 12:42). The best way to catch souls is to seize the sinner by the heart and help him see the profound deceptions of his dreadfully deceitful self, so that he may awaken, become concerned, and betake himself to Christ. Directions given at the national synod, held at Wesel, A.D. 1568, agree with this. Synod proclaimed:

All things should be directed to these two principal objects of the gospel, namely, faith, and the conversion of the soul to God. To this end the preachers of the gospel shall make it their only aim to promote the true mortification and quickening of man. They shall labor in their discourses, as far as practicable, to penetrate into all the hidden recesses and refuges of the souls of their hearers, not being content with dwelling upon gross improprieties, but seeking to expose, to expel, and in the most effectual manner to extirpate the secret hypocrisy of the heart — that seed plot and foul pool of pride, ingratitude, and all ungodliness.

The sacraments they shall administer with great reverence and care, that the covenant of God be not profaned.

Without enlarging, it must be said that in the exercise of Christian discipline, ministers must be exceedingly faithful, considerate, and resolute. They should continually bear in mind that this trust is committed to them and that as ambassadors of Christ they are to discharge it in His name. They must be occupied not with their own business but Christ's. They should continually remember that the Lord Jesus looks upon them and carefully notices how zealous they are in discharging their duty. They should continually consider that upon the use of the keys of the kingdom depend the salvation and condemnation of precious souls. The rulers should be examples to the flock in their walk and their words (1 Pet. 5:3); they should love the truth and seek after wisdom, that their "profiting may appear to all" (1 Tim. 4:15). Surely, if we attentively consider the importance of these duties, we find the greatest reason to exclaim: "Who is sufficient for these things?"

You who are elders know that your office is equally weighty and your duties great. Your office, like that of ministers of the Word, has been instituted by God in His church. You, like they, have been called. If you would faithfully discharge the duties of your office, you should exercise your senses in the Word of God and the government of His church. Above all, you must be sanctified and endued with divine grace, for an ecclesiastical office without spiritual life helps neither our own soul nor the edification of others.

It is therefore your duty to use the key of God's Word to investigate your spiritual state. It is your duty to take heed to the whole flock and to feed it (Acts 20:28), to have special regard for the conduct of its members, and to be continually watchful over the entire congregation to instruct the ignorant, "warn them that are unruly, comfort the feebleminded, support the weak, and be patient toward all men" (1 Thes. 5:14). It is also your duty to see that ecclesiastical discipline is properly exercised against the wicked and offensive. Your duty is to aid and sustain your minister. I shall not enlarge upon this. You assumed those obligations when you were ordained according to the Form. Peruse that Form frequently, I beseech you, and be assured that you, as well as I, must give account at the last day.

The congregation must also conduct itself properly in relation to these keys of the kingdom. My hearers, it is your duty to acknowledge the authority bestowed by the Lord upon His servants and to submit yourselves to them. With Paul, we pray: "Know them which labor among you, and are over you in the Lord...and...esteem them very highly in love for their work's sake" (1 Thes. 5:12-13). You must seriously regard the power of opening and shutting the kingdom, or the remitting and retaining of sins. Listen carefully to the description of those to whom heaven is opened or closed, and consider to which class you belong.

It is the duty of members to warn and exhort one another (Heb. 3:13; 1 Thes. 5:14), as well as to report the unruly who refuse to listen to the exhortations of the rulers of the church, for this is expressly commanded in Matthew 18:17: "Tell it unto the church." Those who are suspended from the Table of the Lord should be tender and penitent, provided the ecclesiastical act be lawful. No one should resist and speak evil to the rulers of the church on account of it, for it is the act of the Lord Jesus. It is performed in His name and by His command. He who resists it resists the Lord Jesus, which is truly a dreadful sin.

To conclude, my hearers, be informed that by nature you are subject to sin as well as the curse and wrath of God, and that the kingdom is shut to you. But I also open to you the kingdom of heaven. God has provided His Son as a Surety. He proposes Him to you as a propitiation through faith in His blood to declare His righteousness. He can save to the uttermost those who come to God by Him. I invite you to come to the Lord and His goodness to experience His grace, peace, and mercy. "We pray you in Christ's stead, be ye reconciled to God" (2 Cor. 5:20). Turn ye, turn ye, from your evil ways, for why should ye die? If you turn to Jesus, come to Him, and receive Him to be justified and sanctified by Him, He will not reject you, for whoso cometh to Him He will in no wise cast out (John 6:37).

But will you not come to Him? Do you continue ignorant and at ease in sin, unconverted and unholy? In the name of the Lord, I declare to you that you shall die. God's wrath rests upon you. You shall find yourselves thrust out (Luke 13:28). But to you who are sensitive and humble because of your sins, who mourn on account of and strive against them and would fain be delivered from them, and for this purpose flee to Jesus and also follow after holiness, to you I announce in the name of Christ that your transgressions are forgiven and that the Lord will no longer be angry with you or rebuke you. Do you fear lest you find yourselves deceived and the door shut against you? Jesus will never shut the door that He has opened but will administer to you an abundant entrance into His heavenly kingdom where you shall ever be with the Lord. Amen.

— 4 —

The Righteous Scarcely Saved

"And if the righteous scarcely be saved, where shall the ungodly and the sinner appear?"

— 1 Peter 4:18

"Things of value are not to be obtained without difficulty" says an ancient proverb. The truth of the proverb is evident in acquiring natural things such as diamonds and pearls, but it is equally true in acquiring spiritual things, such as wisdom and virtue. The more virtues that we possess, the more lovely we are in the eyes of God, angels, and men. These virtues are therefore highly extolled by Solomon (Prov. 3:13-19). Nothing is more beautiful, more valuable, or more lovely than the spiritual and heavenly things that are with God in Christ. But, oh, how great the difficulty with which they are to be obtained! That will not be done without conflict, for "The kingdom of heaven suffereth violence, and the violent take it by force."

That truth is illustrated by the merchant who sold all that he had to purchase the pearl that he found, as well as by the man who, upon finding a treasure hid in a field, sold all that he had to buy that field. Paul teaches the same great truth when he says, "Know ye not that they which run in a race run all, but one receiveth the prize? So run, that ye may obtain." What is the prize to be contended for? It is the incorruptible crown of glory at the end of the course, the salvation kept in store for the children of God in heaven. Salvation here is compared to a crown because victory is given to believers in heaven over all their enemies. They are delivered from all conflict, toil, and pain, whereas here on earth, they find themselves in a vale of tears and in a way of tribulation.

This truth plainly appears in the inspired words of 1 Peter 4:18, "For Christ also hath once suffered for sins, the just for the unjust, that he might bring us to God, being put to death in the flesh, but quickened by the Spirit." The apostle declares that the righteous are saved, although scarcely, in the midst of many conflicts and through much difficulty. In the words that precede our text, Peter speaks about the doleful end of the ungodly, unbelieving, and disobedient. To show the end of the righteous and the wicked, he declares in our text that such shall not be the lot of the righteous but that they shall, although scarcely, be saved, while the ungodly and sinners shall perish. He connects these words with the word *and*, saying *"And* if the righteous scarcely be saved."

The text suggests two subjects for consideration: first, the state of the righteous — that they are saved, yet scarcely — and second, the wretched state of the ungodly.

Who Are the Righteous

We will concentrate here on the first part, that the righteous are scarcely saved and the difficulty a child of God has in attaining salvation. We'll first consider the persons who are righteous, then what is declared of them, and finally the manner in which they are saved. "Righteous" is one of various honorable titles conferred upon the children of God in His Word. Moses, Job, Abraham, Zacharias, Elizabeth, and others are called righteous, but, according to Isaiah 26:2, so is every child of God. In their collective capacity they are referred to as "the generation of the righteous" and "the righteous nation." The righteous of whom Peter speaks in our text are not entirely perfect and without sin. Oh, no! For such are not to be found among the descendants of Adam. As Solomon said, "There is not a just man upon earth." Every righteous person must confess this with shame, grief, and sorrow. This is the sad truth that Paul complains of when he says, "I find then a law, that, when I would do good, evil is present with me." This is also the lament of the church. To be sinless is the prerogative only of the Second Adam "who knew no sin."

The righteous mentioned in the text also do not live in such thorough compliance with the law that it can be said of them, "Do this and thou shalt live." Oh, no! For Scripture plainly teaches, "By the deeds of the law there shall no flesh be justified" (Rom. 3:20). As Job asks, "How should man be just with God?" and David declares, "If thou LORD shouldest mark iniquities, O Lord, who shall stand?"

The righteous here are not people like the Pharisees who seek to justify themselves and regard themselves as righteous. Rather the righteous here have the following characteristics:

- They are righteous in Christ. In themselves, these people are ungodly and destitute of that righteousness needed to stand before God in the judgment. Yet they have received the righteousness of the Lord Jesus offered in the gospel, through which they stand acquitted at the divine tribunal from the guilt of their sins and their punishment and are granted eternal life.

- They live righteously. The righteous conduct themselves agreeably to this righteousness and do what is right and proper according to the law of God. They are filled with the fruits of righteousness.

- They know they are righteous. The righteous are justified in their own consciences through their good works and are conscious of that holy frame of mind, which is a fruit of their uprightness and faith. The Spirit of God bears witness to them that they are children of God.

• Others see them as righteous. The lives of the righteous are so holy that they are recognized as such and are justified as righteous in the consciences of others. These believers are children of God who are in covenant with God. They are spoken of in the text in contrast to the ungodly.

The Salvation of the Righteous

"To save" means to preserve, to free, to deliver from evil, and to bring into a state of security and happiness. Saving may refer to temporal deliverance, as in Matthew 8:25, when the disciples said, "Lord, save us: we perish"; to some mortal disease, as in James 5:15, which says, "The prayer of faith shall save the sick"; or to severe persecution and great affliction, mentioned in verses such as Matthew 24:22. Usually, however, saving in the New Testament refers to the salvation of the soul to eternal life. Our text makes no reference to the temporal welfare or bodily deliverance that the righteous sometimes experience. Consider Noah amid the waters of the flood, for example, or Lot at the destruction of Sodom, the three companions of Daniel in the fiery furnace, Daniel in the den of lions, and Peter in prison. All are examples of righteous people who were delivered from danger in accordance with the promise "The Lord delivereth them out of their afflictions." No, "saved" in our text should be understood as spiritual deliverance or the eternal salvation of body and soul as opposed to damnation. As damnation involves the highest evil, so salvation involves the highest good, which is communion with God here in grace and hereafter in glory. It is that salvation or great good that no pen can describe or no tongue express. We can only say with David, "Oh how great is thy goodness which thou hast laid up for them that fear thee" (Ps. 31:19). This salvation is enjoyed by the righteous, for to be righteous is the way of salvation.

This is true because the righteous are acquitted from guilt and exposure to divine wrath and made heirs of eternal life. They are thus saved in hope. That is what Paul means when he says, "Who shall lay anything to the charge of God's elect? It is God that justifieth." So also David pronounces the man blessed to whom the Lord imputes righteousness without works. This perfect righteousness can stand in the divine judgment. The church responds by saying, "I will greatly rejoice in the LORD."

The righteous are in Christ by faith and are justified in Him. As Habakkuk 2:4 says, "The just shall live by his faith." Believers are justified, Scripture says, "For he that believeth on the Son hath eternal life." The righteous are also sanctified by the Spirit of God to do righteousness, follow after righteousness, and walk in all the ordinances and commandments of the Lord. Since without holiness no man shall see the Lord, it follows that those who partake of holiness shall certainly see the Lord.

The righteous are godly persons, not only in this life but in that which is to come. It is then certain that the righteous are saved, and they alone.

The Manner in Which the Righteous are Saved

Although the righteous are saved, they are scarcely saved. That does not mean that the righteous could fall from that state and come short of salvation, as the Roman Catholics and others teach. Rather, scarcely here means difficulty rather than uncertainty, for the salvation of the righteous who are justified by faith in Christ and sanctified by His Spirit is, according to God's promise, secure, certain, and unchangeable. The righteous have been chosen from eternity. Therefore Paul says, "The foundation of God standeth sure, having this seal, the Lord knoweth them that are his" (2 Tim. 2:19).

"Scarcely" also does not mean that believers continually doubt and and are uncertain about their salvation, for, as

Paul said, "I know whom I have believed, and am persuaded that he is able to keep that which I have committed
unto him against that day" (2 Tim. 1:12). He also wrote,
"For I am persuaded, that neither death, nor life, nor angels, nor principalities, nor powers, nor things present, nor
things to come, nor height, nor depth, nor any other creature shall be able to separate us from the love of God which
is in Christ Jesus our Lord" (Rom. 8:38-39). Believers are
therefore instructed to make their calling and election sure.

According to the original Greek text, "scarcely" here refers to difficulty. This is also how it is used in Acts 14:18,
which says, "And with these sayings *scarce* restrained they
the people, that they had not done sacrifice unto them."
Only a great effort on the part of Paul and Barnabas to refuse the offered homage is what prevented people from
sacrificing offerings to the apostles as gods. That is also
how the word is used in Acts 27:16: "And running under a
certain island, which is called Clauda, we had much *work* to
come by the boat," in other words, "We obtained it, but by
a desperate effort." Thus we speak of something "scarcely
obtained" as secured only by much trouble, labor, and pain.
That is how the word is to be understood in our text. The
righteous are saved, but *scarcely*, that is, with great toil and
effort, through many conflicts, afflictions, distresses, ago-
nies, temptations, and chastisements. That is what the Lord
Jesus means when he says, "Strive to enter in at the strait
gate." We cannot enter that narrow gate except by striving
— even pressing violently toward it. The remarkable passage Matthew 7:13-14 teaches that the way of life heaven-
ward is exceedingly narrow. All of one's life must be
regulated by the law of God. That demands a strict and
precise service.

How the Righteous are Saved

The righteous are scarcely saved, or with difficulty, because:

1. They must be born again. God cannot save unless He first spiritually awakens those who are by nature dead in trespasses and sins. Truly, the same power is needed for the regenerating and recreating of sinners that was required for creating the whole world. But it is needed even more for regeneration because during creation nothing opposed God, whereas the sinner harbors enmity against God. As Scripture says, "The carnal mind is enmity against God." In such a way, the righteous are scarcely saved. If sinners are to be saved, they must realize that believing is the only work that God requires of them. God does not allow a sinner to bring to God such exalted imaginations of himself and his words and actions that he acted as if he were God Himself. Rather, that proud, high-minded man must be so torn, so humble and small in his own eyes, that he falls prostrate before God as if he were a beggar who lies in the dust as a worm, supplicating God's grace.

Judas chose the rope rather than to believe in such a way. Oh, what is required to remove from such a person such false dependence on his own righteousness and such security in resting in it? What is required to drive him naked, bereft of all things, lost, helpless, and desperate to the feet of Jesus? Only through Christ will the sinner be reconciled to God. Only through His perfect righteousness will the sinner be rescued from destruction and eternally saved. It is hard to desire Christ and nothing but Christ. It is toilsome to daily follow after Christ and not to rest until we find Him. If a person believes, the arm of the Lord must be revealed to him. The work of faith shows the exceeding greatness of the power of God. As Paul says, "According to the working of his mighty power, which he wrought in Christ, when he raised him from the dead." Therefore are the righteous scarcely saved.

2. They must repent. This act of the soul includes turning from sin to holiness, from Satan to God, from self and all creatures to Christ. How great a work this is for one

who is so much in darkness that he is darkness itself, who cannot find the way of life and is unable and unwilling to return to it, who is so blinded by self-love that he regards his evil heart as good, who so cherishes delusion that he cannot nor will not abandon it, who is a willful captive in the snare of the devil, and who is a child of wrath and an enemy of God. What is required to arrest such ungodly, heedless sinners in their way and to rouse them from their lethargy? What is required of one who has forgotten and despised God, who has made God his enemy, and who has nothing but the expectation of eternal wrath to bring him to God to realize and enjoy His favor and love? Will not such a person ask, "How can I, an enemy and hater of God, become reconciled to Him? If I appeared in His holy presence, would He not immediately throw me out and cast me into hell? How could God delight in saving a sinner such as I am?" It is very difficult to bring a sinner to exercise confidence in God. But without that confidence, he cannot be led to repentance. Thus, he is scarcely saved.

3. They must be made holy. Without holiness, no man shall see the Lord. What a work this is! What energy and skill the Holy Spirit must use to sanctify the elect sinner, for the sinner is unclean and loathsome within and without. From the crown of his head to the soles of his feet, he is unsound. He must be sanctified in all that he does and leaves undone, yield his members as instruments of righteousness, and forsake all things — cutting off a right hand and plucking out a right eye to abandon his dearest bosom sins. He must also be inwardly sanctified, his heart entirely transformed, and the image of God impressed upon it. He must be holy in all his motives so he will glorify God in all things. Oh, how great a work this is to sanctify a heart accustomed to sin, vanity, and folly and to impart true wisdom to it! Nothing less than divine power is adequate to do this. Therefore is the sinner scarcely saved.

4. They must deny themselves. Jesus said, "If any man will come after me, let him deny himself, and take up his cross, and follow me." The old man with his fleshly affections and lusts must be crucified. He must yield his understanding and make it captive to the obedience of Christ. He must renounce his will. He must abandon his sinful inclinations, lusts, pleasures, reputation, possessions, friends, and be willing for Christ's sake to lose even his life. As Christ said, "If any man come to me, and hate not his father, and mother, and wife, and children, and brethren, and sisters, yea, and his own life also, he cannot be my disciple." How hard this is for a sinner whose heart is a stone! Yet it must take place. Therefore is the sinner scarcely saved. He must be so heavenly minded that he is willing to part with all that is seen for that which is unseen. Like Paul, the sinner must count all things dung for the excellency of the knowledge of Christ. He must despise the favor of men; the treasures, riches, and delights of the world; and seek only those things which are above, where Christ is, thus exalting the Lord Jesus above ten thousand and proclaiming Him to the world. But oh, the magnitude of such a work! Therefore, he is scarcely saved.

5. They must love God above all. They must love their neighbors as themselves, blessing those who curse them, doing good to those that hate, and praying for those who persecute. But how difficult it is to love, especially one's enemies. Therefore, the sinner is scarcely saved.

He is saved with great difficulty in much the same way as it is very difficult for someone who is deadly sick to accomplish anything. An Ethiopian can't change his skin or a leopard its spots any more readily than those accustomed to do evil can do good. Like the dead who contribute nothing to their own restoration to life, the righteous are mortally helpless. As Paul says, "I am carnal, sold under sin." Therefore, the righteous are scarcely saved.

The fickleness of man adds to the difficulty. For some who are convinced by God to forsake their sins and change their conduct may yet prove unfaithful to their resolutions. They do not continue steadfast and believing but turn once more to folly. Their sorrow is like a morning cloud that soon passes away. Therefore is the sinner scarcely saved.

6. God sometimes withdraws from them. The righteous are saved with difficulty because God sometimes forsakes them. He does not do that forever or entirely, but only for a time until He once more restores His comforting grace. But when such grace is withdrawn, the church complains: "The LORD hath forsaken me, and my Lord hath forgotten me" (Isa. 49:13). The Lord, their light and the strength of their life, withholds His help for a time, permitting His children to be subjected to the assaults of their enemies. He hides from them His lovely countenance, appearing to be angry with them, writing bitter things against them, and acting as their enemy. In response, the sinner goes through a season of complaint and lament, of asking and seeking, conflict and wrestling. Job, David, and Asaph experienced such times. The unconverted man knows nothing about such times; he knows nothing of this lost communion with God and nothing of the sweetness of that communion, since he never enjoyed it in the first place. Is it any wonder the righteous are scarcely saved?

7. They must endure conflicts with Satan. The devil goes about as a roaring lion. He is clever and deceitful and is ever plotting to draw believers from God and to destroy them. To this end, he shoots his fiery darts at them to lead them into sin and prevent what is good. He tries to fill their minds with blasphemous thoughts to sift their faith, to extinguish their love, to weaken their hope, and to reduce them to despondency and doubt. They must arm themselves against him, according to Ephesians 6:10-18, but that is done with great difficulty.

What makes it so difficult is that the world in which they live is so wicked. They are surrounded by people of wickedness who act as instruments of Satan. For what Satan cannot do himself, he does through his subjects. He rules the children of disobedience and urges them to destroy the godly, sometimes by treacherous flatteries — by representing in fair colors the beauties, pleasures, honors, and riches of the world to entice their souls — and at other times by assailing them with vile slanders, rebukes, lies, and malicious threats. The righteous can suffer much at the hands of the ungodly for Christ's sake, enduring evil report and good report. They must rise superior to this, though with difficulty.

8. They struggle with their own wickedness. Their evil and depraved nature continually threatens to lead the righteous astray. As Scripture says, "The heart is deceitful above all things, and desperately wicked." Also, "Man is tempted, when he is drawn away of his own lusts, and enticed." The heart, which is a pool of iniquity, tends continually to sin. It continually sends forth sin. Therefore, the heart must be diligently guarded. The old man must be crucified and our members, which are upon the earth, mortified. The body must be brought into subjection and no provision made for the flesh to fulfil its lusts. The righteous must be constantly wrestling, watching, and praying against sin with tears, sorrows, and complaints. Like Paul, they cry, "O wretched man that I am! who shall deliver me from the body of this death?" (Rom. 7:24). This constant strife is one more reason why the righteous are scarcely saved.

9. They endure so many afflictions. The righteous are frequently and grievously assailed. As the Bible says, "Many are the afflictions of the righteous" through which they must enter the kingdom of God. Who can count all the calamities that the righteous experience in this vale of tears; in person, family, estate, calling, honor, and good name? What sickness, poverty, disquietude, dishonor, violence, slander, and persecution they suffer! Scarcely is one

evil past before another arises. Innumerable evils compass them about. How difficult this is for the flesh.

Add to that the deep distress and bitter agony of soul that arises because of sin. That is the greatest evil the righteous are asked to endure. As the psalmist says, "The troubles of my heart are enlarged: O bring thou me out of my distresses." In speaking of the attainment of salvation, the Word of God uses expressions that signify toil, labor, and concern. It says, "Work out your own salvation with fear and trembling," for example, and "Strive to enter in." Such speech suggests a warrior who contends with many mighty foes. A child of God must strive against numerous enemies and mightily assault the kingdom of heaven. He must run the Christian race, follow after perfection, and wrestle after godliness. Such language is drawn from the combatants in ancient games. It implies the great valor of a hero armed from head to foot so he may prove victorious in the conflict and carry away the crown of life.

We are also required to watch, stand fast in the faith, quit ourselves like men, and be strong. We must fight the good fight of faith, being steadfast, unmovable, and always abounding in the work of the Lord. All these expressions suggest that those who are saved are saved, not easily, but through great conflict and with much effort and weariness. This is because of the unworthiness of their best works, the contest between the flesh and spirit, the depravity of their hearts, the narrowness of their way of life, the difficulties of their required duties, the insufficiency of their righteousness, and the strict demands of their righteous Judge.

Do you understand, dear readers, how the righteous are scarcely saved and with so much difficulty? We must not esteem salvation lightly. Unless we would oppose the Word of God, we must acknowledge that salvation is quite different from what's supposed by most men who hope to be saved; for they imagine that their hearts are all right and that they shall be saved provided they avoid outward, gross sins, live honest and correct lives, perform the external duties of godliness, and diligently pursue their own business. Oh wretched men! Can that be true godliness and the narrow way of life? No! Outwardly forsaking sin, pursuing virtue, and living correctly is only what the heathen practice. For, as the Savior said, "Do not even the publicans so?"

Although God has declared in His Word that something more is necessary to salvation and that the way to heaven is exceedingly narrow, men, notwithstanding, form so light an opinion of salvation and imagine that they shall easily acquire it. They do not carefully examine whether they are righteous and are not concerned whether they are in a state of grace and have an interest in Christ but satisfy themselves with a bare and unfounded persuasion and depend on the external propriety of their conduct. They rely on the fact that they are baptized, that they have confessed their faith, that they partake of the Lord's Supper, that they attend the house of God, and that they read His Word. They rely on these things. In the meanwhile, they busy themselves with earthly good, entertaining not the slightest doubt that they shall be saved. This they regard as certain. Know, oh vain man, that thou shalt not thus attain salvation. These things must indeed be done but are not in themselves sufficient. The Spirit of God declares through Peter that the righteous are but scarcely saved. Do you expect so easily to secure it? Oh, no! You lamentably deceive yourself and greatly err. The god of this world has blinded your mind and holds you captive in his snare. While you promise yourself heaven, let me assure you that you shall obtain hell. Listen, I pray you, to the declaration of the Author of all truth, "Not every one that saith unto me, Lord, Lord, shall enter into the kingdom of heaven; but he that doeth the will of my Father which is in heaven."

The Wretched State of the Ungodly

Oh careless and unconverted sinners who have no concern about the state of your souls and yet imagine that you will be saved, who, I pray you, persuades you that you will so readily obtain heaven? I beg you, judge for yourselves. Would Peter without reason have said that the righteous are but scarcely saved? Would the Lord Jesus have improperly described the way of salvation as so narrow? If you would be saved in your carnal, vain, worldly, and careless state, through so superficial a service, it would not be true that we are scarcely saved. We would we saved without difficulty. Your way of life surely does not conform to divine requirements. If you can be saved in your carelessness, did not the disciples, martyrs, and the most eminent saints act foolishly in doing so much and living so precisely? Those believers were greatly concerned about their salvation. Is it possible, then, that you can pursue a heedless course and yet be saved? Do not let your deceitful heart lead you astray. Do not willfully close your eyes and persist in imagining that you can so easily be saved. Most certainly, your deceitful heart turns you aside; you feed upon ashes, you are hastening to eternity with a lie in your right hand.

Must not a regenerate Christian daily pour out to God so many ardent prayers and utter so many agonizing supplications, shed so many bitter tears, be so distressed and concerned about his sins, find it necessary to strive so manfully against them, and also be compelled to endure so many temptations and afflictions? Can you then, by one heartless sigh to God and a little superficial service, become an heir of salvation? Oh, no!

But, you ask, is anyone saved who does not experience such conflict? No, none! This conflict is more the lot of some than others, but every believer has some experience with it. Such a believer, I do not doubt, will find the workings of his heart described in the foregoing exposition. Do not suppose, however, that mere conflict earns the salvation of the righteous. Oh, no! By pure sovereign grace it is the way to salvation, for God leads His children through conflict and conquest.

You might ask, "If this is so narrow a way, I dread to enter it, for who could live like that?" Remember, it is only for a time. The sufferings of this present time are not to be compared with the glory that will hereafter be revealed to the children of God. Is the labor great? The reward is still greater. Is the contest severe? The victory is more glorious. Though the battle lasts awhile, the glorious result is certain. If you truly desire salvation, do not let these things frighten you. If you knew what joys would be found in the way, you would, with Moses, consider the reproaches of Christ greater riches than all the treasures of Egypt. What's more, this way will not always be marked with distress and difficulty. Oh, no! The anger of the Lord endures but for a moment, whereas in His favor is life. Weeping may endure for a night, but joy comes in the morning. The children of God may rejoice that they have more joy in their hearts than the ungodly when their corn and wine increase. As Psalm 119:14 says, "I have rejoiced in the way of thy testimonies, as much as in all riches." A true child of God will tell you that in the midst of all his tribulations, he would not barter his condition for thousands of worlds. He would say, "If a man gave me all the substance of his house for this condition, I would utterly despise it."

Do you want to be like that? Or will you continue to pursue your sinful course and imagine that you will still be saved? Do not entertain such a notion. Abandon that soul-destroying delusion. Do not deceive yourself with such false hope, I beseech you. Awaken before you find it too late and discover that you have deceived yourself. How astonishing that you can go on so securely and without fear while the righteous are so scarcely saved. Do you imagine that you are righteous? Tell me, I plead with you, what reason do you have for such presumption? The Pharisees imagined the same but were mistaken.

Some people equate righteousness with a kind of civil righteousness, which means living in accord with the laws of the land without injuring or wronging anyone, giving everyone his due, and doing what is equal and just. This conduct is good and constitutes honorable living, but it does not define a righteous Christian. A true Christian is convinced that he is by nature, through original and actual sin, deserving of condemnation; that he daily increases his guilt and therefore is a child of wrath. In addition, he knows that he is unable to deliver himself and will not deliver himself because he is an enemy of God.

Do you contemplate this teaching with sorrow and concern? Has it filled you with anxiety and led you to despair of effecting your own salvation? Are you convinced of the holiness and justice of God? Do you have such views of what you deserve that you could justify God if He cast you into hell? Have you seen that God cannot forgive your sins without continuing the threatened punishment? Has this made you hunger and thirst after the righteousness of the Lord Jesus? Has your heart gone out after Him and nothing else? Are you convinced that you are in absolute need of Him? Have you become so supremely concerned about Jesus that you might be reconciled and made at peace with God through Him, thus obtaining the favor of God to live in communion with Him? Have you, to this end, fled for refuge to the Lord Jesus and surrendered yourself to Him?

Do you desire sanctification by virtue of the merits of Christ that you may lead a holy life? Have you experienced this, and do you daily experience it? Has it been, and is it still true, that you seek reconciliation on account of your sins and betake yourself to the Lord Jesus by prayers and supplications? Do you try to glorify God in all your conduct and by correct behavior edify your neighbor, thus working out your own salvation with fear and trembling?

Then you are happy indeed. But oh, how small is this beginning of new obedience? How often do your actions show the contrary?

You who still hold on to your own righteousness are depending for God's acceptance on the goodness of your hearts or your good intentions. You still rest upon the external duties that you have performed, and doing your best. You who securely pursue this course are putting off the evil day. You are walking according to the course of this world, indulging the lust of the flesh, the lust of the eyes, and the pride of life, which are not of the Father but of the world.

You who refuse to follow the appointed way of salvation marked out by God are unwilling to live so strict and careful a life and walk in the way of tribulation. You say, "The way of the Lord is not equal." You say, "Therefore let us break their bands asunder and cast away their cords from us, for what profit is it that we should serve God and keep His ordinances and walk mournfully before Him?" You are inclined to ridicule distressed souls, call their experience idle fancy, and regard it unnecessary to live circumspectly.

Consider at length how miserable your state is. Oh, that you would see the awfulness of your condition. As long as you are not one of the righteous, you are subject to the wrath of God and the curse of the law. To you, God is an angry Judge. If you continue in this state, you will certainly be lost; for if the righteous are but scarcely saved, you will not be saved at all.

Oh sinner, can you hear this without being concerned? I beg you, think how regrettable your condition will be when you lie upon your sick bed with death in view, and your conscience finally awakes and tells you that you are not one of the righteous. You will then open your failing eyes and brokenly exclaim: "Oh, how I was deceived. How I have found through sad experience that the way to heaven is a narrow way. How can I enter that way? It is too late. The door is closed and I am left without hope. Oh wretched me, to have despised the way of salvation! Now I will be forced to learn through sad experience what I was unwilling to believe before. Oh, dreadful eternity!"

Let me therefore continue trying to persuade you before this sad experience becomes yours. If you ask, "What shall I do?" I will say, search for a correct, clear, and heartfelt knowledge of your sins and of your lost state before God. Recognize your complete helplessness and inability to deliver yourself. Know that you will perish unless the Lord saves you with His sovereign grace. Pray to God, asking Him to impress this on your mind so you may be dismayed and concerned about it and be driven as one lost to the Lord Jesus. With hearty self-condemnation, flee for refuge to Him. Surrender yourself to Him, knowing you are an ungodly person in danger of damnation and in desperate need to be justified, sanctified, delivered from sin, and glorified. Do not rest until you come to this point.

To this end, you must earnestly call on God in prayer and supplication. You must, with Paul, count all things loss and dung that you may win Christ. You must forsake all the vanities and sinful associations of the world. You must be diligent in the use of the means God has provided, such as reading the Word of God and listening to the preaching of that Word. You must also be deeply impressed with your helplessness, so that through the use of those means you may look to the Lord for His Holy Spirit. Go forward with this, I beg you. Do not rest until you are in Christ.

Think much about your miserable state, too. Consider how soon you may die and how you must then appear in the judgment. If you have not been converted in this life, you will be lost. Remember, the Lord is willing to help poor sinners who come to Him in great earnestness. On Christ's behalf, I beg you, take this to heart, that in the Day of Judgment it will not be held against you. Oh, that the Lord, by His Spirit, would impress this on your mind so that you might be converted.

By contrast, how blessed are the people of the Lord who are truly righteous. Of them we may say, "Blessed is the nation whose God is the LORD, and the people whom he hath chosen for his own inheritance"; for "Who shall lay any thing to the charge of God's elect?" They can expect great good, for they are partakers of the Triune God. Of them we may say, "Happy art thou, O Israel: who is like unto thee, O people saved by the LORD!" Truly their happiness is so great that it cannot be expressed, although it is not yet fully known or experienced. They can nonetheless exult, saying, "Beloved, now are we the sons of God, and it doth not yet appear what we shall be: but we know that, when he shall appear, we shall be like him; for we shall see him as he is."

They may be lamps despised in the eyes of those who are at ease in this world, but they are precious in the eyes of the Lord. They may not have much in this life, but they have a wonderful future. They may have to endure much tribulation to enter into the kingdom of God. They may experience what Israel lived through in the wilderness, for this world is also a howling wilderness through which all must pass on the way to the heavenly Canaan.

Therefore, O children of God, do not think it strange that many afflictions come upon you. You have heard that the righteous are scarcely saved. Let this sustain you under your crosses, whether of body or soul, since this is the Lord's usual method with His children. Otherwise, how could it be said, "Comfort ye, comfort ye, my people, saith your God. Speak ye comfortably to Jerusalem, and cry unto her, that her warfare is accomplished"? If the people of the Lord experienced no sorrow and conflict, why would they need comfort?

What else should we expect when we read of those who continually serve God before the throne, "God shall wipe away all tears from their eyes," but that they also suffered sadness and sorrow and shed tears of distress. Be of good courage, then, the Lord will not allow you to be tempted above what you are able to bear. In every temptation, He will also provide a way of escape.

Remember that when the Lord makes you suffer affliction, He does that for your highest good, for He chastens those He loves so they may partake of His holiness. Reckon with Paul that the sufferings of the present time are not worthy to be compared with the glory that will later be revealed. Bear in mind that the time is short, for these light afflictions, which are only for a moment, will work out for you a far weightier glory.

Eventually the Lord will deliver you from all afflictions. When you die, He will bring you into blissful fellowship with Him. You will be with Him forever and will never be separated from Him. Your sorrow will be turned into joy, for the Lamb in the midst of the throne will feed you. He will lead you to the fountains of living waters, where God Himself will wipe all tears from your eyes. Amen.

— 5 —

The Miserable End of the Ungodly

"Where shall the ungodly and the sinner appear?"
— 1 Peter 4:18

The unregenerate and the regenerate differ greatly from one another in the following manner:

- In nature and disposition. The unregenerate are darkness, whereas the regenerate are light in the Lord (Eph. 5:8).
- In conduct and walk. In the Dutch translation of Philippians 3:18, Paul describes the unregenerate as those who "walk differently" from the renewed and godly whose conversation is in heaven. The way in which the godly walk is the straight and narrow way, which is indeed a toilsome way but is nevertheless a way of righteousness, a holy way.

  "The way of life is above to the wise, that he may depart from hell beneath," says Proverbs 15:24. But the ungodly walk according to their own fancy, their own desire, and after the imagination of their hearts in the way of perverseness. This is a broad way and easy to the flesh. It appears good to the eyes of the ungodly, but it is, nevertheless, the way of death which leads to destruction.

- In how they handle adversity and affliction. The ungodly who are called to endure divine judgment murmur against the Lord, saying His ways are not equal (Ezek. 18:25). By contrast, the righteous humble themselves under the Lord's hand, are silent in affliction, justifying

God and praising Him. As Psalm 39:9 says, "I was dumb, I opened not my mouth." Likewise, Micah 7:9 says, "I will bear the indignation of the LORD."

• In how they die. Oh how great is the contrast between the righteous and wicked when called to die! They both must come to an end, but what a different end! The end of the righteous is joy and eternal glory, whereas the end of the ungodly is woe, wretchedness, and condemnation (Ps. 37:38; 1:6). This is what our text, 1 Peter 4:18, declares: "Where shall the ungodly and the sinner appear?" We have already explained the first part of this verse, which sets forth the state of the righteous. Now we will study the miserable end of the ungodly. In explaining this part of the text, we will concentrate on two points: the persons (the ungodly and the sinner) and their miserable state (where they shall appear).

The Ungodly and the Sinner

Some scholars believe that Peter refers here to two classes of persons. They think that the ungodly mentioned here are those who are without God. They are the unbelieving heathen who live without God in the world and without the God of the covenant. They are strangers to the covenant of promise. Sinners, by contrast, are unholy, nominal Christians who confess God with the mouth but deny Him with their works. The ungodly are those who sin against God, whereas sinners are those who sin against their neighbor.

This distinction has no sure foundation, however, since the words *ungodly* and *sinner* are often used interchangeably in Scripture. For example, *ungodly* in Romans 4:5 refers to sinners, and *sinners* in Luke 15:1 is linked with publicans, which is how the heathen are described in Galatians 2:15: "We who are Jews by nature, and not sinners of the Gentiles." Sometimes *sinners* are all who do not serve, honor, and obey God. As John 9:31 says, "We know that God heareth not sinners: but if any man be a worshipper of God, and doeth his will, him he heareth."

Thus, in 1 Peter 4:18, we may properly understand that ungodly and sinners refer to the same people, namely the unregenerate who are by nature sinners, some of whom sin more than others. But as long as they live in that state and live according to the desires of their unrenewed hearts, they are all ungodly and sinners.

An ungodly person, then, is one who does not know and serve God but lives without God. As we tend to call one who is without concern, unconcerned; one not just in his dealings, unjust; and one who knows no happiness, unhappy; so a man without God is ungodly. Ephesians 2:12 describes such a man as "without God in the world," and in 4:18, "Having the understanding darkened, being alienated from the life of God." The ungodly man has no spiritual life but acts only out of his depraved nature. Because of the corrupt workings of the heart, he is deprived of inward peace and quiet. His constant propensity to evil causes him to be tossed about and subject to constant perturbation and commotion of mind. The sinner also injures, disturbs, pollutes, and corrupts others. As 1 Samuel 24:13 says, "Wickedness proceedeth from the wicked."

Such a person is condemned as unrighteous and without a title to life. For to have a title to life is to be a partaker of the Spirit of life. Therefore an ungodly person is not only without God but also without Christ, as Paul says in Ephesians 2:12. All of this is implied in the word *ungodly* or *wicked*. Since there are so many misunderstandings about this point (for however common the word *sinner* is in Scripture, the force and meaning of it are not always understood), we will show from the Word of God that the Holy Spirit uses the word *sinner* or *ungodly* to mean the following:

1. A person without grace. Such a person is not acquainted with God in His supremacy and in His glorious and amiable perfections. Consequently, he does not admire

or love God. In Jeremiah 12:1, the prophet asks, "Wherefore doth the way of the wicked prosper?" He then describes their character: "Thou art near in their mouth, and far from their reins," that is, they are not sincere, they have no real love for God, they know Him not, they do not act from an inward, spiritual principle. Hence all those who are not renewed and changed by the Spirit of life are ungodly.

2. A disquieted and perturbed person. "There is no peace, saith my God, to the wicked," says Isaiah 57:21. The wicked are dominated by the lusts that war against the soul (2 Pet. 2:11). In being carried forward by those lusts, they become greatly uneasy, especially when this uneasiness convinces them that such a course must end in destruction. Their sins, however, are too agreeable to them and evil too powerful for them. They are therefore frequently uneasy, perturbed, and distressed by the convictions of conscience. They experience terror of death and of the Last Judgment. As Proverbs 28:1 says, "The wicked flee when no man pursueth." Psalms 32:10 adds, "Many sorrows shall be to the wicked."

3. A person who disturbs good order. The ungodly, who are disruptive and anxious, frequently defile and injure others. As Proverbs 4:16 says, "They sleep not, except they have done mischief; and their sleep is taken away, unless they cause some to fall." What a bad example such an ungodly person is; how polluted and corrupt are his words! As 1 Corinthians 15:33 says, "Evil communications corrupt good manners." By vile and contaminating speech, they frequently excite the passions and stir up evil emotions in others. "The tongue...is set on fire of hell," says James 3:6; it is "full of deadly poison" (3:8). David thus says in Psalm 6:8, "Depart from me, all ye workers of iniquity." He adds in Psalm 119:115, "Depart from me, ye evildoers: for I will keep the commandments of my God."

4. A person who is condemned. An ungodly person cannot stand in the Judgment. As Psalm 109:7 says, "When he

shall be judged, let him be condemned." An ungodly man is the opposite of a righteous one, and a righteous man, by virtue of the merits of Christ, is free from guilt and the punishment of sin. He has in Christ a title to life and is sanctified by His Spirit. Therefore, an ungodly person is one who, according to God's law, has no title to life. He is not united to Christ by faith and hence has no interest in His sufferings and obedience. He is therefore guilty before God (Ps. 5:10). As John 3:18 says, "He that believeth not [the Son] is condemned already." He has no part in the righteousness of life in Christ.

Such ungodly persons have not yet become partakers of spiritual life through regeneration but live after the flesh and their own corrupt desires. They are not united to Christ and do not live to His glory. As Paul says in Romans 5:6, "In due time Christ died for the ungodly." There are various types of ungodly persons, however. These include:

1. The grossly wicked. These monsters in human form are dead weights in the world. They are continually immersed in their wickedness and glory in it. As Isaiah says, "they declare their sin as Sodom" (Isa. 3:9). In Romans 3:13-18, 1 Corinthians 6:10, and Galatians 5:19-21, Paul says that by their fleshly works these people clearly show that they are ungodly.

2. People who show external propriety of conduct but are without God. People who live outwardly correct, moral, and unblamable lives and avoid gross sins do not think that they are ungodly. They view only fornicators, whoremongers, drunkards, thieves, and such as ungodly and profane men. Because they are free from such gross sin, they think, like the Pharisee in Luke 18, that they are not ungodly. Yet one who knows and fears the Lord can readily see from their conduct that they are ungodly. As Psalm 36:1 says, "The transgression of the wicked saith within my heart, that there is no fear of God before his eyes." It is as if the psalmist says, "They may think what

they please — I am quite convinced they are wicked; their life and walk testify they have no fear of God."

3. People who assume they are righteous. Some people refuse to believe they are unrighteous. They flatter themselves by assuming they are righteous, but Christ warns them in Matthew 9:13: "I am not come to call the righteous." Such people are offended at being called ungodly, but in the language of the Holy Ghost this is what they are.

The Jews who said that God was their Father were such people. The Lord Jesus demonstrated to them that they had no part in God but were ungodly and of their father the devil. They were so offended at this that they tried to stone Jesus (John 8:41-44). When the Lord said to them that they were blind, didn't know God, and were alienated from the life of God, they resisted, saying, "Are we blind also?" (John 9:40). Likewise, ignorant, nominal Christians regard as uncharitable any suggestions that they may not be in fellowship with God and Christ. Their actions exhibit no life with God.

4. People who only look righteous. Some people outwardly look righteous, but inwardly they are spiritually dead (Rev. 3:1). Outwardly they have escaped the pollution of the world and appear to be living a godly life. They behave as if they were God's people (Ezek. 33:31), but in reality they are ungodly. They have no title to life in Christ, they do not walk with the Spirit, and they are strangers to communion with God. In a word, they are hypocrites. We must therefore understand that the ungodly in our text refers not only to people who live in open and gross sin but also to all unconverted, natural men who, however much adorned with civil virtues and proper conduct, are not yet united to Christ. They are not sanctified by the Holy Spirit and have no title to life.

Our text adds, "sinner," not to say that an ungodly man is not a sinner, but to better express the nature of man. All men are sinners because they are transgressors of the divine law and destitute of the holiness required by God in His law. But ungodly here also means the impenitent sinner who takes pleasure in sin and continually wanders from the right way. He lives in sin and has contracted a sinful habit. His calling, as it were, is sin. He is therefore deservedly called a sinner.

This is true of each unconverted person, since everything he does is not for the glory of God. Though he does not always sin, yet he does not hate sin. He may avoid some sins, but not from love and fear of God as much as because he lacks the opportunity, disposition, means, or calling to do them.

Furthermore, the sins that he commits rule in him; he lives with delight in them. Like Ahab, he is sold to do evil (1 Kings 21:20).

Where They Shall Appear

When the apostle asks where the ungodly and sinners shall appear, we should not suppose he is doubting, much less denying, that they shall appear before the judgment seat of Christ. Rather, that is presupposed, as in verse 5 of this chapter and in 2 Corinthians 5:10, which says, "We must all appear before the judgment seat of Christ." In addition, verses 14 and 15 of Jude say, "Behold, the Lord cometh with ten thousand of his saints, to execute judgment upon all, and to convince all that are ungodly among them."

Thus, when Peter asks, "Where shall they appear?" he suggests the sad and awful end of the ungodly, as stated in verse 17. The situation is like that of a criminal who, being summoned before a tribunal, is examined, convicted, and condemned. When Peter asks, "Where shall he appear?" he is suggesting that, unlike the righteous, the ungodly shall not be able to stand in the judgment but be judged and condemned. Psalm 1:5 expresses it this way: "Therefore the ungodly shall not stand in the judgment, nor sinners in the congregation of the righteous."

The miserable condition of the ungodly or sinner prohibits him from going anywhere either in this life or in the divine judgment to come with comfort or boldness. As Proverbs 11:31 says, "Behold, the righteous shall be recompensed in the earth: much more the wicked and the sinner." Other places that the sinner cannot go without fear and terror include:

1. Before God in prayer. John 9:31 says, "We know that God heareth not sinners," and Proverbs 15:8 that an unrighteous person's sacrifice is "abomination to the LORD." Proverbs 28:9 adds, "He that turneth away his ear from hearing the law, even his prayer shall be abomination." A sinner may offer many prayers, but because they are offered out of mere custom and not through the Spirit, they are not acceptable to God. As the Lord says, "When ye spread forth your hands, I will hide mine eyes from you: yea, when ye make many prayers, I will not hear" (Isa. 1:15). Indeed, as Psalm 109:7 says, even the prayers of the ungodly become sin.

2. Into God's house to hear His Word. Going there is neither profitable to the unbeliever nor pleasing to God. In Isaiah 1:12, God asks, "When ye come to appear before me, who hath required this at your hand, to tread my courts?" He asks this because the sinner's heart is filled with "filthiness and superfluity of naughtiness" (James 1:21) and prejudice against the Word of God. He comes not to do what the Lord tells him but to find fault or to harden his heart. Therefore, the Lord says to the prophet Ezekiel: "They come unto thee as the people cometh, and they sit before thee as my people, and they hear thy words, but they will not do them" (Ezek. 33:31).

3. To the Lord's Table. Oh how wretched when the seal of grace becomes a token of condemnation to the ungodly! God's table becomes a snare to the sinner; he eats and drinks judgment to himself because he discerns not the Lord's body (1 Cor. 11:29), for he approaches unworthily,

without real spiritual life and without suitable examination and preparation.

4. Into death. How shall the sinner stand before death, the king of terrors? It is the place where everything desirable shall cease and everything that is dreadful shall come upon him. Having lived in ungodliness, he shall die accursed. Oh how fearful must be the thought of death to one whose only care is in this life! Oh how dreadful when death shall seize him! So it was with Belshazzar when he saw the fingers of a man's hand writing upon a wall. As Daniel 5:6 says, "Then the king's countenance was changed, and his thoughts troubled him, so that the joints of his loins were loosed, and his knees smote one against another."

5. At the Last Judgment. How shall the sinner appear at this time? It is true, he shall rise again but only to shame and everlasting contempt (Dan. 12:2). He will appear in the judgment, but as a goat at the left hand where he will be unable to endure the strict scrutiny of the omniscient Judge and the just judgment of the Almighty. When called to give account of every idle word he has spoken, his mouth shall be stopped, and the Judge shall pronounce upon him the fearful sentence, "Depart from me, ye cursed, into everlasting fire, prepared for the devil and his angels." He will then "go away into everlasting punishment" (Matt. 25). Hell, the place of the damned, has been prepared for him that he may live there forever.

The sinner will not be able to stand on account of the vindictive justice of God. Oh how awfully miserable is he who must appear there! How shall his laughter be turned into mourning, his brief prosperity be paid for with a never-ending curse. When he appears there, he will howl for sorrow of heart, gnaw his tongue, and gnash his teeth in inexpressible anguish and pain. He will cry to the mountains and rocks, "Fall on us" (Rev. 6).

This is a necessary consequence. For if the righteous be but scarcely saved, the ungodly and sinner shall certainly perish, as the apostle concludes. A righteous person differs as much from the ungodly and sinner as heaven differs from hell, as light differs from darkness. Their ends, therefore, are exceedingly different. If a righteous person must endure so much affliction, what can the ungodly who still lives in his sins expect? If he who loves God experiences so much suffering and sorrow, why shouldn't one who hates God and is His enemy suffer? If it pleases God to visit and chastise His children, the objects of His favor, for their infirmities, how shall He not avenge Himself upon His adversaries for the sins and evil deeds they committed all the days of their lives?

As Solomon writes, "Behold, the righteous shall be recompensed in the earth: much more the wicked and the sinner." An ungodly person is without God. He is alienated from the life of God and neither fears nor serves Him. Therefore there is no consolation or salvation for him. A sinner living in sin will have no part with the righteous; for "what fellowship hath righteousness with unrighteousness?...or what part hath he that believeth with an infidel?" (2 Cor. 6:14-15).

Where then shall the ungodly and sinner appear in the hereafter, since in this life he refuses to come to God? God calls such a one to blissful communion in Christ, but the ungodly says by his deeds, if not by his words, "Depart from us; for we desire not the knowledge of thy ways" (Job 21:14); "cause the Holy One of Israel to cease from before us" (Isa. 30:11). The holy Jesus invites the sinner to come to Him; but the sinner will not come (John 5:40). He has greater love for sin and the world. God calls him to repentance, but he continues to reject God. God calls him to tears of sorrow, but he remains at ease in his vain delights. Since he does not strive, he will not enter in; since he does not assault the kingdom of heaven with violence, he cannot take it. Since with full strides he pursues the broad way so delightful to him, he has nothing to expect but everlasting destruction. This is sure.

Where They Shall Truly Appear

It follows from the vindictive justice of God, who will by no means clear the guilty and who can have no communion with the sinner, that he will therefore condemn and punish the sinner. As David says in Psalm 5:4-6: "For thou art not a God that hath pleasure in wickedness: neither shall evil dwell with thee. The foolish shall not stand in thy sight: thou hatest all workers of iniquity...the LORD will abhor the bloody and deceitful man." Is not the righteous scarcely, narrowly, and with much toil and labor saved? Then the ungodly and sinner has nothing to expect but eternal condemnation.

From these things, we see the sad and wretched end of unconverted, ungodly sinners. It is also plain that though the ungodly are prosperous, their prosperity is vain and temporary. Their happiness is short, and their joy is but an illusion which ends in everlasting anguish and grief. However well they seem fortified against calamities of every kind, they have suspended over them an unexpected and most awful desolation by which they shall perish. David could therefore say: "Fret not thyself because of evildoers, neither be thou envious against the workers of iniquity. For they shall soon be cut down like the grass, and wither as the green herb" (Ps. 37:1-2). The worldly rank, reputation, power, and wealth of the ungodly may be great, but if we go into the sanctuary and consider their end, we will see how God sets them in slippery places and casts them down into destruction. As Psalm 73:19 says, "How are they brought into desolation, as in a moment! They are utterly consumed with terrors."

Behold then, the awful state of the unconverted. Take notice, ungodly sinners who find your pleasure in sin and are without fear and concern. Behold here the awful and miserable state in which you are before God. You who have not realized you are lost, have not been freed from your own righteousness, your own strength, and your good works, and therefore have not yet become a partaker of the righteousness of Jesus Christ; you, who are not yet born again, have not experienced a saving change in heart and life, but continue in the old man, the old, corrupt nature, and therefore still live in sin, hear this sad message: Woe unto you! it shall go ill with you. If the righteous are scarcely saved, where shall you appear? It is true that you shall appear in judgment before the great God, the omniscient, almighty Judge. But you shall not be able to stand in the judgment; you will be condemned. Oh consider this, I beseech you: when your Judge shall rise up, what will you answer Him? (Job 31:14). How will you vindicate yourself against all that shall be brought against you? Everything shall witness against you: all the means of grace and all the sermons you have heard. The numerous warnings, exhortations, and instructions you have enjoyed shall condemn you and deprive you of every excuse. All the mercy and patience of God and all His benefits which should have led you to repentance will aggravate your sins. The law will curse you (Deut. 29:27). So will the gospel (1 Cor. 16:22). So will your own conscience, which will be compelled to assent to all these things and set your sins in order before your eyes. Furthermore, the Spirit of God, whose motions and strivings you have so long resisted, will then become your enemy.

Oh sinner, where will you appear? What will you reply to all these accusations at the Judgment? Think for a moment what you will say when you are required to give account for every idle word (Matt. 12). When condemned, you will immediately be banished from the presence of your Judge. You will not be able to stand before God, for He hates all workers of iniquity (Ps. 5:5). He will publicly say to you, "Depart from me, ye that work iniquity" (Matt. 7).

How little do you now realize the dreadfulness of being

separated from God, who is the greatest good! The enjoyment of the gracious presence of God, which the saints experience in this life, is more precious to them than the whole world. Even though they are now favored with but a glimpse of His countenance, they exclaim, "In his favor is life" (Ps. 30:5). Indeed, as precious as life may be, the saints can still testify that the lovingkindness of God "is better than life" (Ps. 63:3). If they are deprived of this, they are perplexed, disquieted, and troubled. As the psalmist says, "Thou didst hide thy face and I was troubled" (Ps. 30:7).

Think then how fearful it will be to be forever deprived of perfect communion with that blessed God. Oh how dreadful will be the loss of divine favor! Where will you appear when you shall be delivered to devils? When they drag you away to hell, no one will be able to help you. Everyone will forsake you. It will be too late to look for help. Oh, my heart shudders as I imagine in what condition, in what distress and hellish agony the poor sinner will be when he perceives that he is forever forsaken by God, by Christ, by angels, and by saints, and finds himself in the company of devils who will torment him. Before him, he will see an angry Judge; around him, devils who are ready to execute divine vengeance; within him, a gnawing worm; above him, a closed heaven that will refuse him entrance; beneath him, a gaping hell that will devour him. This will be the place where the ungodly and sinner will appear and remain forever. Oh wretched eternity! Oh eternal wretchedness!

Readers, are your hearts not affected by these things? When David, a man after God's own heart, thought upon the judgment, he exclaimed, "My flesh trembleth for fear of thee; and I am afraid of thy judgments" (Ps. 119:120). Can you hear this without holy concern? Are you not impressed by a subject of eternal worth, which so intimately concerns you? I understand the reason for this strange phenomenon. So deluded is mankind that when a person reads about the ungodly in the Word of God, he supposes that it refers only to the openly and abominably wicked, such as blasphemers, profane swearers, murderers, thieves, whoremongers, drunkards, and similar persons. Those who are free from such gross sins and whose lives are somewhat characterized by orderliness and external propriety of deportment are presumed to be good Christians and godly persons, even if they do not have the slightest indication of grace and spiritual life. In the ordinary associations of life, they are honorable in character, but they are, nevertheless, ungodly and sinners. The Spirit of God, whose decisions should guide our judgment, describes as unconverted all who are not in communion with God, united with Christ, and sanctified by His Spirit. This is so even though they are distinguished by proper demeanor in their associations with others and attentive to the outward forms of religion. All who are still in their natural, unregenerate state are, without distinction, ungodly and sinners, as we have now shown. Oh that it were suitably felt!

Satan devises to deceive and persuade the unconverted that they are not so wicked; that others are far more evil and sinful than they; that their works are not so corrupt; that it is others, not they who are reproved and threatened by the preacher; that they possess many virtues; that their state is not so miserable; and that ungodly persons are only abandoned wretches who are guilty of open and gross crimes and who are punished by the magistrate. Surely, they are not such. By this vile deceit of Satan, the edge of the sword of the Spirit is blunted and prevented from penetrating. It effects no saving change. Hence it is

1. Men are not brought to reflection and knowledge of themselves. When they hear from others or read in the Word of God "What hast thou to do to declare my statutes, or that thou shouldest take my covenant in thy mouth?" (Ps. 50:16); "The sacrifice of the wicked is an abomination to the LORD" (Prov. 15:8); and similar expressions, they are not at all affected. They see only the rudest classes of man-

kind in these texts, not themselves. They do not apply the texts to themselves and hence remain insensible.

2. They reject repentance. Portions of Scripture, however moving, fail to move sinners. Consider Ezekiel 33:11, which says, "As I live, saith the Lord GOD, I have no pleasure in the death of the wicked; but that the wicked turn from his way and live: turn ye, turn ye from your evil ways; for why will ye die, O house of Israel?" Or Romans 4:5, which says that God "justifieth the ungodly." Or Isaiah 55:7, which promises, "Let the wicked forsake his way, and the unrighteous man his thoughts: and let him return unto the LORD, and he will have mercy upon him." The ungodly and sinners read and hear such passages without being moved. They do not believe the words, and they do not believe that they are ungodly and sinners. Therefore they remain unconverted and unjustified.

3. They continue in their sin. They go on securely and unconcerned in sin, in opposition to all warnings, threatenings, and divine judgments, however fearful. Let it be said to them: "Woe unto the wicked! it shall be ill with him" (Isa. 3:11). Let the fearful declaration thunder in their hearing: "The curse of the LORD is in the house of the wicked" (Prov. 3:33). Let them hear: "But after thy hardness and impenitent heart treasurest up unto thyself wrath against the day of wrath and revelation of the righteous judgment of God; who will render...indignation and wrath...tribulation and anguish upon every soul of man that doeth evil" (Rom. 2:5-9). Such admonitions do not disturb them. They do not fear such warnings and have no compassion on themselves because, alas, they have a faulty understanding of an ungodly person and refuse to acknowledge themselves as such.

Oh sinner, if this truth were now revealed to your soul, which is so composed and comfortable, what fear and concern would then arise in your heart. How you would cry to God day and night to be merciful to you!

Should we then indulge in flatteries and say to you that it may yet be well with you — that you have performed many good acts and that there are worse sinners than yourself? Shall we say that since you are baptized and have made a profession of religion or that you attend the public service of God's house that you may be of good cheer? Could that make you happy?

Certainly not. We would be daubing with untempered mortar (Ezek. 13:14) if we said so. The Word of God declares that natural men who do not have the Spirit, are alienated from the life of God, and are strangers to communion with Christ are ungodly and unconverted sinners. Shall His Word have no effect upon you? What advantage would it be to you if we deceived and destroyed you? How he who is misled and deceived at length will forever reproach and curse him who has thus dealt with him. As Proverbs 24:24 says, "He that saith unto the wicked, Thou art righteous; him shall the people curse."

You admit the Word of God is true and that it shall judge us. The Word offers many characteristics of the ungodly and the sinner by which we are to examine ourselves and determine whether we are such, including:

1. An ungodly and a sinner commits sin. 1 John 3:8-9 says, "He that committeth sin is of the devil....Whosoever is born of God doth not commit sin." He that is of the devil is certainly ungodly and is known to commit sin. Now you who commit sin without inward opposition, struggle, and conflict; who find satisfaction and delight in sin; who are not humbled on account of it and ashamed before God after committing it; who do not sincerely mourn it and are not tenderly affected by it, saying, Oh! "what have I done?" (Jer. 8) or "Woe unto me that I have sinned" and are not desirous of reconciliation and sanctification — you most certainly are ungodly and unconverted sinners.

2. An ungodly person has no title to life. However externally correct in his conduct, an ungodly person is not

united to Christ, is a stranger to communion with Him, and therefore has no title to life. If your life is not fixed upon Christ as Surety, if you do not receive Him for justification and sanctification and do not long after Him and look unto Him, if you are not busy praying to Him that you may be justified through Him, it is apparent that you are an ungodly, unconverted sinner.

3. An ungodly person is without grace. Such a person is destitute of spiritual life and is therefore unregenerated and no partaker of the divine nature. However fair your exterior, you are an unconverted sinner if you are not changed without and within, effectually loosened from things here below, and attached to things divine and heavenly.

4. An ungodly person is not at peace. Isaiah 57:21 says, "There is no peace, saith my God, to the wicked." Proverbs 28:1 adds, "The wicked flee when no man pursueth," for they have no peace with God, with conscience, or with others. They are anxious and fearful of natural dangers. A threat, a fierce look, or a contagious disease can make them afraid. And how easily disturbed they are at the thought of death. How restless they become under God's affliction! They live in disagreement with others and corrupt them with their anger, their impurity, their slander and backbiting, their covetous desires, and with any other ways that opportunity offers. These are true marks of the ungodly.

5. The ungodly hate godliness. However proper they appear, the ungodly are at heart haters and opponents of the narrow way of godliness. "They that forsake the law praise the wicked," says Solomon in Proverbs 28:4. Although they may practice some virtues, that is not out of true love or virtue because they hate true goodness. The righteous find joy in doing good, but doing good is a burden to the ungodly. Like the ancient Jews, they proclaim, "What a weariness!"

If only you would believe and see how wretched is your condition and its consequences. If you had a correct view of your corrupt and wretched state, how you would loathe yourselves and your sins. If you desire salvation, we beg you to forsake the broad way in which you have been walking and the lifestyle practiced by mankind. Forsake ungodliness. Let your past life suffice in fulfilling the will of the flesh in the indulgence of your sinful lusts. You must cease from sin and seek to rule your lives in the time you have left according to the will of God. To this end we must do the following:

- Forsake our former sinful lives. We must lament, hate, and flee the way we used to live. The sins that were once agreeable and satisfying to us must now be bitter to our souls. They must fill us with grief and sincere sorrow. We must weep over them with tears of agony, manifesting regret that we have provoked God with so many sins. With sincere hearts we must acknowledge and confess our sins before the Lord, saying with David, "I acknowledged my sin unto thee, and mine iniquity have I not hid. I said, I will confess my transgressions unto the LORD" (Ps. 32:5). Oh that our sins were so heavy a burden upon our hearts that sincere regret for them would cause us to seek forgiveness from our Judge! Like David in Psalm 51:1 we would cry, "Have mercy upon me, O God, according to thy lovingkindness: according unto the multitude of thy tender mercies blot out my transgressions."

  This sorrow must be sincere. We must realize that sin is sin because it is contrary to the holiness of God and His law. Therefore, as 2 Corinthians 7:11 teaches, we must proceed with great care, cleansing ourselves of indignation, fear, vehement desire, zeal, and revenge.

- Pursue holiness. It is not enough not to be ungodly. Those who hate ungodliness demonstrate that by becoming religious and godly. They must seek after and perform that which is good. Hating sin and pursuing godliness are inseparably united. As Paul says in Titus 2:11-12: "For the grace of God that bringeth salvation hath appeared to all men, teaching us that, denying ungodliness and worldly lusts, we should live soberly, righteously, and godly, in this present world."

Since we are helpless and cannot overcome our evil and depraved nature on our own, we must ask God for the grace of His Holy Spirit and make use of all means to obtain a clear view and good understanding of the exceeding evil of sin. For however plausible it may sometimes appear, sin is nothing but deformity. Its origin is the devil. He that sinneth is "of the devil." Sin exhibits Satan's character, bears his image, and is the fruit of darkness.

Sin scorns God's majesty and is contrary to His holiness. It despises His goodness, denies His authority, questions His omniscience, and resents His justice. In a word, sin hates God and merits eternal condemnation. It is impossible to see sin as an abomination and a deformity without regarding it with hatred.

We must guard ourselves against the very beginnings of sin. Since sin acquires mastery over us by degrees, we must shrink back with horror from its subtle approach. We must avoid the least and smallest sins if we would escape the greatest. We should also remind ourselves that God who is omniscient sees and hears and notes all things, and that in the coming judgment we must appear before Him to give an account of all we do.

Is anyone now convinced that he has been ungodly and unconverted? Let him not think that it is too late, lest he yield to despair. Still, such a state is better than that of the moral, careless, and secure. All who have ever been saved were once ungodly and sinners. God alone justifies the ungodly (Rom. 4). Whoever would be justified must first see that he is ungodly. God demands of such that they then forsake their wickedness and return to Him (Isa. 55:7).

How moving God's words are to the wicked. Ezekiel 33:14-15 promises, "If he turn...he shall not die." How can you hear this without emotion? Why do you not cast yourself upon your knees in humble confession, saying like

Israel in Psalm 106:6: "We have committed iniquity, we have done wickedly?"

Why are you not driven to the Lord Jesus, who died for the ungodly (Rom. 5:6), with the desire to be justified by His blood and sanctified by His Spirit? He possesses a fullness that adapts to all the needs of a sinner. He is exceedingly gracious and willing to communicate that grace to penitent sinners.

Jesus stands before us with extended arms, inviting sinners and the ungodly to repentance. Oh let him who senses his sins and his state of condemnation before God surrender himself to the Lord Jesus! Let him who senses his helplessness and unwillingness and is convinced of Jesus' all-sufficiency and willingness turn to God. Let him who desires to be reconciled to God through the merits of Christ and to be sanctified by His Spirit go to the Lord Jesus. He that cometh to Him, He will in no wise cast out (John 6:37).

I conclude with the words of the prophet Isaiah, "Seek ye the LORD while he may be found, call ye upon him while he is near: let the wicked forsake his way, and the unrighteous man his thoughts: and let him return unto the LORD, and he will have mercy upon him; and to our God, for he will abundantly pardon" (Isa. 55:6-7). Amen.

SECOND COLLECTION

———

A Small Collection
of Sermons

FROM THE

Old and New Testament

FIRST PRINTED A. D. 1773

PREFACE TO THE DISCERNING READER

Worthy reader, you possibly imagine that the author of the following sermons might have spared his pains, since the church already groans beneath the burden of a multitude of printed discourses. Of this I am well aware, but in this portion of the world there are few in the possession of the ordinary reader; besides, I am the man everyone talks about — beloved by many, hated by many more. Why then should not my friends be permitted to bring to light that which I teach? To this is to be added, that these discourses were delivered after I had been graciously restored from a severe affliction, through which, for a considerable time, I could not discharge the duties of my office. Let it serve as no offense to you, that they are not written according to the rules of the art; much less according to the new and highly fashionable style. I am not ignorant of the needs of the present age, and I am not writing for the learned but for the plain and uneducated. It shall suffice me if I express myself according to the style of the Holy Spirit, in a clear and simple manner, so that I can be understood by all.

The distinguished Herman Witsius, in his *Controversy of the Lord*, enumerates this among the reasons why, at the period of the Reformation, discourses produced more good than they do at present. The preachers, being frequently uneducated men and not knowing how to gratify their hearers with far-fetched or inflated words of human wisdom, sought to reach the heart by speaking the words of God in demonstration of the Spirit and with power.

Some of these sermons are upon texts suggested to me by friends, with the request that I would treat them. For the most part they have been composed when I was not at home, but at North Branch or Raritan; hence there have crept in some things which will demand an indulgent eye. But there will also probably be found in them some things that will be edifying, for "who hath despised the day of small things"?

Be that as it may, these sermons will be forced upon no one. He that is not pleased with them may lay them aside. Truly we live in times so sorrowful that the discourse of Hosea 4 may well be regarded a word spoken in season. The fear there expressed may appear to many as unfounded, but has already, to a great extent, been realized; for since that time judgments have been multiplied, so that I may say, the thing that I feared is come; and what the future shall still disclose is known to the all-wise God alone. It will be nothing desirable unless there be a general turning to the Lord. Oh, that we were wise, and heard the rod and Him who hath appointed it, and submitted to divine chastisements, that the Lord might not withdraw His blessing from us, and make us desolate, and a land not inhabited (Jer. 6:8)!

Farewell, reader. Peruse these discourses without prejudice and for edification; to which end, the Lord graciously vouchsafe His blessing. I seek not praise, I fear not blame.

— Theodorus Jacobus Frelinghuysen

March 2, 1733

— 6 —

The Sins of Youth Lamented

*"Remember not the sins of my youth, nor my trans-
gressions: according to thy mercy remember thou me
for thy goodness' sake, O LORD."*

— Psalm 25:7

Ancient Grecian history (in which fables are often used to
convey many useful moral lessons) teaches that heroic
Hercules, while young, doubted which course to pursue to
find happiness and renown. He was confronted by two females, one dignified in appearance, modestly attired, and
worthy of reverence. The other had a full and fair countenance, ourtwardly happy appearance, and was decked with
ornaments. Each woman commended a different mode of
life. The one woman was Virtue, the other Pleasure.

Hercules, acting out of noble principle, determined to
follow Virtue. By this means he attained a high level of distinction and performed illustrious deeds. This story is not
true, but is the fictional product of some fertile imagination. It was designed to show how young people stand at a
point where two ways meet. The way of pleasure invites
them to walk according to their natural desire. The other
invites them to wisdom and virtue.

The story teaches that the way chosen in youth generally becomes habit. Young people who refuse to listen to the
voice of pleasure and choose the path of virtue are truly
wise. The contrary, however, is too frequently the case. The

majority of young people choose the way of pleasure. When they finally come to themselves in manhood or in old age, they lament their earlier choice. Like the psalmist in our text, they pray, "Remember not the sins of my youth, nor my transgressions: according to thy mercy remember thou me for thy goodness' sake, O LORD."

In the preceding verse, David prayed in general for the tokens of God's mercy and kindness. He now expresses in particular how he desires to experience those tokens. He asks, "Remember not the sins of my youth, nor my transgressions: according to thy mercy remember thou me for thy goodness' sake, O LORD." Let us consider the meaning of three things in this text:

• The deprecation: "Remember not my sins,"
• The supplication: "According to thy mercy remember thou me,"
• The motive: "For thy goodness' sake, O LORD."

The Meaning of Youth

We will first consider the time of life of which the psalmist speaks. We understand youth to mean the early years of man that begin at birth and extend to full manhood. Youth thus refers to all stages of human life before old age. It refers to a small, speechless child, such as Samuel when he was first weaned (1 Sam. 1:24), and elsewhere it refers to those who are older, though not yet in old age. We thus read, "Saul said to David, Thou art not able to go against this Philistine to fight with him: for thou art but a youth" (1 Sam. 17:33) because "youth" refers to young persons from earliest childhood to complete maturity.

Furthermore, when David mentions the sins of his youth, he is using the phrase in an extensive sense. The term includes:

1. Original sin (Ps. 51:7).
2. The sins of childhood. As Genesis 8:21 says, "For the imagination of man's heart is evil from his youth." The first

thing discernible in children is sin and depravity, which expresses itself as anger, revenge, hatred, envy, jealousy, pride, avarice, earthlymindedness, and the like.

3. The sins of late childhood. Sin is often evident in the period of life when boys and girls advance to adulthood. Proverbs 22:15 teaches that "foolishness is bound in the heart of a child." In this stage of life, young people are often stubborn, trifling, inconsiderate, disobedient, luxurious, haughty, vain, prodigal, wanton, and neglectful of duty.

4. The sins of early adulthood. Whether single or married, so long as we are in full vigor and not yet old, these, too, are the sins of our youth.

We may presume that the psalmist David who laments the sins of his youth here wrote these words when he was an old man or was at least a mature man and father. As he sees the temptations to which young people are subject and how inclined they are to evil, he reflects upon his own sins. It is true that all young people are not equally given to excess. Nevertheless, who would not admit that in one's early years one could not be charged with the sins and acts of inconsideration? For this reason, the psalmist prays, "Remember not the sins of my youth."

When Scripture says that God remembers sins, it means that God punishes sins with corporal or spiritual afflictions and chastisements. Job, the man of God, thus complains: "For thou writest bitter things against me, and makest me to possess the iniquities of my youth" (Job 13:26). Likewise, penitent Ephraim cries, "Surely after that I was turned, I repented; and after that I was instructed, I smote upon my thigh: I was ashamed, yea, even confounded, because I did bear the reproach of my youth" (Jer. 31:19).

When the psalmist prays, "Remember not," he is asking God:

- To forgo punishing his sins with corporal or spiritual judgments.
- To spare him the agony of reflecting upon them with self-reproach and distress; rather, forgiving them for the

Lord's sake and granting him comfort and assurance of forgiveness (Ps. 51:3-11).

The psalmist also asks the Lord not to remember his transgressions. Although all sins are transgressions, there is a difference. Transgressions refer to unfaithfulness to solemn engagements and are committed with more or less deliberation and willfulness. The psalmist is thus praying here for forgiveness of both his original and actual sins — those committed in the rashness of youth as well as those which he might have committed through his whole life to the present day. He also does not deny that he voluntarily and purposely committed many.

The Gift of Mercy

The second part of our text, "According to thy mercy, remember thou me," includes a word that was used earlier in the exposition of this psalm. By "mercy," David meant: "According to Thy sovereign grace, through which Thou canst and wilt show favor to the unworthy, even to the hell-deserving, by forgiving their sins, and from the fullness of Thine all-sufficiency granting them grace for grace."

Furthermore, David uses the word with emphasis, pleading, "Remember thou me, O Lord" as if to say, "Oh God, Thou whose honor it is to be gracious to penitent sinners, indeed, Thou who alone canst forgive sins." Micah said it this way: "Who is a God like unto thee, that pardoneth iniquity, and passeth by the transgression of the remnant of his heritage?"(7:18).

David follows those words with a plea, "For thy goodness' sake, O LORD." Scholars believe this alludes to Exodus 33, which describes how Israel sinned and God determined to destroy or forsake His people. Moses interceded for them, and as evidence that he had found grace, pleaded with God to show His glory. Jehovah's answer was, "I will make all my goodness [the same word in the original as we have here] pass before thee, and I will proclaim the name of the LORD before thee; and will be gracious to whom I will be gracious" (Ex. 33:19).

The result was that Jehovah proclaimed His name: "The LORD, the LORD God, merciful and gracious, longsuffering, and abundant in goodness and truth" (Ex. 34:6). Moses later appealed to this Lord of mercy when he once more interceded for Israel (Num. 14:19).

This goodness of God is wondrously great (Ps. 136). It is the ground upon which all believers, after their wanderings and failings, may approach God. Psalm 13:5 says, "But I have trusted in thy mercy." We may call on the Lord God of mercy (Psa. 59:10,17). No wonder that David adds in our text, "For thy goodness' sake," and in the eleventh verse, "For thy name's sake."

In praying for the forgiveness of his sins, the psalmist appropriately appeals to the goodness of Jehovah. Because God is good, He is ready to forgive (Ps. 86:5). We read that after the people of Israel sinned, Hezekiah prayed that the good Lord would pardon them. Scripture tells us, "the Lord hearkened to Hezekiah, and healed the people" (2 Chron. 30:18-20). Ezra 8:22 says the hand of the Lord is upon all those who seek Him for good. Nehemiah 13:31 says the prophet pleaded upon this goodness of Jehovah, saying, "Remember me...for good." And Hosea 3:5 says, "Afterward shall the children of Israel return, and seek the LORD their God, and David their king; and shall fear the LORD and his goodness in the latter days."

The words of our text teach us that youth has special temptations. The young are vain, tenacious of their own opinions, devoted to pleasure, and impetuous in their feelings. They are improvident and fickle because they are destitute of experience. Daily observation confirms this. The reason the multitudes are destroyed is much due to their behavior when they were young. Although all young people are not guilty of excess (for many are kept from much evil by restraining grace or a good education), who would not acknowledge that in his youthful days he was guilty of impropriety? Even David, who feared God from his youth (Ps. 71:5-6), remembered that in his youth he had committed many sins. Recalling them distressed him greatly, causing him to pray, "Remember not the sins of my youth, nor my transgressions."

Second, we may learn that the elect, who are brought to God, are not only convinced of the sins of their youth at their conversion but subsequently become so struck by them that they are distressed and deeply humbled on account of them. This is evident in David, the man after God's heart; also Job (13:26) and Jeremiah, who says, "Surely after that I was turned, I repented; and after that I was instructed, I smote upon my thigh: I was ashamed, yea, even confounded, because I did bear the reproach of my youth" (Jer. 31:19).

What do you think, you listeners who are advanced in years? Have the sins of your youth come to your minds? You will probably say, "Yes, we have thought of those sins and spoken of them." But friends, that is not the issue. Have you so felt those sins that you have come to repent of them? How clearly are you exposed here — you who not only reflect upon the wanton extravagances of your youth with delight but also talk of them with such satisfaction that clearly you have never repented of them. You think you were such heroes in fighting, drinking, card-playing, horse-racing, dancing, acts of licentiousness, and deceiving unsuspecting females.

If you were truly penitent, you would not think of your sins without grief, or speak of them without tears, much like Augustine in his confession. You aged sinners, the very things that should grieve you are what give you satisfaction. You laugh at what should make you weep. This is wrong. You should say with Jeremiah, "We lie down in our shame, and our confusion covereth us: for we have sinned against the LORD our God, we and our fathers, from our youth even unto this day, and have not obeyed the voice of the LORD our God" (3:25).

We also recognize those among you who regard the sins of your youth as so trivial that you excuse them. You misapply the Scripture which says, "When I was a child, I spake as a child, I understood as a child, I thought as a child." What a vile perversion. Read the Dutch annotations, which say, "The apostle compares the knowledge we have in this life with the knowledge of small children."

David's experience was quite different. If you were blessed enough to possess the spirit of true repentance, your experience would be similar to his. But if you persist in your impenitence, be assured that you will once again taste the bitterness of the sins of your youth. God will bring you to judgment (Eccl. 11:9).

This should also convict you who recognize that you lived in an immoral and unruly manner in your youth but suppose that those sins were forgiven because you are no longer practicing such gross improprieties. You know that you have never been suitably distressed and penitent on account of them. Well, God does not forgive sin until we become suitably distressed and penitent on account of them. David, a man after God's own heart who trusted in the Lord from his youth (Ps. 71:5-6), was still affected by the sins of his youth in his manhood.

I beg you, older men and women, to review your lives so that you might perceive the sins that may be charged against you before God. How important it is that you so see and feel your sins that you are constrained with the psalmist to pray, "Remember not the sins of my youth, nor my transgressions: according to thy mercy remember thou me for thy goodness' sake, O LORD" (Ps. 25:7). Do not rest before you have found grace in God's sight and are united with Jesus. Oh that you, like Ephraim, would view the sins of your youth with such shame and sorrow that you would smite against your thigh (Jer. 31:19). But it is time that I direct my discourse to you who are young. As Psalm 119:9 says, "Wherewithal shall a young man cleanse his way?" The question is, how shall a young man and young woman, who are by nature inclined to evil and have before them so many enticements to sin and youthful lusts, be delivered from the power of depravity? How shall they regulate their conduct to keep themselves unspotted from the world so they may live a virtuous and godly life?

The inspired reply? "By taking heed thereto according to thy word." The way for young people to become sanctified and lead godly lives is for them to heed the Word of God, to be much occupied with it, and to use it diligently for every purpose for which it is profitable. This question applies to all men even though few concern themselves with it. It is especially suitable for the young, however; for they are at the turning point of life and are subject to many temptations. God is highly pleased when young people live piously and religiously; this should therefore be their great concern.

You who are young must take this question personally: How shall I cleanse my way? You, who are by nature evil and impure, must be changed and purified. How shall you purify and cleanse your ways? By regulating them according to God's Word. Acknowledge the privilege you have of possessing the Word of God and enjoying instruction in its truths. How diligently should you read that Word and meditate upon it to grow in knowledge and wisdom and walk according to its directions in your choice of companions, recreation, calling, and marriage.

Alas, we have reason to lament that so many young people are concerned about nothing but how to live in pomp and pleasure while they neglect attending the house of God and studying the catechism. They profane the Sabbath. As Solomon says in Ecclesiastes 11:9, they cheerfully walk in the ways of their hearts and in the sight of their eyes. Likewise, Jeremiah writes, "The children of Israel and the children of Judah have only done evil before me from their youth" (32:30). Indeed, I am ashamed and distressed on account of you. Do not live so, my children. "Flee also youthful lusts" (2 Tim. 2:22). "Remember now thy Creator in the days of thy youth" (Eccl. 12:1). Seek the Lord early, in your youth.

By creation as well as baptism, you are obligated to do the Lord's service. As Lamentations 3:27 says, "It is good for a man that he bear the yoke in his youth." It is a necessary, profitable, honorable, and comfortable good. It is necessary because of God's command, "Seek ye first the kingdom of God" (Matt. 6:33); profitable because "godliness is profitable unto all things" (1 Tim. 4:8); honorable because "them that honour me I will honour" (1 Sam. 2:30); and comfortable because those who are converted early are preserved from many evils. In their old age they can comfort themselves, saying like David, "Now also when I am old and grayheaded, O God, forsake me not" (Ps. 71:18).

You should also be influenced by the lives of saints who were godly from youth and who are so greatly esteemed in the Word of God. These include Obadiah, Josiah, Samuel, Jeremiah, Timothy, and others. In addition, history tells us of children, male and female, who served the Lord in their youth.

Objections of Youth

Before concluding this chapter, we shall address some objections that often lay like stumbling blocks in the way of youth:

Question: If God has fixed the eternal state of every man and elected those who shall be saved, passing by the rest, who can resist His will?

Answer: We must make the Word of God, not the decree, our rule, for "the secret things belong unto the LORD our God." God has determined the span of human life; will anyone therefore refuse to eat and drink? At the Day of

Judgment, God will deal with men not according to the decree of election and reprobation, but according to their obedience and piety. He shall "render...every man according to his works."

Question: If, as it is said, "Those who seek early seldom persevere; the young saint is an old apostate," why is it important that children come to the Lord at an early age?

Answer: This question wrongly supposes that it is possible to fall from grace. But when the seed of God is planted in the heart, it will never die. It remains in him. As Solomon says, "Train up a child in the way he should go: and when he is old, he will not depart from it" (Prov. 22:6). It is true that a young hypocrite is an old apostate. But who do we know who truly feared God and yet forsook Him? Obadiah feared the Lord from his youth (1 Kings 18:12) and persevered. David was converted in youth and was a saint in his old age.

Question: Religion is so strict. It is too severe for young people and more suited for the old. Religion is a depressing thing. It stupifies the mind and deprives one of all pleasure.

Answer: Consider who says such things of religion. Are they familiar with it? No, for those who have truly experienced it testify with Asaph, "It is good for me to draw near to God." O friends, the pious see godliness far differently. They speak of what they know as well as what they have seen, proved, and experienced. They proclaim, "The peace of God...passeth all understanding" (Phil. 4:7) and "A day in Thy courts is better than a thousand elsewhere." Sorrows and humiliations do not proceed out of piety, but arise from the lack of it. Religion is the source of comfort and exaltation.

Question: The duties that religion imposes are an intolerable burden. The laws are exceedingly strict and the commands difficult to perform. Demands that conflict with flesh and blood include denying ourselves, loving our enemies, and cutting off a right hand. These are hard sayings, heavy duties. Who can enter this strait gate and walk this narrow way?"

Answer: This is the way to heaven; there is no other. If it were not so, the Bible would not be true. Though the duties of religion are grievous for the flesh, they are not grievous for the spirit. The service of sin is more grievous than any service of Christ. How many are destroyed by drunkenness, debauchery, and excess? How great are the pangs of hatred and the torment of envy?

Question: Upright professors of religion are scorned everywhere. They are called Puritans and schismatics by some, hypocrites and Pharisees by others.

Answer: This is nothing new. Ages ago, there were scoffers in Israel. David was "the song of the drunkards" (Ps. 69:12). The righteous were regarded "as a lamp despised in the thought of him that is at ease" (Job 12:5). Paul was branded a heretic, "a pestilent fellow...a mover of sedition" (Acts 24:5). Christ was called a glutton and winebibber (Matt. 11:19). Shall the disciple then be greater than his Master? We know there will be scoffers in the last days. What if those days have already come? Let him who cannot bear contempt for religion's sake refrain from calling himself a Christian. Furthermore, remember that though the pious are despised by the world, they are highly esteemed by God. "If any man serve me, him will my Father honor," Jesus said. He who is ashamed of Christ should remember what Christ warned: "Whosoever therefore shall be ashamed of me and of my words in this adulterous and sinful generation; of him also shall the Son of man be ashamed, when he cometh in the glory of his Father with the holy angels" (Mark 8:38).

Question: I would be religious if I only knew which religion was the true one. But how shall I, being young, arrive at the right conclusion? One professes one belief, another something else, while a third rejects both.

Answer: This is a great evil that Satan uses to confuse people. But it isn't anything new; it has been present in the church throughout the ages. The Word of God tells us, "There must be...heresies...that they which are approved may be made manifest" (1 Cor. 11:19), so that hypocrites may be exposed. But all differences in religion are not heresies. Those who sincerely receive the Word of God agree that without true repentance, unfeigned faith, and sincere devotion no one can be saved. They all agree that it is necessary to fear God, and keep His commandments, to "live soberly, righteously, and godly" (Titus 2:12). Why do you not yield and forsake your lusts?

Question: Why the haste? There is always opportunity for repentance. God is merciful; He will not reject a penitent sinner even in his last moments. We know that from the thief on the cross.

Answer: What happened to the malefactor is an instance without parallel; it is an instance without command (for where is a command to put off repenting?); it is an instance without promise. It was a case of special mercy, having its reasons in the time of its occurrence. Remember, the other malefactor continued in his sin and remained hardened to it. He did not follow the example of the penitent.

These questions and similar evasions may keep you from committing your life to the Lord. But think, what will you answer in that Great Day? Will you say that you were not called? You cannot say so, for God has called you in many ways. Will you say that you were too young? You cannot say that either, for others as young and younger than yourself have listened to the call. Your duty first and above all is to "seek...the kingdom of God, and his righteousness" (Matt. 6:33).

Will you say there are too many demands upon your attention? That would not do, for there is nothing more important than this. Will you say that you expected more time to perform this duty? Why should you expect something God has not promised? Why should God lengthen your days, which you spend in the service of sin? Why should He do that for someone who refuses to turn to Him during the best time of life? Do you suppose that you would turn to the Lord if your life were prolonged to the age of Methuselah?

Does this affect you? Then consider whom you will blame for your destruction. You cannot blame God, for He has sent His Son into the world to be offered for you. You cannot blame Christ, for He would gather you as a hen gathers her chickens, but you resisted Him. Nor can you blame the Spirit, for He would convince, convert, and sanctify you. But you would not. You have resisted and quenched Him. You also cannot blame ministers of the gospel, for they have set before you life and death; they have shown you the danger of sin and the necessity of holiness.

You cannot say that you had no time to come to the Lord, either, for you had time for acts of wantonness and vanity and sinful diversions. Therefore your mouth will be stopped. You will be forced to take all the blame yourself. As Hosea 13:9 says, "O Israel, thou hast destroyed thyself." Come, then, seek the Lord while He may be found.

If you are old, you will soon die. If you are young, you may soon die. Now is the time for anyone, young or old, to seek the Lord. Can one seek the Lord too early? No. How often do we find old people who lament their misspent time. Let us now bewail our sins and make our calling and election sure. I conclude with the promise, "Those that seek me early shall find me" (Prov. 8:17). Amen.

— 7 —

The Way of God With His People
in the Sanctuary

*"All the paths of the LORD are mercy and truth unto
such as keep his covenant and his testimonies."*
— Psalm 25:10

One of the greatest promises that Jehovah made to His people is found in Isaiah 65:24, which says, "And it shall come to pass, that before they call, I will answer; and while they are yet speaking, I will hear." Two phrases in this verse express the readiness of God to hear the prayers of His people. "Before they call, I will answer" refers to the desires of the heart that are in the soul even before a word is spoken. Since God searches the hearts and the reins and knows the desires contained in them, He frequently grants those desires a gracious hearing even before they are expressed.

"While they are yet speaking, I will hear" means that God will hear and answer the prayers of the pious by assuring them that their desires shall be fulfilled as well as by actually fulfilling their desires. He will avert the evil that threatens them and bestow the desired good.

The Holy Spirit, who excites desires in the children of God, grants the assurance that God hears their prayers. These desires are of God, according to the will of God, and becoming to the character of God. Thus, the Holy Spirit imparts the assurance that such desires shall not be in vain; for, "The eyes of the LORD are upon the righteous, and his ears are open unto their cry. The righteous cry, and the LORD heareth, and delivereth them out of all their troubles" (Ps. 34:15, 17).

Our text offers a striking example and evidence of this assurance. The goodly psalmist had just prayed, "O my God, I trust in thee" (v. 2) and expressed his confidence that prayer would not be in vain. Now he presents a threefold petition: for knowledge of the Lord's ways (v. 4), for guidance in the Lord's ways (v. 5), and for the experience of divine mercy (vv. 6-7). Scarcely have the words proceeded from his lips when the Comforter, the Holy Ghost, assures him that the Lord hears those petitions.

Verse 8, which says "Good and upright is the LORD; therefore will he teach sinners in the way," answers the psalmist's first petition. Verse 9, which promises "The meek will he guide in judgment: and the meek will he teach his way," answers the second. And verse 10, our text, which says, "All the paths of the LORD are mercy and truth unto such as keep his covenant and his testimonies" answers the third petition which was, "Remember, O LORD, thy tender mercies and thy lovingkindnesses; for they have been ever of old. Remember not the sins of my youth, nor my transgressions: according to thy mercy remember thou me for thy goodness' sake, O LORD."

We will study this text in three parts: that which is spoken of, that which is affirmed, and the persons of whom the prophet speaks.

The Paths of the Lord

Some say the fourth verse of this psalm refers to the commands and laws of God, but the first part of verse 10 about the paths of the Lord really means the works of God and His mode of operation. Specifically, it refers to:

- God's eternal decrees and purposes. Proverbs 8:22 says, "The LORD possessed me in the beginning of his way, before his works of old." Isaiah 55:8-9 refers to this as God's counsel and His ways.

• His works of nature and grace. Job 26:14 says of these works of nature, "Lo, these are parts of his ways." Psalm 67:1-2 says of grace, "God be merciful unto us...that thy way may be known upon earth."

• His method of acting and dealing with men. We read that Nebuchadnezzar said, "Now I...praise...and honour the King of heaven, all whose works are truth, and his ways judgment," and in Psalm 77:13, "Thy way, O God, is in the sanctuary." Man has his purposes, plans, and counsels, but the psalmist speaks here of the paths of the Lord Jehovah, whose name here refers to the eternal and gracious purposes of God and their fulfillment.

In the second part of our text, the psalmist goes on to say that "all the paths of the LORD are mercy," or grace (v. 6), which is a sign of God's effectual purpose and powerful inclination to do good to man, manifested in and accomplished through Christ. The word *truth* is also significant here. It refers to the faithfulness of God and the fulfillment of His gracious promises to His children.

Of Mercy and Truth

Our text teaches here that God has planned from eternity to show His lovingkindness, grace, and mercy through the Son of His love. Furthermore, all His dealings work to this end. He has promised this to His people, His performance of this is faithful and true, and all of His methods are revealed in His relationship with His church, even when it might be difficult to detect this from outward appearances.

Psalm 89:1-2 speaks more of this mercy and truth of God: "I will sing of the mercies of the LORD for ever: with my mouth will I make known thy faithfulness to all generations. For I have said, Mercy shall be built up for ever: thy faithfulness shalt thou establish in the very heavens." Verse 14 adds, "Justice and judgment are the habitation of thy throne: mercy and truth shall go before thy face." And Psalm 145:8, 17 adds, "The LORD is gracious, and full of compassion; slow to anger, and of great mercy. The LORD is righteous in all his ways, and holy in all his works."

Some theologians believe this text alludes to Exodus 34:6-7 for in Exodus 33:13 Moses had prayed, "If I have found grace in thy sight, show me now thy way," to which the Lord responded, "I will make all my goodness pass before thee, and I will proclaim the name of the LORD before thee." "Lord" here refers to "The LORD God, merciful and gracious, longsuffering, and abundant in goodness and truth, keeping mercy for thousands, forgiving iniquity and transgression and sin, and that will by no means clear the guilty; visiting the iniquity of the fathers upon the children, and upon the children's children, unto the third and to the fourth generation."

Though all of the ways of God are mercy and truth, they are by no means such to ungodly and hardened sinners. As Deuteronomy 32:4 says, the ways of God are judgment and justice to sinners. His way to them is "in the whirlwind and in the storm.... God is jealous, and the LORD revengeth; the LORD revengeth, and is furious; the LORD will take vengeance on his adversaries, and he reserveth wrath for his enemies" (Nah. 1:2-3). But all His ways are mercy and truth to those who keep His covenant and His testimonies. That is what is taught here.

God's Covenant with the Elect

To understand "Unto such as keep his covenant," we must understand the conditions and requirements of the covenant. By covenant, we mean the laws to which those in covenant with God are bound and to which they say yea and amen when they give assent to the covenant of God. So we read in Deuteronomy 4:13, "And he declared unto you his covenant, which he commanded you to perform,

even ten commandments; and he wrote them upon two ta-
bles of stone."

The word *testimonies* in the text refers to the Word of
God, which is the infallible and only credible testimony of
God that relates things which could not be known without
His revelation. This includes things relating to God,
namely His ways and works, and to the duty that sinners
owe to God. But the term in our text especially refers to
what God testifies in His Word regarding the duties of
those in covenant with Him.

"Keep" in the text, a not uncommon term, means the opposite of annulling or transgressing the commands of God.
Keeping or observing the testimonies of God means hearing them with pleasure as well as reading, searching,
understanding, remembering, loving, and obeying them.
The Word of God clearly and abundantly teaches that the
ways of God are not only merciful and true, but that they
are merciful and true to those who keep God's covenant
and testimonies. For these obedient ones are the object of
God's eternal election and heirs of the blessings of the
covenant of grace. In time they are called into covenant
with God and submit to it. From this flows the confidence
of a good conscience and a dependence upon God for all
things that pertain to life and godliness, such as forgiveness of sins, righteousness, peace, and joy in the Holy
Ghost. It is evident to them that all the ways of God are
mercy and truth, for God cannot deal with the objects of
His favor in any other way than is agreeable with His eternal promises.

Sometimes it seems like God deals differently with his
children. But even then, their afflictions and judgments are
sanctified to their souls. That is only the privilege of those
who keep His testimonies, for they alone are the objects of
God's eternal choice. They alone are in covenant with God.
They are the objects of His regard and are therefore assured of His mercy.

All this is confirmed in the Word of God, which says that the ways of the Lord are mercy and truth to those who are in covenant with Him; who are upright, who believe, and who keep His commandments. All of sacred Scripture supports this, including verses such as "Mercy shall compass him about" (Ps. 32:10; 36:7, 10).

This applies to all the ways of God with His people. For "all things work together for [their] good" (Rom. 8:28). Even chastisements are a token of the love of God (Heb. 12:6-7); however, this blessing is the privilege only of those who keep God's covenant and His testimonies (Isa. 3:10-11).

Believers come into covenant with the Father through the Son. As the Lord Jesus says in John 3:36, "He that believeth on the Son hath everlasting life: and he that believeth not the Son shall not see life; but the wrath of God abideth on him." The Lord's graciousness extends forever to those in covenant with Him. As Psalm 103:17-18, "But the mercy of the LORD is from everlasting to everlasting upon them that fear him, and his righteousness unto children's children; to such as keep his covenant, and to those that remember his commandments to do them."

This verse includes an answer to the suppliant, who prayed earlier (v. 6), "Remember, O LORD, thy tender mercies and thy lovingkindnesses." He is now assured that all the ways of Jehovah are mercy and truth. Had he specifically prayed that God would not remember the sins of his youth, he could assume the certainty of an answer based upon the mercy and truth of God explained in this verse.

That is the teaching of Exodus 34:6-7, for example, in which Moses prays, "Pardon, I beseech thee, the iniquity of this people according unto the greatness of thy mercy" (Num. 14:19). Or Nehemiah 13:22, in which the prophet asks, "Remember me, O my God, concerning this also, and spare me according to the greatness of thy mercy." Or Psalm 51:1, in which the psalmist prays, "Have mercy upon me, O God,

according to thy lovingkindness: according unto the multitude of thy tender mercies blot out my transgressions."

The forgiveness of sins flows out of the lovingkindness
and truth of God, as Psalm 103:3-4, 8-9, 11 teaches. Even
when God afflicts His sinful children, He remains a forgiving God who continues to act with them in mercy and
truth. As Psalm 89:28 says, "My mercy will I keep for him
for evermore." Verses 30-33 go on to say that if God's children forsake His law, "Then will I visit their transgression
with the rod.... Nevertheless, my lovingkindness will I not
utterly take from him."

Such verses teach that all the paths of the Lord are merciful and flow out of the forgiveness of sins. That is true only
of people who keep His covenant and His testimonies to do
them, for the verses teach that God is ready to forgive sins
only of those who are penitent and believing and who turn
to Him. "Seek ye the LORD while he may be found, call ye
upon him while he is near: let the wicked forsake his way,
and the unrighteous man his thoughts: and let him return
unto the LORD, and he will have mercy upon him; and to
our God, for he will abundantly pardon" (Isa. 55:6-7).

God will not forgive men who continue in their sins (Jer.
22:9). When men repent, however, they obtain forgiveness
(Mark 1:4,15; Luke 24:47; Acts 5:31). Therefore Peter said to
the Jews in Acts 3:19, "Repent ye therefore, and be converted, that your sins may be blotted out" (see also Acts
8:22). So the psalmist seems to be saying, "Although your
sins and numerous transgressions and departures from
God in your youth are objects of His aversion, and He
could therefore justly deny you His favor, He will not be
angry with you provided you lay hold of His strength." He
will not be angry for the sake of His name and His eternal
purposes and in accordance with His ordinary method of
dealing with His children, for He graciously promises to
forgive their sins and grant them the tokens of His love
and faithfulness if they come to Him to "obtain mercy, and

find grace to help in time of need." They must come confessing their sins, hating them, and turning from them. They must flee for refuge to the grace of God in Christ Jesus. And, together with a cordial, believing assent to the covenant of God, its promises and its requirements, they must approve them and sincerely desire to observe and faithfully fulfill them.

If your conscience assures you that those are your feelings, why should you not confidently conclude that Jehovah will not remember your sins but will remember you according to the greatness of His mercy for His goodness' sake? Truly, God is good, even to the evil and unthankful. He is good to all of His creatures, "and his tender mercies are over all his works." But He reserves a special goodness for His own people. Hence, we should examine whether we are partakers of that special goodness. God's Word proposes these evidences:

- He is good to those with a clean heart. As Psalm 73:1 teaches, "Truly God is good to Israel, even to such as are of a clean heart." Ask yourselves whether you are clean in heart. Have you ever become so aware of your impurity that you have been afflicted with loathing, grief, and detestation? Have you ever so desired a pure heart that you prayed like David, the man after God's own heart, "Create in me a clean heart, O God"? Have you then gone for refuge to the Lord Jesus, that "fountain opened to the house of David and to the inhabitants of Jerusalem"?

- He is good to those who trust Him. As Psalm 36:7 says, "How excellent is thy lovingkindness, O God! therefore the children of men put their trust under the shadow of thy wings." Ask yourselves whether you have fled for refuge to the grace of God in Christ. Have you fled to Jesus as your Priest, regarding yourself as condemned and helpless not only because of gross transgression but also because your best works are filthy rags? Have you sought righteousness and salvation only in Christ? Have you fled to Jesus as your Prophet, renouncing your own wisdom to be instructed by Him? Have you sought him as your King, to be in subjection only to Him? Do you yearn for the sanctifying as well as justifying grace and mercy of God? Have you rightly sought communion with God, desiring it as your highest good?

• He is good to those who keep His covenant and His testimonies. That is the promise of our text as well as of Psalm 102:17-18. Therefore, ask yourselves if you know by experience what it means to enter into covenant with God. Have you broken your covenant with sin, death, and hell and become acquainted with covenant dealings with God? Have you actually entered into covenant with Him? Baptism and the Lord's Supper do not usher one into the covenant; they are seals only for those in the covenant.

Do you have experimental knowledge of special, secret, heartfelt dealings between the Lord and your soul by which you surrendered yourself wholly, forever, and not only once to God and His service, but daily renewing that surrender? Those who have done so understand the meaning of Joshua 24:15: "As for me and my house, we will serve the LORD" as well as Psalm 73:25-26, 28: "Whom have I in heaven but thee? and there is none upon earth that I desire beside thee. My flesh and my heart faileth: but God is the strength of my heart, and my portion for ever. But it is good for me to draw near to God: I have put my trust in the Lord GOD, that I may declare all thy works." They understand David's words in Psalm 89:15, "Blessed is the people that know the joyful sound: they shall walk, O LORD, in the light of thy countenance." And the testimony of the bride in Song of Solomon 2:16, "My beloved is mine, and I am his." And of Isaiah 44:5, "One shall say, I am the LORD's; and another shall call himself by the name of Jacob; and another shall subscribe with his hand unto the LORD, and surname himself by the name of Israel." And also of Paul in Acts 27:23, "For there stood by me this night the angel of God, whose I am, and whom I serve."

Have you experienced the significance of these inspired declarations? Do you regard all the commandments of God, without exception, as good? Do you choose to obey His commandments? Do you keep His testimonies? Do you observe His requirements? Do you ask what the Lord will have you to do, as Paul asked in Acts 9:6, and Samuel in 1 Samuel 3:10?

You who are ungodly and unconverted must realize that the ways of God are indignation and wrath to every soul that does evil. Your sins remain unpardoned and are treasured up to add to your condemnation. Woe unto you; God's ways for you are judgment and justice. His truth and faithfulness can only cause you terror, for they verify all the threats of His Word. What will it help you to experience much of the goodness of God in this life if in the meantime you are not led to repentance by the riches of God's goodness, long-suffering, and forbearance? For if you persist in your sin, you will treasure up to yourselves "wrath against the day of wrath and revelation of the righteous judgment of God" (Rom. 2:4-5). Oh that you were partakers of God's special goodness! Oh that you would seek refuge in the free grace of God in Christ!

Realizing the paths of God are goodness and truth should encourage the concerned and support the despondent. If you are convinced of your wretched state and would like to be reconciled to God, do not be kept from coming to Him. If you are weary of sin and sincerely desire to draw near to God through Christ, then come. The Lord is not unmerciful, cruel, or inflexible, but good, as He promises. He runs to meet sinners, as we learn from the parable of the prodigal son (Luke 15). The unchangeable God does so to all who turn to Him. He calls, He invites, He knocks, He presents Himself to you, and He promises that those who come to Him will in no wise be cast out (John 6:37). Then do not remain at a distance because of fear.

The words of our text should console and invigorate you who are upright believers, dear people of God. God's mercy and truth are the foundation upon which you may continually summon courage to return to the Lord (Hos. 3:5; Ps. 13:5). The Lord is the God of mercy; therefore, you are guilty of injustice towards God if you regard Him as evil, uncompassionate, unwilling to listen to your pleas, and angry in not immediately delivering you from affliction, threatened or real, or granting the desires you pray for.

You should be ashamed, for you dishonor God with such thoughts. God is merciful and true; His ways are mercy and truth. Acknowledge those perfections and glorify Him. Have you sinned? Are you in affliction? Convince yourself that God is merciful and faithful. Humble yourself before Him as a little child, as David did (Ps. 131:2).

If a poor soul asks, "How can I believe that the Lord's paths are mercy and truth to me? I suffer so many afflictions, both in soul and body, that the ways of God to me appear to be indignation and wrath." I answer that, it may appear to be so to you, but that is only for now. Later you will see that all things have worked together for your good (Rom. 8:28); that God is merciful in the midst of wrath; that He will not be angry forever but delights in mercy (Jer. 3:12), chastising those whom He loves (Heb. 12). His wrath will endure for only a moment, for there is life in His favor. "Weeping may endure for a night, but joy cometh in the morning" (Ps. 30:5).

The truth and faithfulness of God, the Amen, should also console you, dear children of God, since you can thus assure yourselves that He will never forsake you and will keep all His promises to you. Let this serve as an encouragement to you. For although we are unfaithful, God remains faithful. "He cannot deny himself," says the apostle (2 Tim. 2:13).

The weak believer who laments, saying, "How can I comfort myself with the faithfulness of God when I experience no fulfillment of the promises? I ask but do not receive." My response is that we must not limit the Holy One of Israel as the wicked Jews did (Ps. 78:41). God has His own time; if He tarries, wait for Him. Wait upon the Lord and keep His way because He will surely come; He will not tarry (Hab. 2:3).

However strange and mysterious the paths of God may appear to you, you shall one day reflect and find that all have been mercy and truth to you. Then you will be able to say with the psalmist, "I will sing of the mercies of the LORD for ever: with my mouth will I make known thy faithfulness to all generations. For I have said, Mercy shall be built up for ever: thy faithfulness shalt thou establish in the very heavens." Amen.

— 8 —

God's People: Signs and Wonders

"I am as a wonder unto many;
but thou art my strong refuge."
— Psalm 71:7

Jonah 4:6 tells a remarkable story. When the prophet Jonah was overcome with impatience and oppressed with heat, Jehovah prepared a tree or plant for his protection. Jonah greatly rejoiced in the shadow of that plant. We shall not investigate at length the nature of this vegetable growth. Scholars do not agree about what it was, since, according to linguists, the Hebrew word used for this growth is not found elsewhere in Scripture. Some think it was a wild pompion or gourd; others, a plant that rises so high that it sometimes surmounts and covers structures. Others think it was a wild vine. The early church father Jerome, who could not find an appropriate Latin word for this vegetation, used one that means ivy.

Regardless of what the growth was, it gave the prophet joy. The joy lasted only a short time, however, for God sent a worm the next day that attacked the plant. The vine withered.

The incident shows how in ancient times God would indulge in such ways with the holy prophets and men of God, offering them signs and wonders. For example, Isaiah 20:3 tells us that the Lord asked Isaiah to walk naked and barefoot three years "for a sign and wonder upon Egypt and upon Ethiopia." He also appointed Ezekiel, saying, "I have set thee for a sign unto the house of Israel" (Ezek. 12:6); and "I am your sign" (v. 11).

The words of our text show how David was used by the Lord. "I am as a wonder unto many," David says. While in danger of being surprised and attacked, the prophet testifies of his trust in God alone. He prays for speedy deliverance from wily and cruel foes, according to the favor shown him in times past, even from his youth. This gives him unceasing reason to praise God's name (vv. 1-7).

The words of our text include David's confession about himself as well as his relationship with God. We shall thus study the text in two parts:

• David's confession about himself and how that confession is a light to others, and

• David's confession about Jehovah, thanking Him for what He has been and still is to David.

David's Confession About Himself

The person in the text refers to himself as "I." Although the name of David is not found in the title of the psalm, we believe that he wrote the psalm because the contents, style, and phrasing are so similar to that of David's other inspired songs. Who David was is well known. He was a son of Jesse of the tribe of Judah; was born in Bethlehem; was a prophet and king; and was a sweet psalm writer in Israel. The Spirit of the Lord spoke through him and put His word on his tongue. David was the type of king who foreshadowed the Messiah, who would later be referred to as "God's servant David" (Ezek. 34:23-24).

David's confession about himself is "I am as a wonder unto many." A wonder or miracle is an event that is beyond the power of man and is contrary to nature. The Bible relates many such wonders: the budding of Aaron's rod (Num. 17:8); fire falling from heaven (2 Kings 1:10); the earth opening up to swallow Korah, Dathan, and Abiram

(Num. 16:30-32); Balaam's ass speaking (Num. 22:28); the walls of Jericho falling down (Josh. 6:20); an iron swimming (2 Kings 6:5-6); water flowing from a rock (Num. 20:11); the forty-day fasting of Moses and Elijah (Ex. 34:28; 1 Kings 19:8), and many others. God used such signs, wonders, and miracles to confirm the messages of the prophets and apostles.

When David says he is "a wonder to many," he is saying that God has done such great and strange things in and through him that he has become a wonder to others. If we examine the life of David, we find this to be true. For he was a wonder to many when he was a boy and slew the giant Goliath; and when he overcame the lion and bear, delivering the sheep out of their mouths (1 Sam. 17). He was a wonder when he was only a shepherd and was appointed king (described by Asaph in Psalm 78:70-71); and after being anointed king, performed so many mighty deeds that people sang of him, "Saul hath slain his thousands, and David his ten thousands" (1 Sam. 18:6-7). He was a wonder in being delivered out of so many dangers and hazards. For he had many, powerful foes, such as Saul and his adherents Doeg, Ahithophel, and Absalom, who pursued him like he was a partridge, seeking by every means to deprive him of the kingdom as well as his life. Yet he continued to stand, which is in every respect a wonder of preservation and deliverance.

Add to this all the distresses and temptations this pious man endured, which led him to exclaim, "Deep calleth unto deep at the noise of thy waterspouts: all thy waves and thy billows are gone over me" (Ps. 42:7); and "For innumerable evils have compassed me about: mine iniquities have taken hold upon me, so that I am not able to look up; they are more than the hairs of mine head: therefore my heart faileth me" (Ps. 40:12). David's afflictions were many, yet the Lord graciously delivered him out of all of them. He may thus be viewed as a wonder unto many when he testifies, "Many, O LORD my God, are thy wonderful works which thou hast done, and thy thoughts which are to us-ward." Surely his numerous escapes, his deliverance from spiritual desertion, his support in mental discouragements, his consolation amid sorrow, his restoration from so many disorders of soul make him a wonder (Ps. 4:1; 18:17).

David was a wonder of God's sovereign grace as a prophet and king. But he was also a wonder as a child of God, because, in spite of his sins and grievous falls in the matter of Uriah and Bathsheba, he was not forsaken by the Lord. His sins were forgiven him upon his repentance and confession.

Scholars believe that this part of the text follows from what is said in the previous verse. Thus David becoming a wonder to many is a result of the wonderful deliverances and protections that God continually favored him with since human conception. By such signs and wonders the people of God might be taught to believe in God, to firmly adhere to Him, and not to doubt a similar result of their trials. In this respect Isaiah and Ezekiel are also called wonders (Isa. 20:3; Ezek. 12:6).

Scholars note that the Hebrew word for wonder can also mean "monster." David could be called a monster, since many people in Israel in the time of Saul looked upon David with astonishment and horror. Because of the numerous sufferings he endured, they supposed God must hate him. David tells us that in verse 11 of our Psalm. Shimei cursed David as one hated (2 Sam. 16:5), and David regarded himself as "a dead man forsaken" (Ps. 31:12).

As our text says, David was a wonder "to many." The original word for "many" can also mean "great," signifying individual as well as collective magnitude. In saying that he was a wonder to many, David included those who were godless and graceless. David frequently complained of the great and the rich who taunted and persecuted him. In Psalm 69:12, for example, he says, "They that sit in the gate speak against me." The Word of God teaches and experience confirms that such people are usually graceless and have the least knowledge of the way of God with His people.

David's Confession About God

"But thou art my strong refuge" begins with a word that indicates an antithesis to what preceded it. The person the psalmist confesses is so important that He is referred to as "thou." He who is a place of "strong refuge" to the psalmist is none other than the Lord God, Jehovah (v. 1). He is the One David earlier describes as "rock...my fortress" (v. 3); "my God" (v. 4); "my hope, O Lord GOD...my trust" (v. 5). No wonder, then, that he thankfully acknowledges God with this illustrious confession, "My strong refuge."

Each word in this phrase has a special emphasis. A refuge is a strong and well-fortified place surrounded with walls and entrenchments to which people flee for security. We flee to castles, elevated places, and rocks for protection against enemies, the heat, or rising floods. God is likened to such a place. "Ye have shamed the counsel of the poor, because the LORD is his refuge," says Psalm 14:6, meaning the Lord is a secure place of resort, a rock, a tower, a shadow, protection, and a means of causing consternation to foes. Psalm 57:1 adds another image to that place of refuge, saying, "In the shadow of thy wings will I make my refuge." Isaiah 25:4 says the Lord is "a refuge from the storm, a shadow from the heat."

The Lord is properly called a refuge because in Him is everything that we seek in a refuge. In Him we are preserved from all danger and evil. As Psalm 91:1 says, "He that dwelleth in the secret place of the most High shall abide under the shadow of the Almighty."

In our text, David thankfully acknowledges the grace, faithfulness, and preservation that he has experienced at the hand of God. He is not just naming God's attributes but confessing them. Such is the testimony found here and elsewhere in Scripture of those who trust in the Lord (read Psalm 40:2; 61:4; Isa. 63:7-14), since in all their extremities and distresses they flee in prayer for refuge to God. In such a way criminals fled to the horns of the altar, and those who unintentionally committed murder fled to a city of refuge to escape an avenger of blood. All who seek refuge do so because of the promise of the divine command, "Trust in him at all times; ye people, pour out your heart before him: God is a refuge for us" (Ps. 62:8). They are assured that God will provide them deliverance and protection. As Psalm 50:15 says, "Call upon me in the day of trouble: I will deliver thee."

The people of God experience this daily in accord with Psalm 46:1-2. God is a sure hiding place, a strong refuge. He is not only strong, as His name El signifies, but He is the strength of His people (Ps. 18:1). He is strong, mighty — yes, almighty — a secure, sure refuge. For God is excellent in counsel and mighty in works. He is a good refuge because He exercises His strength for the good of His people. As Jeremiah 16:19 says, "O LORD, my strength, and my fortress, and my refuge."

Knowing this in general is of little value. The child of God is privileged to apply such knowledge to himself in particular. That is what David does here by using the word *my*. There is no more comforting word in Scripture, for it implies the following:

- It is a word of faith. It is expressed in texts such as "The LORD is my shepherd; I shall not want" (Ps. 23:1) and "My Lord and my God" (John 20:28).

- It expresses approbation and assurance. Consider "My beloved is mine, and I am his" (Song of Sol. 2).

- It suggests satisfaction and joy. A pious woman I know was in distress and affliction. She read Psalm 18, finding the word *my* nine times, each of which was sweeter than the preceding. She was so comforted and refreshed by the word that she spent the whole day in thanksgiving and adoration of the love of God in Christ.

• It implies confidence. Those who use the word do so knowing who God is and what He does for them for their strength and protection. If the Almighty is for them, who can be against them? They can come to Him and find in Him a secure hiding place. *My* implies special confidence, for God's children are assured that their covenant God is willing to help them.

Some who read this text may say to themselves, "You may with propriety apply these words to yourself, for you also have been a wonder to many, both in your sufferings and deliverances; for if the Lord had not been a strong refuge to you, you would long since have perished in your affliction." Of this I shall say nothing for fear that you might think that I want to be likened to David. I know full well that I am not a king or prophet or son of a prophet but only a poor servant of Jesus Christ.

In addition, if I mentioned all that has happened to me and all that I have experienced, where should I begin? Where would I end? Perhaps I would say something was a wonder, which you would not believe. What would you say if you heard that the preacher is a wonder to himself?

Enough. It is time that I apply these words more directly to our minds. For in addition to saying that David, Isaiah, or any other eminently pious person are signs or wonders, Scripture also refers to all truly gracious persons in the Old as well as in the New Testament as such. As Isaiah 8:18 says, "Behold, I and the children whom the LORD hath given me are for signs and for wonders in Israel." Jesus Christ, the Messiah, uses the same words in Hebrews 2:13.

The ways in which true believers are signs and wonders include the following:

1. In how few there are. In comparison with the ungodly, the number of the godly is so small that the disciples of Christ are as signs and wonders in Israel. They are called

a "little flock" in Luke 12:32. Matthew 20:16 says, "Many be called, but few chosen." And Revelation 3:4 says there are "few names even in Sardis."

2. In how they are changed. They are wonderful displays of how God works perfection in them as He changes them from darkness to light, from death to life, from being carnal to becoming spiritual, from ungodliness to godliness. Such change is as great as being raised from the dead. A believer is such a wonder that natural men are led to say, "Oh how this man has changed. How different he is from what I knew before!"

They who were once fools and knew nothing of spiritual things are changed into divines who are capable of teaching and edifying others. "Wilt thou shew wonders to the dead?" Psalm 88:10 asks. Yet the Lord performs such wonders in dead sinners. Therefore the state of grace is called "marvelous light." The work of grace that David refers to here can also be called the work of providence. As Psalm 139:14 says, "I will praise thee; for I am fearfully and wonderfully made: marvelous are thy works; and that my soul knoweth right well."

3. In how they endure affliction. True believers are wonders because of the many afflictions, temptations, conflicts, wrestlings, desertions, falls, and risings that they must endure. Because of who they are and how God deals with them, they are subject to many dangers. But they also experience many wonderful deliverances and escapes. Therefore, when a pious soul carefully examines this subject, he must burst forth saying, "Wonderfully, oh Lord, hast Thou borne me! Wonderfully, oh Lord, hast Thou gone before me! Wonderfully, oh Lord, hast Thou stricken me! Wonderfully, oh Lord, hast Thou delivered me! Wonderfully, oh Lord, should I now conduct myself! How wonderfully should I now shine forth! How wonderfully, oh Lord, should I now please Thee! But, alas, how far is it from being the case."

One person's experience in such things may be greater than another's. But all "must through much tribulation enter into the kingdom of God" (Acts 14:22), being compelled to strive (Luke 13:24) and to do violence (Matt. 11:12); for the righteous are scarcely saved (1 Pet. 4:18).

4. In how God chooses them. True believers are signs and wonders of God's long-suffering and sovereign grace. For He has passed by so many and adopted them as His children. He has refused the rich, the noble, the mighty, and the wise, choosing the poor, the despised, and the obscure (1 Cor. 1). He has frequently honored with His favor the vilest of mankind. Harlots and publicans, according to the Savior's own words, went in before Pharisees and scribes (Matt. 21:31). Are they not a wonder?

5. In how they are regarded by the world. They are signs and wonders because they are an offense to the world and in many ways are condemned and persecuted by it. Is it not a wonder that the children of Zion, who are precious because of the glory that God has bestowed on them and are thus worthy of all honor, are so despised and scoffed at, made such a spectacle, and regarded as filth by the world?

God provides comfort, however. Scholars believe that Isaiah 8:16, which says "Bind up the testimony, seal the law among my disciples," indicates that Christ comforts and strengthens the prophet against the malice of evil men by His own example. It is as if God is saying, "Am I called in my own person in the discharge of my public ministry to experience contempt at the hands of men? Let it not seem strange to you, oh Isaiah, that the same is expected of you." Isaiah goes on to say, "The children whom the LORD hath given me are for signs and wonders" (v. 18) and, "Many are averse to us, and hate us, because their ungodliness is reproved by us."

Are you such a wonder, my friend? You may be a wonder to many who are not pious. You may be a wonder of God's long-suffering; that He has not yet destroyed you, that He has not cut the thread of your life, that He did not cast you into utter darkness long before this, that He has not struck you down in the very act of sin, that He has not sent fire from heaven upon you, that the earth has not opened its mouth to swallow you alive. But unless the wonderful riches of God's goodness have led you to repentance, you are now treasuring up wrath to yourselves (Rom. 2:5).

Are you a wonder because you remain unconverted despite all the means of grace, because you are learning nothing, because you continue ignorant even of the judgments that God is sending upon this earth? Have you forgotten the earthquake that recently threatened to destroy us? Are you a wonder because you see and hear of people dying but you still persist in the way of your heart as if you had made a covenant with death and hell? In this respect, you give us much occasion to wonder, but you lack what makes the people of God truly a wonder.

Alas, even among Christians of the Reformed Church there are people who are notorious, not as David was because of how wonderfully God dealt with him, but because of their ungodliness in lying, deceiving, fighting, drinking, cursing, swearing, lewdness, and other abominations. God grant you the blessedness of experiencing that change for good that would truly make us wonder.

We would also ask, Is the Lord your strong refuge? You might respond, "Why do you ask this? Where else should we go?" My friends, it is one thing to say this and another to practice it. Paul describes believers as people who have fled for refuge to the grace of God in Christ. Have you ever been confronted in every direction by foes and surrounded by enemies? Have you been as affected by your spiritual state as those who fled from pursuers to the horns of the altar or the cities of refuge? Have you then run to Christ to hide in Him and to be concealed from the wrath of God? Have you then laid hold of the strength of God? Oh, that the wonderful long-suffering and goodness of God would convince you to put your trust in God and exclaim, "How excellent is thy lovingkindness, O God!" (Ps. 36:7).

It is time for me to speak to the gracious ones. Do not be surprised that you are a wonder to many and that the world regards you as wonderful. Let it not seem strange to you that you are a terror to the evil. You are a wonder to yourselves; a wonder of forbearance, of sovereign grace. What a wonder that God should have looked upon me — one so vile, the chief of sinners — showing me His wonderful preservation, care, and deliverance. Surely you may indulge that wonder without restraint, extol the sovereign grace of God, and show forth praise to One who has called you out of darkness into His marvelous light.

Be concerned, now, that you may also be a wonder of godliness. You will find yourself in many circumstances and experience many events that bring you to exclaim with David, "The troubles of my heart are enlarged: O bring thou me out of my distresses." Remember, then, to go for refuge to your strength, your high tower.

As David says, "Thou art my strong refuge." Should you not say so? God is your covenant God. You have never experienced evil at His hands; indeed He has frequently been your refuge, for can you not say, "Hitherto hath the Lord helped me"? Consider the past. What wants and dangers have you experienced in which He did not help, redeem, and deliver you? If a child is in distress, does he not run to the arms of his parent? Truly, the Lord of Hosts is with us in all storms.

Whatever your distress, whatever the dangers you are experiencing, even though all things seem against you, do not fail to make Him your refuge. As Proverbs 18:10 says, "The name of the LORD is a strong tower: the righteous runneth into it, and is safe." Meditate frequently upon how God helped you in the past. As Psalm 77:11-12, 14 says, "I will remember the works of the LORD: surely I will remember thy wonders of old. I will meditate also of all thy work, and talk of thy doings. Thou art the God that doest wonders." What wonder you will experience when you review God's wonderful dealings. What great things you will tell the Lord when you come to Him, especially when the Lord "shall come to be glorified in his saints, and to be admired in all them that believe." He will show His wonderful power and goodness in the glorifying of His believing people (2 Thes. 1:10), and you will sing with the psalmist, "Blessed be the LORD: for he hath showed me his marvellous kindness in a strong city" (Ps. 31:21); "a city which hath foundations, whose builder and maker is God." Amen.

— 9 —

The Man of Sorrow

*"I am the man that hath seen affliction
by the rod of his wrath."*
— Lamentations 3:1

There are many distinguished songs in Scripture. There is
the song of Moses and the children of Israel (Ex. 15:1-19), of
Miriam and the women of Israel who rejoiced after being
delivered from Pharaoh at the Red Sea (vv. 20-21), of Deborah
and Barak (Judg. 5), of the Virgin Mary (Luke 1:46-55), of
Zacharias (vv. 68-69), and of Simeon (Luke 2:29-32). The Song
of Solomon is the only book in the Bible that is called a song.

Scripture includes lamentations as well as songs. There
are lamentations over the death of Saul and Jonathan (2
Sam. 1), over the destruction of the city of Tyre (Ezek. 26),
and over the princes of Israel (Ezek. 39). But an entire book
of Jeremiah is called Lamentations. Though we are uncertain about when the book was written, its name helps us
understand the nature of its contents, namely, lamentation
over the devastation of Jerusalem.

In the second chapter of Lamentations, Jeremiah utters
doleful complaints about the miserable state of Jerusalem
and the desolation of the Jewish people. He reminds the
people of the causes of their afflictions and calls them to repent of their sins with earnest prayer. In Lamentations 3:1,
our text, the prophet laments the condition of the Jewish
people. Let us examine this text in two parts:

- The experience of the prophet, and
- The cause of the affliction.

The Prophet's Experience

The one who speaks in our text is the prophet Jeremiah, the son of Hilkiah. "I am the man," he says. Other words the Hebrews use for the word *man* include Adam, alluding to his origin; *Enosch*, the afflicted one; *Isch*, a person of respectability or distinction; or, in our text, as *Gebe*, which properly signifies a man as the first, most eminent, mightiest of the human race.

The prophet does not mean himself when he speaks of man but of the whole church that constitutes one body. This is the "man that hath seen affliction." The original word for affliction is derived from a root word which means to be humbled or to be oppressed; to be made poor, meek, and afflicted. Afflictions thus means trials, distresses, judgments, and miseries. They include three different types:

1. Spiritual affliction. These afflictions affect the soul. They arise from the hiding of God's face, the sense of God's wrath, and from the kind of sin of which Job, Heman, David, and other pious men so bitterly complain.

2. Christian affliction. Christians suffer these for the sake of the gospel.

3. Corporal affliction. These afflict the body and the outward man. The apostle Paul speaks of them as human or common to man (1 Cor. 10:13). They can proceed directly from the hand of God or indirectly from the hand of man. Those that proceed from the hand of God are either general or special afflictions. Christians suffer general afflictions, such as hunger, pestilence, and war along with the inhabitants of the land in which they live. Special afflictions, such as sickness, weakness, poverty, or bereavement are suffered personally in connection with one's husband, wife, children, and dearest friends.

Afflictions that come upon us through men are, again, either common disasters, such as war and the evils which are associated with it; or special, which are inflicted by those we are associated with in life, as, for example, the sufferings and maltreatment that a husband must endure from his wife, or a wife from her husband, or one neighbor from another. The prophet has seen all of these afflictions with his own eyes in others and has experienced them himself, for his afflictions and miseries were many. For his faithful rebukes he has suffered so much from kings, priests, false prophets, and common people that he is forced to exclaim, "Woe is me...a man of strife and a man of contention to the whole earth" (Jer. 15:10)!

The miseries that Jeremiah experienced included reproach (Jer. 15:15) and deceit, "Come,...let us smite him with the tongue" (Jer. 18:18). So many people slandered him that he complains, "My sighs are many, and my heart is faint" (Lam. 1:22). In addition, he was ridiculed (Jer. 20:7), was in danger of being murdered (Jer. 18:22), was punished with stripes (Jer. 20:2; 37:15), and was harassed and apprehended (Jer. 26:9). In the court of the prison where he daily received a piece of bread, he was falsely accused (Jer. 37:21) by men who said, he "seeketh not the welfare of this people, but the hurt." He was cast into a pit where he sank in mire in which he would have died had not Ebedmelech the Ethiopian rescued him (Jer. 38). After he was rescued, Jeremiah was committed to the court of the prison, where he remained until Jerusalem was captured. Then he was carried with the rest of Israel into captivity.

Jeremiah could truly say, "I am the man that hath seen affliction." In addition to physical afflictions, he experienced afflictions of the mind, which so distressed him that he cursed the day of his birth (Jer. 20:14). He resolved to speak no longer in the name of the Lord, and God's Word burned like a fire shut up in his bones (Jer. 20:9). Scripture does not say how Jeremiah died, but ancient writers say that as a reward for his faithfulness, he was stoned to death by wicked Jews in Egypt.

The prophet also witnessed the afflictions of others. He watched them endure days of trouble, judgments, the destruction of the city, the destruction of the temple, and the devastation of the whole land by the king of Babylon. He watched as they were carried off into seventy years of exile with its accompanying evils, privation, suffering, pestilence, and the dispersion of the people. He writes in agony, "If I go forth into the field, then behold the slain with the sword! and if I enter into the city, then behold them that are sick with famine! yea, both the prophet and the priest go about into a land that they know not." The temple and the house of the king were burned with fire and the walls were broken down. King Zedekiah was carried off to Babylon and his children and nobles slain. The bronze, silver, and gold vessels of the temple were carried away (Jer. 14). When the prophet foresaw these things, he could only exclaim, "My bowels, my bowels!" (Jer. 4:19). He describes all of this with bitter grief and profound mourning in the book of the Lamentations, saying, "Thy breach is great like the sea: who can heal thee?"

The Cause of His Affliction

The second part of our text, "by the rod of his wrath," speaks of a rod. *Schevet*, the original word for rod, is sometimes translated stick, staff, or scepter, and signifies a shoot from the stock or root of a tree.

A rod is used for discipline, punishment, and chastisement. It is used in this text in a figurative sense to mean punishments, afflictions, and judgments. The word is fittingly used here, for as a rod cannot inflict a stroke or move itself unless it is lifted, so it is with the judgments of God's hand (Jer. 15:2). As a rod is used for discipline and amendment, so also are judgments. "Blessed is the man whom thou chastenest, O LORD, and teachest him out of thy law," says the psalmist (Ps. 94:12). As a rod hurts and inflicts pain, causing uneasiness and distress to those it is used against, so the judgments of God cause pain and distress to those they are levied against (Heb. 12:11; Micah 6:13). As the rod is raised through anger, wrath, and displeasure, so are judgments, punishments, and troubles proofs of God's wrath. The text thus connects the rod with God's wrath or anger. As Isaiah 10:5 says, "O Assyrian, the rod of mine anger." Or Isaiah 57:17: "For the iniquity of his covetousness was I wroth, and smote him."

We might say, "I am the man that hath seen affliction" because we live in times of adversity, trouble, and distress. Many people die, going to their long home as mourners go about the streets. Let no one suppose that I would liken myself to Jeremiah. I am not a prophet or a son of the prophets. Yet to some extent I can also say, "I am the man that hath seen affliction." I have seen an awful flood in which thousands of men and animals were destroyed. I have lived through a time of famine. I have seen fearful hailstorms in which the windows of houses and churches were broken in pieces, trees shattered, and the increase of the earth destroyed. I have lived through a time of pestilence in France and Germany. I have seen terrible hurricanes in which churches, houses, barns, and forests were violently blown to the ground; I have lived in a time when villages were burned to ashes and desolated by war. Today I experience the affliction of seeing so many people, especially the young, die of smallpox and other contagious diseases.

I have suffered affliction in such measure that for a long time I was so weighed down by the divine hand that I could barely discharge my ministerial duties. But who can talk about his own tragedy without tears? If I tried to do that, sorrow would overwhelm me. How often I have been compelled to make the complaints of Job my own. I shall bring these remarks to a close with the words of David: I am indeed afflicted, "yet the Lord thinketh upon me."

Your Afflictions

Not one of us is free from afflictions. We are all subject to various trials and miseries. Both the righteous and the wicked suffer. But what is your attitude under affliction? Have we remained insensitive to the Lord's ways?

That is why the Lord has just reason to say, "I have smitten them, but they have not mourned." You who have been afflicted with smallpox, what have you learned? In spite of drought, loss of employment, storms, and hurricanes in which we have suffered for a long time, our attention is scarcely directed to the objects so prominently held up to view.

People cannot help but be affected by those who have been maimed, crippled, distressed, affected by conflict of mind, impaired in their mental faculties, poor, and the like. But where is our true compassion? We are like those who saw the man who had fallen among thieves. With the priest and Levite, we pass by on the other side (Luke 10). Who thinks of people in bonds as if he himself were bound with them? Who weeps with those who weep (Rom. 12:15)? Oh readers, let us realize that we are afflicted because of sin. For "man that is born of a woman is of few days, and full of trouble."

When afflictions come upon us, let us first, admit that we deserve them. Second, we must recognize the hand of God in them and humble ourselves under them (1 Pet. 5). Third, let us not be unresponsive but say with the church, "I will bear the indignation of the LORD" (Micah 7:9). We must "be afflicted," as James 4:9 says. And we must not rebel but turn to the Lord. Let us weep and mourn and make preparation for death in obedience to the command, "Set thine house in order; for thou shalt die, and not live." *Hodie mihi, oras tibi* — today me, tomorrow thee.

Oh that our heads were waters and our eyes a fountain of tears that we might weep day and night for a breakthrough in the daughters of my people! I conclude with Psalm 41:1, "Blessed is he that considereth the poor: the LORD will deliver him in time of trouble." Amen.

— 10 —

The Lord's Controversy
With His People

"Hear the word of the LORD, ye children of Israel: for
the LORD hath a controversy with the inhabitants of
the land, because there is no truth, nor mercy, nor
knowledge of God in the land. By swearing, and lying,
and killing, and stealing, and committing adultery,
they break out, and blood toucheth blood. Therefore
shall the land mourn, and every one that dwelleth
therein shall languish, with the beasts of the field, and
with the fowls of heaven; yea, the fishes of the sea also
shall be taken away."

— Hosea 4:1-3

A judge does not condemn or punish a criminal until the
man's offense has been distinctly and convincingly presented to him. So also the righteous Judge of the whole
earth, the only lawgiver, deals with sinners who cannot endure His divine decision.

Scarcely had our forefathers disobeyed the covenant
when the Lord cited their offenses before His tribunal, convicted them of their dreadful apostasy, and pronounced
judgments and punishments upon them (Gen. 3). This
happened with the first generations of men (Gen. 6) as well
as with the inhabitants of Sodom and Gomorrah. How
long did the Lord rebuke the children of Israel in the wilderness, particularly at Massa and Meribah, where they

tempted and proved Him? How many times did He convict them of rebellion and murder? For forty years He struggled and pleaded with them to convict them of sin. Eventually He swore in His wrath that they would not enter into His rest (Ps. 95).

In the same manner Jehovah deals with the people in our text. First, He calls them before Him to debate their cause; to sit in judgment over them, to convict them of their abominations, and to hear their defense. He then summons them before His tribunal. Finally, He announces their well-deserved punishment. Our text can be studied in four parts:

- The preface: "Hear, O Israel"
- The Lord's controversy
- The occasion of that controversy, which includes Israel's sin of omission (there was no truth, mercy, or knowledge of God in the land) and its overt sin of evil (swearing, lying, killing, stealing, committing adultery, and a multitude of such aggravated crimes that "they break out, and blood toucheth blood")
- The threatened punishment

Hear, O Israel

The preface of this text refers to the children of Israel, who are usually known as the descendants of Jacob (Hos. 12:3-5), but here it specifically refers to the ten tribes of Israel in contrast to Judah (see Hos. 4:15-17). God calls these children to hear the Word of the Lord. All exhortations, promises, and threats are considered to be the Word of the Lord, and rightly so, because Jehovah is their author. These teachings are sure and irrevocable because they serve as a rule to the people of God and because Jehovah reveals Himself in them as Jehovah — One who is true, faithful, holy, and just.

God calls His children to hear. This is a common introduction to the message of the prophets. It suggests what the prophet might have said: "Do not think that I speak from my own impulses or reprove and threaten you with judgment because I hate you. No, I am the mouth and servant of the Lord. You are not hearing my word but the Word of the Lord. Hear ye heavens, and give ear, thou earth, for the Lord speaketh. Hear, O my people (Ps. 81:8). O earth, earth, earth, hear the word of the LORD (Jer. 22:29)." The prophet might have added that they should hear with their ears but also with attention, reverence, faith, and obedience.

God's Complaint

Israel is summoned here to listen to the Lord's controversy with the people of Canaan as well as the children of Israel. In earlier passages, such as Hosea 2:1-2, believers are asked to contend with their adulterous mother. Nehemiah contended with the nobles, but here the prophet says the Lord Himself has a controversy, or complaint. The original word for controversy suggests not only a plea or lawsuit between two parties, but also an open and just accusation brought against a criminal before a judge. It includes a punishment and is thus more than a mere reproof.

Other parts of Scripture also speak of God contending with His people. In Genesis 6:3, Isaiah 1:18, Jeremiah 2:9, 29, and our text, the phrase refers to God's self-justification and determination, by reason of the offense against His majesty, to inflict appropriate punishment. Thus the Lord's controversy is not just with words but with deeds and inflictions, as mentioned in verse 3 of our text and in Hosea 2:3. That controversy is also suggested in 1 Samuel 25:39, when David says, "Blessed be the LORD, that hath pleaded the cause of my reproach from the hand of Nabal." And in Amos 7:4, when the Lord declares that He will "contend by fire."

In our text, the Lord has a controversy with the inhabitants of Canaan. He will no longer deal with them in exhortations and reproofs through the prophets but will pronounce judgment upon them. He will not condemn them without a formal trial and without hearing their defense, however; for although all offenses are open before Him, yet the Lord will never pronounce judgment against sinners until He has first heard what they would testify against Him (Isa. 5:3; Micah 6:2-5).

The Reason for God's Complaint

God has a controversy with the children of Israel, first, because of their sins of omission, or their absence of virtues. Specifically, His charges include:

1. There is no truth in them. The Hebrew word for truth, *emeth*, signifies agreement between the judgment and the object it relates to. In man, this generally refers to righteousness, holiness, and uprightness of life. Particularly it refers to the virtue of matching our words with our intentions as well as faithfully doing what we say we will do.

2. There is no mercy in them. The word for mercy is *hesed*, which can also be translated as compassion or goodness. It generally means an earnest love or an inclination to do what is good for another.

The Psalms describe pious people as those who are good, merciful, godly, and kind because they have surrendered themselves to the Lord and His service. "I remember …the kindness of thy youth," Jeremiah 2:2 says, referring to people who indulge in acts of kindness to their fellow men. Eleazar, Abram's servant, asked for mercy when he said: "And now if ye will deal kindly and truly with my master." David showed mercy to Saul's house for Jonathan's sake. The children of God are called to be kind and merciful persons. They consult the best interest of their neighbors, they do good to the poor and afflicted, they do good even to their enemies.

3. They have no knowledge of God. No rational creature, much less a godly person, who has the Word of God can be destitute of knowledge. We must thus understand that

what our text refers to here is a correct and truly saving knowledge of God as He has revealed Himself in His Word, which includes faith, love, and obedience. This is not the kind of knowledge that even devils possess. Rather, it is true knowledge that is based on the Word of God and is accompanied by faith as well as love for God and our neighbor. As the Dutch annotations say, "Understand here a correct, true, saving knowledge of God, regulated by His Word, and coupled with faith and love to God and our fellow man." (See Jeremiah 9:24; 22:16; 31:34; 1 Samuel 2:12; 1 John 2:4.)

Those who do not know God do not acknowledge, reverence, fear, and obey Him. Nor do they keep His commandments. This evil extends to every class of people in Canaan, Hosea says. Therefore there is no knowledge "in the land."

There was no faithfulness or truth in the prophets and no kindness between rulers and their subjects. The kingdom and the priesthood were so corrupt that there was no knowledge of God in priests, people, and the whole land. Everyone was corrupt.

It is true that there were still some pious people — although few — at that time, for even in the most corrupt times the Lord preserves a holy seed (Rom. 11:2-3; 9:5). But those who were good and merciful were so few that they could scarcely be found (Micah 7:1; Ps. 12:1).

In addition to the sins of omission, the people of the land were committing sins of commission. These included abominations such as:

1. Swearing. The original word for swearing refers to cursing ourselves or others or wishing evil from God upon others as well as uttering an oath with curses. To swear, then, is to ask out of malice or fierce anger temporal or everlasting evil upon ourselves or others (Acts 23:12; 2 Sam. 16:5-6).

2. Lying. This is speaking against our judgment or better knowledge in civil or religious things. As Hosea 7:13 says, "Though I have redeemed them, yet they have spoken lies

against me." To lie is to say what is contrary to fact and better knowledge or to declare as truth what is not true. Lies include:

- Pernicious lies, which we use to injure our neighbor.
- Officious lies, which we use to promote our own or another's advantage.
- Lies of pleasure or inconsideration. We use these for gossip or entertainment. But all lies, without exception, are evil (Ps. 5:6; Eph. 4:25; Col. 3:9).

3. Killing. This includes violent murder as well as acts done against authority and out of hatred or evil passion that assault, wound, or injure the body of another. Killing can be committed in thought, word, looks, and deeds, as we have seen in a previous sermon on the sixth commandment.

4. Stealing. This means taking property from another and appropriating it to ourselves, contrary to the will of the other person. This is forbidden in the eighth command, "Thou shalt not steal."

5. Committing adultery. This means defiling the bed of another and having carnal knowledge of someone we are not married to. This is forbidden in the seventh command, which we will preach about this afternoon.

All these sins are forbidden by the law of God and include severe denunciations and penalties. It is for such sins that the judgments of God came upon the inhabitants of the land (Rev. 9:21). These sins were multiplied so much that the prophet says, "They break out and blood toucheth blood."

"Break out" means to increase with violence and to spread forth with a sudden, mighty infestation (Gen. 28:14). The verse thus suggests, "They break out without measure with all manner of abominations (as robbers and enemies break through interposing barriers) without fear of God's laws, institutions, and regulations. They so multiply their evil doings that they cannot be subdued or restrained by human or divine law. They are like rapidly rising floods that violently and without control burst through dikes and dams."

"Break out," the Dutch annotations say, suggests a flood that bursts forth because of the violence and abundance of water. It also suggests robbers and enemies that are so violent that they erupt with all kinds of abominations, regardless of the laws and ordinances of God.

We find another application of the word in verse 10.

"And blood toucheth blood" in Hebrew literally says, "bloods touch bloods." The word *blood* here has been explained in various ways. Some think it means the thoughts of Jewish masters are directed to murder and the flow of blood, which was common in Israel at that time. Others think blood refers to sinful, forbidden marriages with close relatives. Still others think blood refers to various capital offenses that were continually multiplied or heaped up by the children of Israel, resulting in such a complication of evils that one sin followed another.

The last interpretation is plausible, since Scripture compares sin to blood-guiltiness (Ps. 51:14), and the spilling of blood is considered a grievous crime. Blood is the foundation and instrument of lust, and is thus the cause of sin. Blood provides substance and food for lust, wrath, and other depraved feelings.

But "blood" is more often used in Scripture to mean the shedding of blood through murder. As Psalms 51 and 106 say, "Deliver me from bloodguiltiness." The accusation "blood toucheth blood" in our text thus repeats or exaggerates what preceded it. The meaning then, is this: "The whole land is defiled and filled with blood. One murder or violent death follows another; scarcely has one incident of bloodshed occurred before another takes place. They have shed blood upon blood."

Punishment for the Land and Its Inhabitants

The Lord thus pronounces a sentence upon the sinful

land and its inhabitants. "Therefore shall the land mourn," He says. The land refers to Canaan and its inhabitants. They will mourn, meaning that they will manifest their grief and sorrow by outward signs and indications, whatever they might be. Technically, a land cannot mourn, but figuratively it can mourn if it becomes so desolate that it makes its inhabitants mourn. As a land or earth is said to laugh when it is so adorned, beautiful, or faithful that it stirs its inhabitants to joy (Isa. 35:1-2), so its people will mourn when the place is so desolate, uncultivated, and unfruitful that it can only create anguish in its owners and inhabitants (Isa. 3:26; 24:4; Joel 1:10; Amos 1:2).

What naturally follows, then, but the "languishing," or pining away of the inhabitants of the land? To languish is to fail and swoon away from lack of strength (Ps. 6:3; Lam. 1:12). Our text indicates how massive this languishing or swooning or utter exhaustion will become. Not only the inhabitants of the land, but the beasts of the field and fowls of heaven will languish because of the sins of men. Even the fish of the sea will be taken away, for when the waters are dried up the fish must perish.

We know that great abominations were found among the Israelites and that the punishment God threatened them with came to pass, for these things are written in the books of Kings and Chronicles as well as by Joel and Amos, fellow prophets and contemporaries of Hosea. The fearful wars that the ten tribes waged are recorded in 1 Kings 14:30 and 2 Chronicles 13:17. In response to all of that, murders broke out in the land of Israel, blood touching blood. Swearing, lying, and stealing abounded, as recorded in Amos 2:6-7.

Punishment for Our Land and Its Inhabitants
Even as the land of Canaan was guilty of these sins, so are we in our land with its inhabitants. The Lord thus has a

controversy with the inhabitants of our land. Our land as well as the church are devoid of the following virtues:

1. There is no truth in them. They show no regard for words, promises, bonds, or oaths. To where has fidelity fled? No one can depend on anyone's word or promise. Truly, the words that Isaiah wrote in the time of Israel can be applied today: "And judgment is turned away backward, and justice standeth afar off: for truth is fallen in the street, and equity cannot enter. Yea, truth faileth; and he that departeth from evil maketh himself a prey: and the LORD saw it, and it displeased him that there was no judgment" (59:14-15).

2. There is no mercy in them. There is no zeal for the honor of God or for the good of one's neighbor. No one shows generosity, either in the house of God or to support the poor and needy.

3. There is no knowledge of God. What profound ignorance exists in the midst of all the means of grace. How few are able to recite the fundamental truths of religion! Where is true knowledge that is connected with the graces of love, humility, and self-denial? Some people have knowledge, but it is not sanctified knowledge. They have knowledge but do not practice it. They do not know the meaning of "If ye know these things, happy are ye if ye do them" (John 13:17). They profess God, but they do not acknowledge Him when they deny Him with their works (Titus 1:16). We thus have earned this reproach of Paul: "Some [we may say many] have not the knowledge of God: I speak this to your shame."

The inhabitants of Canaan as well as the church and our land today not only live with the absence of virtues, but also with the presence of the following abominations and transgressions:

1. Cursing. How often is the name of God profaned by cursing and swearing around us! What horrible oaths are belched out! Where are the people who fear the name of God?

2. Lying. Lying is so common that no conscience is made of it.

3. Murder. There is much murder around us in the literal sense, but even more is committed in the eyes of God. What malice, envy, and revenge abound! How numerous are the envious Cains, rancorous Esaus, morose Nabals, and revengeful Lamechs.

4. Stealing. How the land is filled with thieves, with workers of unrighteousness who use all their ingenuity and find all their pleasure in defrauding their neighbor, thus appropriating to themselves that which is not their own.

5. Adultery. This land contains many adulterers, whoremongers, and impure persons. We shall speak more about that later today.

Every iniquity is practiced with an uplifted hand among us and breaks out daily. Piety is scarcely to be found anywhere. Who can think about these things without sighing and tears? Who can contemplate without sorrow the wounds of the church and the corruption of its members? Truly, we have reason with the prophet Micah to exclaim, "Woe is me! for I am as when they have gathered the summer fruits, as the grapegleanings of the vintage: there is no cluster to eat: my soul desired the first ripe fruit. The good man is perished out of the earth: and there is none upright among men: they all lie in wait for blood; they hunt every man his brother with a net" (Micah 7:1-2).

No wonder that our land and its inhabitants have long been afflicted with hurricanes, hail storms, dry summers, and severe winters, in which many beasts have died. In addition, we have suffered malignant diseases, business slowdowns, decay of commerce, unfruitful seasons, and unfavorable harvests, so that almost everyone complains. But who can object to that when he considers his sins? Truly, unless people begin turning to the Lord, they should fear that the land will mourn. Read Zephaniah 1:2-4.

Punishment for Us

Six conditions give us reason to conclude that there is nothing desirable suspended over either our land or church:

1. Corruption is widespread.

2. God has been warning us. If the Lord has punished so many Christian churches in other lands, why do we think that we shall escape His wrath? For a long time God has been pouring out His judgments like vials upon the church. If these things are done in a green tree, what shall be done in the dry? Happy is he who by the faults of others learns to correct his own (Zeph. 3:6-7).

3. He has given us signs and wonders. If we have wandered so far away that the miseries of others cannot teach us wisdom, God has given us other tokens of His displeasure. He has sent us signs in heaven and upon earth. Our wonderful God shows wonders in heaven and signs upon earth, such as blood, fire, and vapor of smoke. He shows forth lightnings with terrible thunders, turns the moon into blood and the sun into darkness. Whoever knows history is aware of how often strange events have preceded revolutions or the subversion of states. A storm or tempest that flattens barns and churches; the dreadful lightning and thunder that caused devastation to houses, churches, men, and beasts; that strange and wonderful light throughout the land that almost converts night into day, how awesome and how terrible each is!

I do not encourage you to become superstitious of the signs of heaven. Nor would I encourage you to be a second Duke of Alvas who, when asked by the king of France for his opinion of the terrible comet that was making its appearance, replied: "Sire, I have had so much to do upon earth that I have had no time to look to heaven."

I will not try to explain these signs, either. However, I do agree with the old and established opinion that such signs in the heavens are premonitions of changes in the affairs of earth. And I agree with the early church father Tertullian, who said, "All these things are indications of God's approaching displeasure; which to the utmost, it is our duty to proclaim, preach, and endeavor to avert by our prayers."

4. The punishment is building. From the earliest times, God would warn His people before inflicting them with blows. Did He not do that with Egypt and Pharaoh? Was not this His method with the Jews whom He first smote and then consumed? For confirmation, scan the dreadful passage of Leviticus 26:14-33. It says that warnings will not be repeated forever. With each one God says, "If you do not now repent, tomorrow I will smite with sevenfold greater force." What does this mean with respect to how you earn a living? What about how you may be affected by contagious diseases? What about weather conditions, which are so dry, then so wet? What can all of this say to us but MENE, MENE, TEKEL, UPHARSIN (Dan. 5:25)?

5. God may punish the church. Since God is withdrawing His Spirit from us, He may be planning something unusual for us as a people and a church. He might be planning to remove from us the candlestick of the gospel, to turn our land into darkness and the shadow of death.

When God destroyed the first temple, He removed the glory of the God of Israel from His people. He stood upon the threshold, then finally forsook the city, whereupon the prophet was commanded to depart. Since we can likewise clearly perceive the withdrawal of the Spirit, is it not time to wake up, and, like the two disciples, plead with the Lord Jesus to abide with us (Luke 24:29)?

Nothing can be worse than when God says to His people, "Pray not," and takes from them the spirit of prayer. The prayers of the pious support the land. Today no one is expressly forbidden to pray, but we are lacking in zeal, tenderness, and engagedness in prayer. Oh New Netherlands, what will become of you if the pious do not pray for you?

Oh Lord, our God, who dwells in the heavens, Thou

canst help us by powerfully turning us to Thyself; we beseech Thee, do not depart from us. For Thy name's sake, be gracious to us.

Oh my friends, wake up! What else can I say but "Hear the Word of the Lord"? Listen to its teaching and reproof. We warn you for your good. The counsel of Daniel to Nebuchadnezzar is our counsel to you: "Wherefore, O king, let my counsel be acceptable unto thee, and break off thy sins by righteousness, and thine iniquities by showing mercy to the poor; if it may be a lengthening of thy tranquillity" (Dan. 4:27).

Cursing, lying, adultery, licentiousness, stealing, and similar sins must no longer be found among us. Each of us must search his ways, mourn over, and depart from his sins. Each has done his part toward inflaming the wrath of God, so each must work to extinguish it. A holy reformation and change must take place among us, for this is the only way to sustain a sinking land. When God says so plainly: I will rend and depart; I will bear away, and there shall be "none to deliver," we must resolve like Israel to say, "Come...let us return" (Hos. 6:1).

I beseech you beloved, by the mercy of God, by the blood of Jesus Christ, by your spiritual and temporal welfare, by the love you bear wife and children, by all that you hold dear, turn to the Lord. Fall at His feet. "Kiss the Son, lest he be angry," today, while ye hear His voice. Do not put off till tomorrow what must be done today "before the decree bring forth" (Zeph. 2:2).

I conclude with the words of Paul: "For the grace of God that bringeth salvation hath appeared to all men, teaching us that, denying ungodliness and worldly lusts, we should live soberly, righteously, and godly, in this present world" (Titus 2:11-12). Amen.

— 11 —

The Children of God Preserved From Self-Exaltation by Trials

"And lest I should be exalted above measure through the abundance of the revelations, there was given to me a thorn in the flesh, the messenger of Satan to buffet me, lest I should be exalted above measure."

— 2 Corinthians 12:7

The poet Claudian once wrote, *"Tolluntur in altum ut lapsu graviore ruant,"* which means, "They are raised on high that they may be brought down with greater force." The idea here is that the wicked are exalted prior to their grievous destruction.

There are many examples of this in sacred Scriptures, such as Pharaoh, king of Egypt, who was brought low by being torn from his throne, then was drowned in the waters of the Red Sea; and of Saul, who was searching for his father's asses when he was exalted to the position of king over Judah but then was humbled by being deprived of his kingdom and rejected by the Lord. That was also the lot of the proud and blasphemous Sennacherib, king of Assyria, who was slain by his sons; of Nebuchadnezzar, who was cast from the throne of his kingdom, deprived of his glory, and driven from men to dwell with the beasts of the field; and of his son, Belshazzar, whose kingdom was taken from him before he was slain (Dan. 5). King Herod was exalted as he sat in royal apparel on the seat of judgment, but he was then smitten by an angel of the Lord and eaten of worms till he gave up the ghost.

History also includes examples, such as James II, who was elevated from a duke to king but subsequently was forced to resign the throne in favor of his son-in-law, William III.

Such examples teach that men are frequently exalted that they may suffer a more dreadful fall. Furthermore, the greater their elevation, the more they are in danger of self-exaltation. Since the children of God are encumbered with the flesh, it is also possible for them to fall into the sin of pride. We learn this from the account of the pious king Hezekiah, whose heart was lifted up before his kingdom was destroyed.

To prevent such self-exaltation in believers, God sends affliction upon them. As our text says, Paul was given a thorn in the flesh, "lest he be exalted beyond measure."

The passage prior to the text contains an account of how the apostle was favored with an extraordinary revelation and heavenly vision (vv. 1-4), how he applied it to himself (vv. 5-6), and the consequence of that vision, which includes a grievous affliction upon Paul. Such was the excellence of the revelation that he was given a thorn in the flesh, "the messenger of Satan to buffet me" in order to preserve him from the pride by which he was in danger of being carried away.

To understand our text, we will study it in three parts:
- Paul's thorn in the flesh
- Where the thorn came from
- The purpose of the thorn

Paul's Thorn in the Flesh

The thorn that the apostle complains about here is an incredibly heavy and painful affliction. The Greek word for this thorn literally means a sharp stake, a thistle, or a ragged or thorny fragment of wood that is jabbed into the flesh or bones. It is similar to what is mentioned in Ezekiel 28:24, which says, "And there shall be no more a pricking brier unto the house of Israel, nor any grieving thorn." Such a thorn causes great pain and distress until it is removed. The apostle uses the term figuratively to describe something that is causing him extreme pain or bodily affliction.

He also refers to the affliction as "an angel of Satan." An angel is a messenger, or emissary, and Satan is an adversary. Satan himself is an evil angel, but "a messenger of Satan" appears to refer to one of the fallen angels sent forth by Satan, the superior or chief of evil angels. Matthew 25:41 refers to such a hierarchy when it mentions "the devil and his angels."

We thus understand by this that the devil, with God's permission, is the means or instrument that is used to torment and afflict Paul. Such was also the case of David in 1 Chronicles 21:1. It was especially so of God's servant Job (1:9; 2:2, 6-7). Indeed the apostle Paul can be regarded as a kind of second Job. We readily see how the work of the devil is a thorn in the flesh to him. It was extremely painful and distressing to him, even as it was to Job, especially when we consider how Satan might have tormented Paul with memories of his former ungodly life and conduct. This affliction may have led Paul to agonize about his previous life and suffer, like the brothers of Joseph, the pain and gnawing of conscience (Gen. 42:21).

When the text says Satan's angel "buffeted" Paul, it does not mean that the messenger literally struck Paul with his fists, as it does in Matthew 26:67 and 1 Corinthians 4:11. Rather, the term is used figuratively here and refers to being treated contemptuously or ignominiously. Being struck with the fist is thus a great indignity, insult, and affront (see 1 Peter 2:20). The apostle uses the word *buffet* here to say that the messenger of Satan uses himself and his instruments to bring disgrace and contempt upon Paul, both in his person and office (although without success). The word *buffet* is used in the general sense of showing contempt (1 Thes. 2:2; 1 Cor. 4:11).

The terms thorn in the *flesh* and messenger of *Satan* may be used separately or together, but the verse here includes both the idea that the messenger of Satan caused the thorn in the flesh as well as that the thorn itself was the messenger of Satan.

Let us now see what Paul means by this thorn in the flesh and messenger of Satan; that is, what this thorn was and how the messenger of Satan buffeted him. On this subject, there are almost as many opinions as men. Truly this text might be included with other things in the epistles of Paul that Peter says are "hard to be understood."

We shall offer some opinions even though it is impossible to call any of them definitive. Even Augustine acknowledged that he did not know with certainly what Paul meant by this thorn and messenger of Satan. What we do know, however, is the following:

1. The thorn was something in the flesh of the apostle that caused him constant uneasiness, even severe pain.

2. Satan, by divine permission, was the instrument that caused this affliction, or at least aggravated it. But exactly what this thorn or affliction was is difficult to determine. Some think the thorn was bodily weakness, such as a pain in the head or weakness of the kidneys. Others thought that the apostle, like Timothy, was afflicted with a weak stomach. Basil and other early church fathers guessed that the thorn was some disease inflicted by the devil, as in the case of Job. Others disagreed, saying the apostle nowhere complains of sickness.

3. Some believe the thorn represents the conflict between the flesh and the spirit. It is a symbol of the remains of Paul's corrupt nature, which he so dolefully laments (Rom. 7). But this is common to all the regenerate.

4. Chrysostom, Theophylact, and others believed the thorn represented special enemies, persecutors, oppres-

sors, backbiters, and slanderers of the apostle. Like so many goads and sharp stakes, they continually opposed his holy endeavors. Scripture compares such ungodly persons with briars and thorns. For example, consider Jotham's parable of a bramble (Judg. 9:14-15), and Numbers 33:55, which says that the Canaanites would be like pricks and thorns to the Israelites. They "shall vex you in the land wherein ye dwell," the passage says. Accordingly, Paul could be referring to Hymenaeus and Philetus (2 Tim. 2:17-18), Alexander the coppersmith (2 Tim. 4:14), Diotrephes (3 John 9), and others who sought to have preeminence over him.

5. Beza believed the thorn stood for the heaviest afflictions, both of body and soul, that were brought upon the apostle through the instigation and buffeting of Satan.

6. Others believed that Paul was literally buffeted by a messenger of Satan.

7. Still others, both ancient and modern expositors, many of whom were Roman Catholic, thought the thorn represented evil desire or temptation to lust. Others rejected this, observing that Paul had the gift of continence. In addition to having lawfully avoided such temptations, he was already old when he wrote of this thorn.

8. One distinguished divine believed the thorn was a certain disease that physicians referred to as *morbus hypochondriacus*. He believed this because the disease deeply penetrates the flesh, causing much uneasiness and a thousand imaginary troubles. All of this is due to physical obstructions, a lack of animal spirits, and impurity of the blood. No disease could be more of an affliction than this; none could so rob life of comfort or so humble the mind. The disease is caused by numerous cares and anxieties, intense application of mind, and much watching, all of which were exceedingly abundant in Paul.

He who is afflicted with this disorder may with difficulty pursue his vocation even though he may be brought low by it. This is indicated in our apostle who, notwithstanding his affliction, continued faithfully to discharge the business of his office. The disease also causes daily suffering, although occasionally there can be some relief from it. When this disorder was most severe in the apostle, the messenger of Satan aggravated his trouble and buffeted or afflicted him with tormenting sensations. It was much like what happened with the lunatics in the New Testament who, during the time of the full moon, experienced great distress because of natural causes but were even more afflicted by Satan, who took advantage of this aggravation of their malady (Matt. 4:24).

That God now should sometimes use Satan to bodily afflict His children is not altogether strange, since He did so in the case of Job, who was a man of distinguished piety (Job 1:1). How this happens exactly, we do not know. All we have is conjecture.

Let each one of you decide which interpretation is closest to the truth. But it is acceptable as well if some say they do not know the real meaning of the expression, since the apostle himself does not reveal what it means. As one expositor of Scripture says, "The things which are manifest let us recognize, and what an apostle has left in obscurity let us leave in obscurity." It will be safest to form no definite conclusion on the subject but to explain it in a general manner, assuming as certain that:

- Since Paul was favored with wonderful revelations that exalted him, the thorn was sent as a special remedy to preserve him from pride. Furthermore, something more is intended here than common temptations which are spoken of in Numbers 16:29 or 1 Corinthians 10:13.

- The thorn was a truly grievous affliction; the apostle was so disturbed and distressed by it that he "besought the Lord thrice," that is, many times (v. 8), to be relieved of it.

Some divines believe this passage speaks in general of those many and diverse afflictions to which the apostle, to his humiliation, was subjected, such as persecution, false apostles, and various offenses by which he was hotly and constantly pursued. Indeed, Paul describes the effect of such trials as being pierced with thorns and smitten with the fist, because he suffered such vexation, pain, and contempt that he felt as if his flesh had been torn with thorns and his face had been beaten with a fist.

The apostle uses similar descriptions in Romans 9:2, which help us understand that the sore evil that he speaks of in our text not only caused pain to his body but trouble to his soul. Furthermore, the devil had a special hand in this, for the thorn caused the apostle to struggle with a special corruption or temptation of heart. Christ was subjected to such a temptation, and so was Paul.

Where the Thorn Came From

Our text says the thorn was given to Paul. The apostle acknowledges that the thorn was a gift that was given to him by God to humble and restrain him. Rather than to view it as a reason to murmur against God, he views it as a means by which it can be used for the glory of God and the good of His people (Phil. 1:29).

Truly it is an act of distinguished love on God's part to bridle, restrain, and preserve His people in a state of humility. "There was given to me," Paul says, indicating that God, not the devil, was in control. God was the author of the trial but He permitted Satan to effect it to carry out Paul's humiliation. This tempter was given to Paul, Jerome says, to repress Paul's pride.

Indeed, all afflictions proceed out of the providence of God; for according to His sovereign will, God uses the devil as well as ungodly men to try and chastise His people. Note how Shimei cursed David. That did not happen without God's control. We can apply this also to the messenger of Satan, since Satan can do nothing without God's permission (1 Kings 22:22; Job 1:12; 2:7; Matt. 8:31-32). Furthermore, no matter how grievous this thorn was to the poor apostle, it was meant for his good; for God chastens those whom He loves.

The Purpose of the Thorn

Paul was given the thorn, as he says, "Lest through the abundance of the revelation I should be exalted above measure." He repeats the phrase "Lest I should be exalted above measure" at the end of the verse. Paul was favored with many significant revelations. By nature man is prone to self-exaltation, especially when he has received eminent gifts from the hand of God. Such special favor can lead us to entertain extravagant ideas of ourselves. A believer can be so carried away by pride when made the object of special divine manifestations that he readily forgets himself and begins to speak and act in an unbecoming manner.

After Nadab and Abihu saw the Holy One of Israel, they brought strange, unholy fire to the altar. The Lord thus smote them and they died (Lev. 10:1-2). Moses adds, "This is it that the LORD spake, saying, I will be sanctified in them that come nigh me, and before all the people I will be glorified." We thus see that even when very pious men fall, they are humbled to be preserved from further pride. Elijah, for example, was a distinguished but timid man of God. Moses was a great man, but he too had his weaknesses. Paul was marked by the distinction of having been caught up into the third heaven, or paradise. But in order that the apostle, who was a weak man encumbered with depravity, might not become elevated or puffed up (for knowledge puffeth up), either by regarding himself as greater than the other apostles and other teachers, or by underestimating others and regarding them as inferior to himself, or by allowing others to entertain too high an opinion of himself, God in His good pleasure brought upon Paul an affliction, leading the apostle to say, "Lest I should be exalted above measure."

In such ways God will suppress all pride in His children. And no wonder, for self-exaltation is an evil by which they can easily be overcome. We see evidence of this even in the pious Hezekiah, whose "heart was lifted up: therefore there was wrath upon him" (2 Chron. 32:25). "God resisteth the proud," says 1 Peter 5:5, and Luke 16:15 adds that they are an abomination to Him. God punished the sin of pride in our first parents, in Pharaoh, Nebuchadnezzar, and others. He will also bring it to subjection in His children, in whom He delights. The spirit of self-exaltation is by nature an act of injustice towards God because it appropriates to ourselves that which belongs to God. God will thus do what is necessary with His children that they shall not exalt themselves; He not only forbids it in His Word but also uses instruments, sometimes of the most grievous kind, which can be heavy and diversified afflictions, as we have seen in Paul.

These afflictions produced the desired effect; for the apostle was humbled by them in these four ways:

1. He frequently prayed to God for deliverance (v. 8).

2. He was submissive to God's answer (v. 9).

3. He learned to accept his infirmities, saying, "Most gladly therefore will I rather glory in my infirmities, that the power of Christ may rest upon me" (v. 9).

4. He learned to take pleasure in them.

Psalm 119:130 says, "The entrance of thy words giveth light." We leave it to you to determine whether the exposition of the apostle's text helps you understand what it means. But here are some of the lessons it offers:

• That all things, within or without, that painfully affect or disquiet us, proceed from the hand of God. The apostle plainly teaches this when he says, "There was given...me a thorn in the flesh, the messenger of Satan to buffet me, lest I should be exalted above measure." The story of pious Job teaches the same lesson.

• That even the most holy men are not exempt from the

temptations and buffetings of Satan. Even Christ was tempted. So was Peter (Luke 22) and now Paul. Therefore Peter warns, "Be sober, be vigilant; because your adversary the devil, as a roaring lion, walketh about, seeking whom he may devour."

• That God allows such difficulties to happen to His children for their good. Paul specifically says that the thorn or messenger of Satan was given to him so he would not be exalted by the abundance of revelation that God had granted him. Likewise, God frequently lays crosses upon His people to wean them from the world, to prevent them from sinning, to keep them humble, to produce holiness in them, to drive them to God, to stir them to pray, to stimulate them to work out their salvation with fear and trembling, to assure them that the love of God will increase, and to lead them to depend only upon His grace. Truly "whom the LORD loveth he correcteth" (Prov. 3:12; Heb. 12:6; Rev. 3:19).

Although the thorn in the flesh caused great trouble and distress to the pious apostle, he learned to bear it with patience, recognizing that the Lord was using it to preserve him from self-exaltation. Thereafter, he also held himself in little esteem because he was firmly persuaded of the love of God towards him. For in answer to his thrice-uttered prayer, he was given this assurance, "My grace is sufficient for thee" (v. 9). In this the apostle Paul may be regarded as an example and pattern of lessons that may apply to the whole church of Christ in general and to each believer in particular, namely:

1. They too may be given thorns in the flesh. They may be given tribulations, persecutions, assaults, and vexations from the ungodly enemies of the truth. This is implied when the church is seen as a lily among thorns (Song of Sol. 2:2). The church is like a lily because of its fragrance and beauty, but it stands among thorns because it is called to endure fierce persecution and trying afflictions.

2. They may be given messengers of Satan to buffet them. Though they may not have to endure what Job or Paul did, they are nonetheless called to endure contempt, taunting, mockery, and abuse by word or work from Satan's instruments because they are godly, pious, and believing. Truly such painful and contemptuous treatment are buffetings of Satan, which proceed out of the old enmity between the seed of the woman and that of the serpent (Gen. 3:15).

3. The children of God, even those who have much light, much grace, and much experience, may fall into the sin of entertaining exalted thoughts of themselves. They may become proud like Hezekiah, whose heart was lifted up (2 Chron. 32:25); like David, who numbered Israel (1 Chron. 21:1); and like Peter, who, not long after eating the Lord's Supper with the Lord Jesus, became puffed up with vain glory and fell into the hands of Satan (Matt. 26:31-33). Therefore God visits them with many afflictions, both spiritual and corporal.

4. No one among the children of men is free from trouble, perplexity, and adversity, for, as Job 14:1 says, "Man that is born of a woman is of few days, and full of trouble." What happens to one happens to all. Afflictions are as common with the righteous as they are with the wicked. In every time, God's judgments have been present in the world.

Friends, every one of you is afflicted in one way or another. But have afflictions humbled, changed, and brought you to God? Alas, how many people are like Pharaoh, whose heart was hardened by the judgments of God; like Israel, who revolted even more after she was stricken (Isa. 1:5); and like those who, instead of humbling themselves and acknowledging their faults, murmur and complain. The apostle Jude describes such people in verse 16. 1 Peter 5:6 warns, "Humble yourselves...under the mighty hand of God, that he may exalt you in due time." Oh that the judgments and afflictions we are afflicted with would have such a desirable result as in Manasseh who, when the Lord brought him into difficulty, earnestly "besought the LORD his God" (2 Chron. 33:12). Or as with the prodigal son who, when reduced to such extremes that he nearly perished with hunger, said, "I will arise and go to my father, and...say unto him, Father, I have sinned against heaven, and before thee" (Luke 15:18).

To this, let me add the example of the pious, such as the church in general, which responds to the Lord's afflictions by saying, "I will bear the indignation of the LORD, because I have sinned against him, until he plead my cause, and execute judgment for me: he will bring me forth to the light, and I shall behold his righteousness" (Micah 7:9).

Consider also how David responded to difficulties, saying, "Before I was afflicted I went astray: but now have I kept thy word" (Ps. 119:67). Likewise, Christ, when abandoned by the disciples who fell asleep instead of keeping watch with Him, prayed the more earnestly (Luke 22:41). Or Jonah, who slept in the ship but cried out to God when he was in the belly of the fish. All of this teaches the importance of the divine command, "Is any among you afflicted? let him pray" (James 5:13).

Children of God, learn from the example of Paul and from the Lord Jesus, who equally felt the sharp thorns of persecution and enmity from the Jews; who experienced the temptations of Satan (Matt. 4); and who suffered his buffetings. In like manner you must become conformed to the ways of God (Rom. 8:29).

Are you called to endure temptation? Are you suffering affliction? Are you struggling against a special conflict? Do not become discouraged, but "Count it all joy when ye fall into divers temptations" (James 1:2); for God remains your friend. He calls His dearest children to suffer thorns in the flesh. Your trials are not by chance. They were given to you by God, who has good reason to inflict them, namely, to suppress your pride and to humble you. What Christian does not want to be humble? Truly, how frequently we pray, "No greater good be granted me than that I be made humble and little in my own eyes." To this end, we must expect thorns and buffeting.

I conclude with the words of Paul, "And we know that all things work together for good to them that love God, to them who are the called according to his purpose" (Rom. 8:28). Amen.

— 12 —

The Believer's Well-founded Expectation of Future Glory

"Nevertheless we, according to his promise, look for new heavens and a new earth, wherein dwelleth righteousness."

— 2 Peter 3:13

"Behold, I make all things new," promises the One who sits upon the throne (Rev. 21:5). Thus everything that receives a new essence or form receives it from God, who sits upon the throne. The renewal of the earth, after a dreary winter, during a delightful spring in which nature assumes a new look, is the work of God. As Psalm 104:30 says, "Thou renewest the face of the earth."

The renewal of the Church through the abolition of the old covenant and the establishment of the new (Heb. 8:13) also comes from the One who says, "Behold, I will do a new thing" (Isa. 43:19). The renewal of the mind, by which the elect put off the old man and put on the new, becoming new creatures in Christ Jesus to do good works, is also from the One who promises, "A new heart also will I give you" (Ezek. 36:26). The giving way of an old year to the new is also from the One who says, "The day is thine, the night also is thine: thou hast prepared the light and the sun" (Ps. 74:16). And the passing away of the earth that we inhabit to make way for the new heavens and a new earth is from the Almighty, who promises it, as we learn from our text.

In the passage that precedes our text, the apostle Peter discusses the instability and destruction of the world, which will eventually be consumed by fire (vv. 7, 10, 12). He then writes about the permanence of believers who shall remain after that event. That figurative language sets the context for the words of our text, which are especially appropriate for today, since through the goodness of God we are about to begin a new year. Oh that we might be given a new spirit that we might "walk in newness of life" (Rom. 6:4).

We shall examine this text in three parts:
- The expectation of new heavens and a new earth
- What is contained in this new place
- The basis of this expectation

The Expectation of New Heavens and a New Earth

Peter taught that the heavens would pass away with a great noise. The question thus arises, "What shall we have therefore?" (Matt. 19:27). Is something better, something more lasting reserved for us?

Yes, our text says. God will give us "new heavens and a new earth." This is implied by the word *nevertheless*. Although this world will experience a mighty change, we can look for new heavens and a new earth. Although the heavens and earth that we now see will pass away, everything will not come to an end. "We" to whom God is longsuffering and who will come to repentance; we who have been holy and godly in conduct (v. 11); we who have obtained a precious faith with true believers (2 Pet. 1:1), we "look for" this new heavens and earth.

To look for, or expect, is to direct one's attention to a good that we do not yet possess (Matt. 11:3). The word suggests patience. When the apostle says, "We look for," he does not intend that we merely expect, as if the outcome may be doubtful or based on insufficient grounds, but with assurance that what is expected shall come to pass.

What do we expect? As Peter says, "New heavens and a new earth." Expositors do not agree about the meaning of this phrase. Opinions differ, even among the orthodox. Some say the phrase refers to the new kingdom of Jesus which will reign upon earth before the Day of Judgment. It describes the blessed state of the church upon earth that we can expect before the end of the world.

Others believe it means that the heavens and earth will pass away by being reduced to ashes, and a new system will emerge. Still others think that the heavens and earth will only be changed and purified in their qualities, which means that "new" really means "renewed." Finally, some think this phrase refers to the dwelling place of the glorified saints in heaven, a place of glory and bliss, otherwise called the heavenly country, where the pious will live after they pass from this earth (Heb. 11:16).

We will not test these opinions to see which we should approve and reject, since this matter does not affect the foundation of our faith. What we can say with confidence is that this text teaches:

- That the new heavens and new earth are different than the heavens that now exist (v. 7), which shall pass away with a great noise, as well as to the present earth (vv. 10, 12). John thus says, "The first heaven and the first earth were passed away" (Rev. 21:1).
- That the heavens and earth that we now know shall not remain the same but will be changed in state and appearance.
- That the new heavens and new earth will not appear before the judgment, that is before the Second Coming of Christ.

With this in mind, our opinion is that the new heavens and new earth refer to the future state and place of the children of God after this life. It is where they will dwell after the Day of Judgment in their whole persons, soul and body. It is the blissful and illustrious condition that is reserved for the elect at the coming of the Day of the Lord. It is that exquisitely delightful heavenly habitation, here called "new heavens and a new earth" and elsewhere called the "new Jerusalem" (Rev. 21:2).

These heavens and earth are "new," not in substance and not absolutely new, for they have existed from the foundation of the world (Matt. 25:34). Rather they are new in the sense that the heavens and the earth shall be delivered from the curse of sin and restored to the state of perfection in which they were created by God, if not more truly, yet more gloriously (Rom. 8:21). They are new in the sense that heaven will be occupied by new inhabitants, or saints, in whom the Lord Jesus will be glorified, and by believers in whom He will be admired (2 Thes. 1:10). They are new in the sense that they will shine with new glory and luster ("renewed," as the Dutch annotations say), and new in terms of occupying a new place, since Christ will come again, then take them to Himself, that where He is they may be also (John 14:3).

The renewal begun in the children of God here will be completed in the "new heavens and earth" by the granting of new and far more illustrious qualities and benefits, such as:

- A new place to live: their Father's house.
- A new body, which is no longer vile, but like the glorious body of Jesus Christ (Phil. 3:21).
- A new society, the innumerable company of angels, in answer to the promise, "I will give thee places to walk among these" (Zech. 3:7).
- A new happiness and new blessedness so great that the prophet writes, "For since the beginning of the world men have not heard, nor perceived by the ear, neither hath the eye seen, O God, beside thee, what he hath prepared for him that waiteth for him" (Isa. 64:4). Our Savior also speaks of it when He says, "I will not drink hence-

forth of this fruit of the vine, until that day when I drink it new with you in my Father's kingdom" (Matt. 26:29).

The saints who are no longer occupied with the groveling pursuits of this earth will then be given a new work of serving the Lord day and night in His temple and exclaiming: "Blessing, and honour and glory, and power, be unto him that sitteth upon the throne, and unto the Lamb for ever and ever" (Rev. 5:13). They will do this in the new heavens and new earth, gloriously described in Revelation 21:1, "And I saw a new heaven and a new earth: for the first heaven and the first earth were passed away; and there was no more sea."

Many questions could be asked here, such as, "Will the earth then be inhabited, and, if so, will God then create other human beings?" It is not reasonable to think that the earth will be inhabited, for "there shall be no more sea." Yet the earth will not be created in vain; rather, as eminent Reformed divines believe, the saints will have such a ready ability to transfer themselves from one place to another that they will sometimes visit the new earth, where they can delight in glorifying God.

What Is Contained in This New Place

Although it is true that there is righteousness in the pious, it is more consistent with the construction of our text to apply the words "wherein dwelleth righteousness" to the new heavens and new earth. In these, righteousness will dwell, for nothing but pure righteousness and glory will be found in them. A contrast is thus established between the present, in which ungodliness and unrighteousness exist, and the future, in which righteousness alone shall be found. The apostle does not say that it is, or shall be, but that it "dwells" there, thus expressing its substantial nature and its permanence. It shall be there, not for a time, but forever. This is not a vain hope, but one that is well-founded, as taught by the last portion of our text.

The Basis of This Expectation

Scripture contains many prophecies in which God promises new heavens and a new earth. Isaiah 65:17 says, "Behold, I create new heavens and a new earth: and the former shall not be remembered, nor come into mind." Isaiah 66:22 adds, "For as the new heavens and the new earth, which I will make, shall remain before me, saith the LORD, so shall your seed and your name remain."

It is true that this promise refers to the state of the church in the New Testament, which is now beginning to be fulfilled but will be totally fulfilled at the end of the world, when all things will become new. As the Dutch annotations say of Isaiah 65:17: "This, indeed, partially took place at the first coming of Christ, by the preaching of the gospel, and the gift of the Holy Ghost, who was richly communicated to believers under the New Testament, but shall not take place fully, until the second coming of the Lord, when His church shall be taken up to heaven. This expectation, therefore, is firm and well founded, resting as it does upon the infallible Word of God." That is also the meaning of these words written by the apostle John, "And he that sat upon the throne said, Behold, I make all things new."

Surely God's children have a glorious hope in seeking not only a present but also, and especially, a future good. They have good grounds to look for new heavens and a new earth, which include the glorious liberty of the children of God, the adoption of children, the redemption of their bodies, and the blessed hope of righteousness — with one difference. In the order of divine operation in the work of grace, glorification follows sanctification, whereas here God's children are changed from glory to glory (2 Cor. 3:18). Sanctification is the beginning of glorification.

What do you think, beloved, are you looking for new heavens and a new earth? If you say yes, do you hope to be partakers of this blessedness? If you again say yes, I ask,

Upon what do you base your hope? Will your hope make you ashamed? If so, you must, while you are here on earth and beneath the heavens, become new creatures (2 Cor. 5:17). As Christ said, men do not put new wine into old bottles. So we also say that the new heavens and new earth are not for those who live in the old man, that is, in their natural state. "For in Christ Jesus neither circumcision availeth any thing, nor uncircumcision, but a new creature" (Gal. 6:15).

Examine yourselves. Are you renewed in the spirit of your minds? Have you received a new heart and a new spirit? I urge this renewal upon you. See it as a mirror in which to view yourself to see whether this work of grace has begun in you.

The Spirit of God describes gracious people as renewed ones. It is clear that they have new light in understanding, since they cannot only be taught the letter of the Word but also have an experimental knowledge of spiritual things and are as convicted of them as if they had actually perceived them through their senses. They see Him who is invisible as greatly to be feared in the assembly of the saints. They see themselves as chief of sinners, Jesus as the fairest of the children of men, the whole world as a fleeting show, eternity as near at hand, and they have respect for the recompense of reward. A new and wonderful light arises in their understanding which before was in darkness. Their will and affections have a new bent, since they now "as newborn babes, desire the sincere milk of the word" (1 Pet. 2:2). They heartily love the Lord as their strength, they labor that they may be accepted of Him, hate every false way or sin, and say to each, "Get thee hence" (Isa. 30:22). They ardently yearn "to depart and...be with Christ" (Phil. 1:23). Ezekiel refers to this as a new heart and a new spirit (36:26). Titus calls it a new and purified conscience, which no longer sleeps but is wakeful and tender and seeks God's face.

If they do not heed God's suggestion, they are inwardly

chastised, but if they obey, the peace of God follows. The blood of Christ thus purifies their consciences. They are marked by a new and hearty service to God because they are no longer content with merely outwardly performing the religious duties of prayer, listening to the Word, and receiving the sacraments, but truly desire to do these in spirit and in truth. If they are not moved by doing such duties, they leave in sorrow. But if they are stirred by them to attention and reverence, they praise God with joy. Paul calls this serving God "in newness of spirit" (Rom. 7:6).

These believers also speak in a new way. They are no longer ashamed of Christ and His words. Rather, godly words like a living stream flow out of their overflowing hearts. They delight in no companionship more than in those who speak to one another in mutual edification. The corn and new wine of divine grace causes the young men and maids to speak. As Mark 16:17 says, "They shall speak with new tongues." They indeed show a whole new way of living and speaking, showing their faith in works, not to be seen by others but to glorify God and edify their neighbor.

Friends, this is that renewed mind of which the Word of God so frequently speaks and which must be found in those who look for new heavens and a new earth. This mind develops with greater speed and exists in greater quantity in one more than in another, but all who are true partakers of grace become partakers of its essential parts through this renewal.

When you measure yourselves by this rule, what is your conclusion? Oh how many are strangers to it! They include:

1. Those who are not acquainted with the nature of this renewal but represent the preaching of it as a new doctrine.

2. Those who explain it in terms of outward things, or as a change of dispensation under the New Testament, or as mere morality, as if it merely meant to be free of gross sins. That is contrary to the teaching of the whole Word of God, which presents it as a renewal of the mind, and the soul as

the seat in which it rises, proceeding outward, not merely in external conformity to the law of God, but in a righteousness exceeding that of the scribes and Pharisees. Alas, that such ones should be found, even in the Reformed Church among those who frequent the Lord's Table, who deride and oppose this renewal, regarding the inward experience and pious discourse of the people of God as ignorance and delusion. Furthermore, if what they hear causes inner turmoil, they resist the influence because they take no pleasure in such a way of life.

Such people remain in the deformity of their natural sinful condition. They are abominable in the eyes of God, regardless of how becoming they are outwardly and how the world admires them. Truly, as John 3:6 says, "That which is born of the flesh is flesh." Such people have no reason to believe they are truly interested in the precious merits of Jesus, the power of which always manifests itself in the renewal of the man (2 Cor. 5:17).

If they have not been renewed, what hope can they truly have of salvation, of arriving in heaven, and of participating in its glory? The place and its inhabitants must be in harmony with each other. Heaven is called the New Jerusalem into which nothing shall enter that defiles (Rev. 21), for God saves us surely "by the washing of regeneration, and renewing of the Holy Ghost" (Titus 3).

Oh that you were brought to examine yourself so that, while confounded and humbled, you would cast yourself before God, who alone can produce in you, according to Psalm 51:10, "A clean heart, O God; and. . .a right spirit." I beg you to earnestly strive after it that you may be renewed (Rom. 12:2). Be changed by the renewal of your mind, "Put off concerning the former conversation the old man, which is corrupt according to the deceitful lusts; and put on the new man, which after God is created in righteousness and true holiness" (Eph. 4:22, 24).

To do this, you should be influenced by:

- The necessity of it. Without renewal, one is not a Christian. Without it, one cannot expect the new heavens.

- The passing of the year. We are about to begin a new year. Will you continue to live from year to year remaining in your old way of life? Why does God put up with you? Why didn't you, like others, die during the past year and pass into eternity? Why were you spared? Is it so that you could continue in your old sins? No, but that you should lead a new life. But if you continue to live without renewal and should leave this world, then you will not have a place in the new heavens and new earth but in Tophet, prepared of old (Isa. 30:33). As Ezekiel 18:31 warns, "Make you a new heart and a new spirit: for why will ye die, O house of Israel?"

  Since righteousness dwells in these new heavens, you must be marked by the practice of righteousness and godliness; for the workers of iniquity shall be cast out (Matt. 7:23). But he who worketh righteousness shall abide in the tabernacle of the Lord (Ps. 15:1-2), for only such ones are accepted with Him (Acts 10:35). Rise up, then, let us follow after righteousness (1 Tim. 6:11), seeking to attain it and exhibit it by yielding ourselves as instruments of righteousness unto God. Righteousness, godliness, and holiness in every form must dwell in believers before they can expect to become part of those new heavens and new earth in which dwell righteousness.

- The glory of renewal. You must be influenced by the glory of this renewed life, for happy are those who partake of it. They have great reason to exclaim with the psalmist in Psalm 103:1, 5, "Bless the LORD, O my soul: and all that is within me, bless his holy name. Who satisfieth thy mouth with good things; so that thy youth is renewed like the eagle's." This renewal is evidence that the Lord has looked in mercy upon you, since without His transforming influence, no renewal can take place. Only He who sits upon the throne can say, "Behold, I make all things new." Only those who are renewed can say, "We are his workmanship, created in Christ Jesus unto good works" (Eph. 2:10).

By this renewal God's children are introduced to an entirely new state. They are brought into actual communion with God by participating in the illustrious blessings of the new covenant, described in Jeremiah 31:33. They acquire the kind of excellent spirit written of in Daniel 5:12. They no longer act in bondage to a spirit of fear but according to a spirit of adoption, whereby they cry, "Abba, Father" (Rom. 8:15). They have a new relationship with the Almighty, who is their Father; the church, who is their mother; believers throughout the world, who are their brothers and sisters; and angels, who are their preservers.

This great change is described in Isaiah 62:2, "Thou shalt be called by a new name, which the mouth of the LORD shall name." This renewal also produces the highest character in those who partake of it, since by it they become as much like God as any creature created by God could possibly be (Eph. 4:24). However insignificant and contemptible they may be in the eyes of the world, they are to be regarded as holy and excellent ones (Ps. 16:3). For, in renewing them, God has made them partakers of the inheritance of the saints in light. As Matthew 5:8 says, "Blessed are the pure in heart: for they shall see God." There, at last, will the renewal begun in them become complete by the addition of new and more illustrious qualities and blessings.

From ancient times it has been the custom among all nations for people to offer good wishes to each other on the first day of a new year. Subjects have done so to their rulers, children to their parents, pastors to their flocks, and friends to each other. Since, during the past year, so many people have gone to their eternal home, causing mourners to go about in the streets, I count it a privilege and joy upon the first day of the new year to look at you, beloved. Some of you are older than me, others my equals in age, and still others younger than me. What gift shall I give you for the new year? You should expect no delicacies for the palate or no silver and gold, for I have none of these. But I do offer you something that comes out of my duty and office and is drawn from the Word of God. I wish you, my hearers, old and young, men and women, a new heart and a new spirit, that you may walk in newness of life. If you receive this as a new year's gift, how happy you would be!

For you, children of God, I wish that you will be strengthened within, that you may benefit from it and go from strength to strength and virtue to virtue until you appear in the heavenly Zion before God, where you will sing a new song, saying, "Thou art worthy to take the book, and to open the seals thereof: for thou wast slain, and hast redeemed us to God by thy blood out of every kindred, and tongue, and people, and nation." Amen.

— 13 —

God's Judgment Upon Corrupt Members of the Church

"And I beheld, and heard an angel flying through the midst of heaven, saying with a loud voice, Woe, woe, woe, to the inhabiters of the earth by reason of the other voices of the trumpet of the three angels, which are yet to sound!"

— Revelation 8:13

Horns or trumpets (Num. 10:1-10) were blown to call the children of Israel to joyful observance of their religious rites before the Lord (Lev. 25:9; 2 Sam. 6:15; Ps. 47:5-6). As Psalm 81:3 says, "Blow up the trumpet in the new moon, in the time appointed, on our solemn feast day." See also Psalm 150:3-5; Matthew 24:31; and 1 Corinthians 15:52.

Horns or trumpets were also used to gather together an army for an expedition against or attack upon an enemy. The sound of trumpets also roused the Israelites, filling them with terror and fear of impending destruction (Judg. 3:27). In the conquering of Jericho, trumpets played a major role. The walls of the city fell down after all the armed men of Israel, who were led by seven priests bearing seven ram horns before the ark, had marched for seven successive days around the city.

In Chapter 13 of Revelation, we read of seven trumpets that herald severe, uncommon, notable, and previously threatened judgments and calamities. Chapter 8, in which our text appears, can be viewed in three parts: first, heaven prepares for the sounding of the trumpets (vv. 1-6); second, the trumpets of the four angels are sounded (vv. 7-12); and third, the chapter concludes with an introduction to the three following trumpets (v. 13). In our text an angel cries woe because of the plagues accompanying those three trumpets.

Two points offer themselves for contemplation:
- Preparation for the announcement.
- The dreadful announcement.

Preparation for the Announcement

Our text begins with John's statement, "And I beheld, and heard an angel." This was as remarkable an occurrence for John as it would be for any of us. Holy men in both the Old and New Testament saw many visions, and so it was with John. Verse 13 says he "beheld, and heard an angel." Angels, which had appeared to many of the pious, also appeared here to John. Angels can reveal themselves, either in the contemplations of the mind, in allowing themselves to be seen with the eye, or in assuming a human body for a time.

Regardless of how the angel revealed itself to John, our text says that John heard and saw the angel "flying." Angels are spirits who are endowed with supernatural motion. They are said to have wings because of their promptness, swiftness, and readiness for universal service. Isaiah 6:2-6, for example, refers to angels as seraphims, or winged ones. Flying in our text indicates the angel's promptness in discharging his commission and the speedy execution of the judgments he announces.

John also saw the angel "in the midst of heaven." We know that there are three heavens in the regions of space above us. The angel John saw flew above the earth so that his voice could be better heard. He speaks in our text with an audible voice, and what he says is amazing. Crying out with a loud voice, he summons the people of God and urges them to prepare for the judgments that will follow.

We know from 1 Corinthians 13:1 that angels speak, but in our text, the angel speaks with a loud voice. This is a distinct, articulate, intelligible sound, characterized by majesty and glory for the purpose of exciting fear, reverence, and awe.

The Dreadful Announcement

What the angel says in such a loud voice is, "Woe, woe, woe to the inhabiters of the earth." Woe is the sound of one who is in great trouble and distress. As Isaiah says, "Woe is me! for I am undone" (6:5). It is also used to announce calamities that are about to fall upon others. For example, Isaiah says, "Woe unto the wicked! it shall be ill with him" (3:11); Zechariah, "Woe to the idol shepherd" (11:17); and Matthew, "Woe unto you, scribes and Pharisees!" (23:13). The word is used to proclaim great and threatening calamities that are temporal, such as "Woe unto them...that give suck" (Matt. 24:19); and eternal, as in "Woe unto thee, Chorazin! woe unto thee, Bethsaida!" (Matt. 11:21).

The word is used three times for emphasis. Such repetition is frequently found in sacred writings. Examples from the Old Testament include: "Sigh...sigh," (Ezek. 21:6); "Wailing shall be in all streets; and they shall say in all the highways, Alas! alas!" (Amos 5:16). Examples from the New Testament include: "Verily, verily," (John 3:3); "Jerusalem, Jerusalem," (Matt. 23:37); and "Saul, Saul, why persecutest thou me?" (Acts 9:4).

Jeremiah 22:29 offers greater emphasis by using a word three times: "O earth, earth, earth, hear the word of the LORD." Likewise, "woe" is used three times in our text. This word, which is used by Christ and His inspired servants, signifies the following:

1. The earnestness of the speaker.
2. The speaker's compassion for the pitiful children of men.
3. The certainty that what is announced will surely occur.
4. The fearfulness and severity of those plagues.

One woe would be swiftly followed by another. As Revelation 9:12 says, "One woe is past; and, behold, there come two woes more hereafter."

The woes are pronounced, John says, "To the inhabiters of the earth." This is especially appropriate because the inhabitants of the earth had become degenerate and very earthly minded. But the woes are also addressed to corrupt members of the visible church, which at that time was scattered and spread over the whole earth.

The text also refers to more soundings of the trumpet of the three angels. Three woes announce the soundings of three angels. Surely calamities would follow that would be far greater than the four that already fell upon the heavens and earth.

We cannot say for sure what these three soundings refer to. The people who lived on earth in the days of Noah definitely experienced a time of woe when the flood came and destroyed them all. The fire that came down from heaven to destroy Sodom and Gomorrah and the neighboring cities was another time of woe (Gen. 19). It was a time of great woe when Jerusalem was destroyed by Titus Vespasian. About four years previous to that event, a man named Jesus, son of Ananias, had walked around the city exclaiming: "Woe to Jerusalem! woe to the temple! and, lastly, woe to me also!"

The words of the text, however, specifically refer to the church of the New Testament which experienced a time of great woe during the ten persecutions of the pagan Roman emperors. Christians had been cruelly tortured and put to death during that era. The seven churches of Asia then experienced a time of woe as the candlestick of the gospel was removed from them and the cities were destroyed by earthquakes.

Now Smyrna alone remains, and all the places where churches once flourished groan beneath a Turkish yoke. It is true that under Constantine the Great there was silence for "half an hour," meaning the church enjoyed relative

peace for a brief time. But that only lasted until 606 A.D.,
when the pope began to exalt himself during the reign of
Emperor Phocas.

The woes in our text may also refer to the troubles that
heretics and antichrists brought upon the church, such as
the corruption of doctrine and cruel persecutions. Such
persecutions prior to the Reformation include the inhuman
butchering of the Waldenses after they were forced out of
their homes and fled as partridges to the mountains. One
hundred years before the Reformation, John Huss and Jerome of Prague were condemned as heretics by the council
of Constance and burned at the stake. And surely the
Church experienced woe under the Duke of Alva in Holland, when hangings, beheadings, and burying alive were
common. The church in France also suffered woe during
the reign of Charles IX, when believers in Paris were mas-
sacred on St. Bartholomew's day, and later, under Louis
XIV, when so many were forced into exile and dispersed
throughout the world.

Woes also afflicted Bohemia, Hungary, Europe, and
other places of the old world that suffered floods, diseases,
famine, poverty, and war. Closer to home, the inhabitants of
our land suffer the woes of many contagious diseases, such
as pox, pleurisy, and bloody flux. All of that confirms the
truth of what Solomon says in Ecclesiastes 12: "Man goeth to
his long home, and the mourners go about the streets."

Beloved, we do not see visions as the apostle John did.
Nor are such visions necessary, for we have the word of the
prophets and apostles which contain this commission:
"Say...to the righteous...it shall be well with him," but
"Woe unto the wicked! it shall be ill with him" (Isa. 3:10, 11).
This solemn task has been delivered to us by the prophets,
Christ, and the apostles. I am thus compelled to say, woe
unto me if I do not announce to you the divine woes. Lest
you think I am unnecessarily alarming you, I will use the
very words of the Holy Spirit. Prepare yourselves, then, for

"Knowing...the terror of the Lord, we persuade men" to believe (2 Cor. 5:11). Woes will surely fall upon:

1. You who are wicked and unconverted. It shall not go well with you (Isa. 3:11). You may prosper for a time here on earth, but in the day of death and in the Last Judgment, you will suffer greatly. As the prophet says, the fruit and reward of your hands shall be given to you. You will be rewarded for your evil works, for tribulation and anguish shall be rendered to "every soul of man that doeth evil" (Rom. 2:9).

2. You who are careless and "at ease in Zion" (Amos 6:1).

3. You who are whoremongers and adulterers. God will judge you (Heb. 13:4).

4. You who are thieves, unrighteous, and slanderers. You will not inherit the kingdom of God (1 Cor. 6:9-10).

5. You who are drunkards. (Isa. 5:11).

6. You who are liars, cursers, swearers, and blasphemers. The Lord will not hold you guiltless (Ex. 20:7).

7. You who are miserly, unmerciful, promiscuous, immoral, and quarrelsome as well as you who are rich and put your trust in possessions, making them your idol. Hear the words of Christ: "But woe unto you that are rich! for ye have received your consolation" (Luke 6:24); and of James: "Weep and howl for your miseries that shall come upon you" (James 5:1).

8. You who are proud. God resists you (1 Pet. 5:5).

9. You who are hypocrites and pretenders, who look good in front of others but whose hearts are false and deceitful. Listen to Christ and tremble (Matt. 23).

10. You who are worldly and indulge in dancing, gambling, horse racing, and sensuality. "Woe unto you that laugh!" (Luke 6:25).

11. You who are hard and insensible. As Proverbs 29:1 says, "He, that being often reproved hardeneth his neck, shall suddenly be destroyed, and that without remedy."

12. You who are affected by nothing. "Except ye repent, ye shall all likewise perish" (Luke 13:3, 5).

13. You who are unconverted and remain unaffected by the means of grace.

According to the divines, you include:

• The entirely ignorant and openly wicked.

• Those who rely upon the external performance of duty and despise what they have learned. These people outwardly seem religious and formally partake of the Lord's Supper.

• Those who give lip service to the truth, whose conversation seems pious, and who have frequently been under conviction but have returned to a state of carelessness. Listen to Christ Himself: "Woe unto thee, Chorazin! Woe unto thee, Bethsaida!" (Matt. 11:21).

Woes, both temporal and eternal, shall come upon every one of you who do not repent. I beseech you, then, before the irrevocable curse (Matt. 25:41) sounds in your ears, repent. Only the penitent, godly, upright, and righteous who continue in well-doing will escape this tribulation (Rom. 2:7). The Lord bless this message to you all, using it for His glory and your salvation. Amen.

— 14 —

The Soul Seeking Jesus

"But Mary stood without at the sepulchre weeping: and as she wept, she stooped down, and looked into the sepulchre, and seeth two angels in white sitting, the one at the head, and the other at the feet, where the body of Jesus had lain. And they say unto her, Woman, why weepest thou? She saith unto them, Because they have taken away my Lord, and I know not where they have laid him. And when she had thus said, she turned herself back, and saw Jesus standing, and knew not that it was Jesus. Jesus saith unto her, Woman, why weepest thou? whom seekest thou? She, supposing him to be the gardener, saith unto him, Sir, if thou have borne him hence, tell me where thou hast laid him, and I will take him away. Jesus saith unto her, Mary. She turned herself, and saith unto him, Rabboni; which is to say, Master. Jesus saith unto her, Touch me not; for I am not yet ascended to my Father: but go to my brethren, and say unto them, I ascend unto my Father, and your Father; and to my God, and your God. Mary Magdalene came and told the disciples that she had seen the Lord, and that he had spoken these things unto her."

— John 20:11-18

"The Lord GOD hath given me the tongue of the learned, that I should know how to speak a word in season to him that is weary: he wakeneth morning by morning, he wakeneth mine ear to hear as the learned."

— Isaiah 50:4

In love the Father sent His Son into the world. In goodness He commissioned Christ to preach good tidings to the meek and poor and to proclaim the acceptable year of the Lord. But the Father knew the nature of the world into which He was sending His Son. It was a world full of wickedness and ignorance. The Father also knew the character of those whom His Son would be dealing with. He thus did not send His Son to the world unqualified. As Isaiah says, God gave Jesus the tongue of the learned, full of wisdom and understanding, that He might know how to speak a timely word to the weary. Grace was poured into His lips, and on Him rested the Spirit of all wisdom and knowledge.

The Lord Jesus revealed this learned tongue in various ways when He lived here on earth. He spoke in a heavenly manner, revealing the secret counsel of God about the salvation of lost sinners. He declared profound mysteries that far exceeded human science and learning. "He taught...as one having authority" (Matt. 7:29), so that people said in astonishment, "Who teacheth like him?" (Job 36:22).

He also revealed this learning in how He applied words and wisdom to the state and situation of people around Him. When He responded to people who opposed Him, He put them to silence (Matt. 22:34). When He addressed bold, arrogant, hardened sinners, He reproved them, calling upon them terrible judgments, such as "Woe unto thee, Chorazin! woe unto thee, Bethsaida!" (Matt. 11:21).

But when He came upon weary, sorrowful, dejected, and disquieted souls, Jesus refreshed and comforted them. That is what the prophets foretold (Isa. 42:1; Matt. 12:20). That was also how He responded after His resurrection to His disciples, the women, and Mary Magdalene. He comforted them as they mourned His removal from their sight. He also revealed Himself to the seeking, weeping Mary, comforting her, as we see in the words of our text.

We had intended to preach on Psalm 23:4, and had been preparing for that, but we changed our mind because

John 20 is more suitable to Easter. It is also a better subject to explore prior to the administration of the Lord's Supper. Oh, that we had Mary's weeping, seeking, loving soul! We shall note two points in our text:

- The appearance of the two angels (vv. 11-13).
- The appearance of Christ to Mary Magdalene (vv. 14-18).

After Christ disappeared from the tomb, His loved ones who continued to love Him wanted to know where His body could be found. They could not rest until they found Him. Among these, Mary Magdalene, a known pious woman, was preeminent. She so loved the Savior that she wept at the tomb.

Mary was comforted at first by the appearance of the angels and later by the appearance of Christ Himself, whom she first did not know but later did when He revealed Himself to her, showing Himself as a merciful and loving High Priest who has compassion on His people. We have discussed this subject at length before and trust that you are not ignorant of it. Let us therefore proceed at once to the doctrine and application of our text, which teaches:

- The soul which seeks Christ will not cease till it finds Him.
- The absence of Christ so disturbs a believer that no one, even ministers and angels, can put him at rest. Believer, can you testify of this? It is so, as well, of Christ's spouse, the church (Song of Sol. 3:1-4).

Our text offers clear proof of the resurrection of Christ. Christ appears to Mary Magdalene, who is the first person to be honored with seeing Him alive after His death. Oh how powerful and burning her love is for Christ! How ardent her desire for Him is after He appears to her! This is what her seeking and asking shows. This is what her overflowing tears prove. Her love cannot be satisfied until she sees Jesus. No words can comfort her; she will continue weeping until she finds her Lord. Only then will she proclaim, "My Lord." We see Mary here as a seeking soul who

will not be satisfied by anything other than the love of the
Lord Jesus.

Come with me for a while to contemplate the exercises
of a soul that seeks and loves the Lord Jesus. Cast your
eyes upon Mary, that lover of the Lord Jesus, as she seeks
Him with bitter tears. Truly, oh communicants, if you
would partake to your advantage and comfort of the
Lord's Supper, you must, like Mary, be a soul that:

1. Sees in Him such beauty and preciousness that from
your heart you say like the bride, "My beloved is white and
ruddy, the chiefest among ten thousand" (Song of Sol. 5:10);
for unto them who "believe he is precious" (1 Pet. 2:7).

2. Seek Him out of the conviction of your misery and
need, knowing that without Him you cannot endure or ever
be at peace. He must be the object of all your joy, all your
rest, satisfaction, strength, and, in a word, all your love.

3. Be set upon not only the salvation that is in Jesus, but
also His person, which is so lovely, holy, and resplendent.
He must be so fair and so precious in your eyes that you
yearn to be with Him and to be united to Him. His sweet
presence and communion must be like life itself to you, for
you are so enamored by Him that without Him you cannot
rest. And no wonder, for you should now see Him as the
true God, the highest good, the brightness of the Father's
glory, and the express image of His person. From eternity
He has in the council of peace willingly presented Himself
as Surety and Mediator and in time assumed the nature of
man, permitting Himself to be lifted up upon the cross.

You now see Him sitting at the right hand of the Father,
crowned with glory and honor, having received all power
and exaltation as "Prince and a Saviour" (Acts 5:31), and
Advocate with the Father. In all these things, you behold
how glorious a Mediator He is. This stirs up your love so
that you constantly meditate upon Him, saying like the
bride, "A bundle of myrrh is my wellbeloved unto me"
(Song of Sol. 1:13).

You also consider the benefits bestowed upon you in the love shown you by Jesus while you were still on the broad road to destruction; when He first drew near to you with cords of love and touched your heart; when He first opened your eyes to your lost, miserable state; when Jesus first showed Himself to you; when He extended His wings of love over you; when you heartily and freely received Him, surrendering yourself to Him; when you wrestled with Him; when you felt His love, realizing the truth of the words, "I have loved thee with an everlasting love: therefore with lovingkindness have I drawn thee" (Jer. 31:3).

Oh, how this prompts love for Jesus! Do you not thus yearn for His constant presence, so sweet and animating? Do you not experience this? Or do you find yourself estranged from Him in a dead, dark, sinful condition, complaining and weeping? Like Mary and the dove of Noah, do you seek but cannot find rest anywhere? Like the poet, you would then be inclined to say:

> *With Mary early I'll arise,*
>   *Visit the tomb with weeping eyes;*
> *With sadness, sighs, and cries I'll go,*
>   *And thus pour forth my heavy woe,*
> *And seek Him till His face I see;*
>   *Bedew the tomb with floods of tears,*
> *My way pursue midst groans and fears,*
>   *Fall down before my Jesus' face,*
> *His precious feet again embrace,*
>   *Nor leave Him to eternity.*

If the Savior asked Mary, "Why weepest thou? whom seekest thou?" she would answer with the church, "For these things I weep; mine eye, mine eye runneth down with water, because the comforter that should relieve my soul is far from me" (Lam. 1:16). And no wonder, for all that is not in Jesus is a burden to a soul that finds in itself only darkness, impurity, sin, and helplessness. Nothing earthly can satisfy such a one; only Jesus can gratify its desires. Such a soul properly seeks Jesus:

1. With humiliation. This includes a contrite, broken, tender, and prostrate heart. Upon such will the Lord look with compassion (Isa. 57:15, 18; 66:2; Ps. 34:18; 51:17).

2. With confession of sin. Like David in Psalm 32, this soul condemns and abhors itself, looking with shame, sorrow, and regret upon its sin. It looks to the Lord, pleading for reconciliation, peace, holiness, and strength.

3. With longing. It looks to Christ as the church does in Isaiah 26:9, confessing, "With my soul have I desired thee in the night; yea, with my spirit within me will I seek thee early."

4. With submission. As Micah 7:7 says, "I will wait for the God of my salvation," presuming not to tell the Holy One of Israel when or how.

The soul does not seek the Holy One of Israel in the tomb, but in heaven, using every means possible to do this. It seeks Him in the house of God, peruses the Scriptures, comes to the Lord's Table, and retires to a private room, where it enters into prayer and meditation. Oh how often it wrestles with its Lord in prayer, secretly crying out with mouth and heart, "O Lord, I will not let Thee go until Thou bless me. Oh, bless me, then, bless me! If Thou art a stranger and speakest roughly to me, yet will I, with Mary, seek Thee until I find Thee."

I think I hear such a soul addressing Jesus from the fullness of its heart, saying, "Oh my fair, my precious, lovely Lord Jesus, in whom alone my soul can find rest; oh most lovely fair One, whose love alone can quicken my soul, come, approach my soul. Turn to me, my soul's friend, my treasure, and soul-satisfying portion! I seek Thee early; my soul thirsts for Thee. Art Thou not the One who lovest me? Who now keeps Thee away? Didst Thou not first prompt my love to Thee? Here is my heart, come live in it, appropriate it wholly. I have become enamored by Thy service; I willingly resign myself to Thee. Oh, that I might live before Thee in greater holiness and in greater delight!" Such should be the plea of those who approach the Lord's Table, for they indicate the true longing of a soul that seeks and loves the Lord Jesus.

What do you think — are you like that? If you compare yourself with such a soul and find yourself unconverted, you must confess it. For you must be like that soul to be welcome at the Lord's Table. Do not approach the table unprepared; for Christ invites only His friends. Anyone else is not welcome.

Oh, that you could be aroused! Seek the Lord, I pray you, while He may be found; call upon Him while He is near. For you cannot be assured of your life for a moment. Avail yourself, then, of the present moment. The Lord may be found right now, but you do not know how long that will last. Right now He invites you to come so that He may offer you His favor and grace. He stands with open arms and waits. Do not let this season of grace — the time in which He may be found — pass you by.

Remember how long He has done this, calling you year after year. Do you dare to ask Him once more to call and invite you to Him? Think of what sad but unproductive lamentations your neglect will produce in hell, when you will no longer be able to respond to His call. If there is anything which will make the gnawing of the immortal worm intolerable, it will be the piercing reflection that the time for finding the Lord has been wasted. To find and enjoy Jesus is heaven upon earth. Why then do you continue to procrastinate? No one who has ever experienced finding Jesus has ever regretted it. You need not shrink from seeking Him; it is not so difficult, so burdensome, so irksome as many suppose. If you seek Him now, you will be comforted forever, finding satisfaction in your weeping. Get up, then, and do not delay. Get to work. Use every means you know to search for Jesus:

- Seek Him in the assembly of His people, whether in His house or in catechism classes.

- Seek Him by studying and searching His Word. Ask about Him wherever you can.
- Seek Him in prayer in your private chamber.
- Seek Him in every way and at every time in which He may be found; today, tomorrow, when you are young or old; in times of affliction; and with all earnestness (Ps. 119:10). Above all, seek the kingdom of God and His righteousness (Matt. 6:33) urgently and constantly (Gen. 32:26).
- Seeking and loving souls, you are entitled to the Lord's Supper. Seek Him at the Lord's Supper. Seek Him there, for there He will be found; there He will eat with you. If Jesus asks you, "What are you looking for? What do you want?," be careful that you tell Him your inmost desires and that you open wide the mouth of your soul. Happy are you if you can truthfully say, "Lord Jesus, I seek only Thee, for without Thee nothing can bring me satisfaction. Whom have I in heaven but Thee? There is nothing upon earth that I desire beside Thee."

Oh that I would hear the kind of weeping that happened at the Lord's Supper in a Scottish church. The tears from old and new members were so prolific that the minister was compelled to say, "Communicants, why all this weeping among you?"

"We weep with Mary, on account of an absent Christ," some replied. Is this the reason for your weeping, poor soul? If so, I hope that you will also experience Mary's consolation. Jesus may be nearer than you imagine, for when Mary was most certain that Jesus had gone away, He startled her by saying, "Mary." She was immediately comforted, saying, "Rabboni."

If one of you says, "I weep with Peter because I have denied Him," let me assure you that you might also experience the happiness that Peter did when the angel said, "Tell his disciples and Peter that he goeth before you into Galilee" (Mark 16:7). The weeping Peter would be comforted. Still another says, "I weep with Christ Himself out of love at the grave of Lazarus. The love of Christ causes me to weep." If this is so, may I say to you what the Jews said, "Behold how, today, the people love Christ."

If you are a believer and you come to Christ with hearty weeping and with a seeking, loving heart, you shall find and enjoy Him, for this is what our faithful God promises. As Psalm 69:32 says, "Your heart shall live that seek God." Likewise, Christ promises, "If a man love me...my Father will love him, and we will come unto him, and make our abode with him" (John 14:23). Amen.

— 15 —

The Soul Covenanting With God

*"And Joshua said unto the people, Ye are witnesses
against yourselves that ye have chosen you the LORD,
to serve him. And they said, We are witnesses."*

— Joshua 24:22

Beloved communicants, today you have renewed your
covenant with God. You have chosen God as your portion,
promising that you will be His servants, that you will walk
in His ways, and you will keep His commandments. You
are witnesses to this, as our text teaches. Although I am not
Joshua, I am adopting his words to say to you, "You are
witnesses that you have chosen the Lord and will serve
Him. Follow then the example of the people of Israel and
say, 'We are witnesses.'"

Joshua 24 contains the leader's last address in which he,
in a moving manner, renews the covenant made with Israel
at Sinai and seeks to impress upon the children of Israel
the obligations they have already assumed to acknowledge
the Lord as their God and to serve and fear Him. In verse
15, Joshua says, "And if it seem evil unto you to serve the
LORD, choose you this day whom ye will serve."

It appears that among the children of Israel were a
number of promiscuous people who had not reached a decision about whom they would serve. Noting the evil of
this, Joshua says to them, "Choose you this day whom ye
will serve." In other words, do not defer your determina-

tion. I ask you now to make your decision about whom you will serve, whether it be the God of your fathers or the gods of the Amorites. Do what seems right to you, realizing that your present and future happiness will be jeopardized if you make the wrong choice.

"Would you know my choice?" Joshua seems to ask, then announces it: "As for me and my house, we will serve the LORD" (v. 15). Joshua is not indifferent to the indecision of the people. The children of Israel had a similar problem in the days of Elijah in not being able to decide whom they would serve. At that time the prophet asked, "How long halt ye between two opinions?" (1 Kings 18:21). So Joshua now urges, "Come, I pray you, to a conclusion whom ye will serve."

The people respond by choosing the true God and repeatedly state that they will persevere in His service. "We will serve the LORD," they say (v. 21). Joshua now reviews that decision, urging the people to remember what they promised. "Ye are witnesses against yourselves," he says. We will note two parts of our text:

- Joshua's proposal to the people of Israel
- Israel's assent

Joshua's Proposal

The person referred to in our text is the pious Joshua, son of Nun of the tribe of Ephraim. He was Moses' minister who was appointed after Moses died to lead the children of Israel into the promised land. He is described in Deuteronomy 34:9 as a man "full of the spirit of wisdom; for Moses had laid his hands upon him." The spirit of Moses rested upon Joshua. He became a godly and excellent man whom the Lord honored by appointing him governor of the people of Israel and asking him to usher them into the sacred land which the Lord God of their fathers had promised to give them as a pledge of heaven. He was a type of

Christ, whose name became Jesus in the New Testament (Acts 7:45; Heb. 4:8).

Joshua was first called Oshea, but Moses named him Jehoshua (Num. 13:16), which means Savior of the Lord, because he was ordained by the Lord to be an instrument in conferring great benefits upon His people. He would deliver them out of the hands of the Canaanites, their enemies. In doing so, he would serve as an illustration of Him who would later be called Jehoshua, or Jesus (Matt. 1:21; Heb. 4:8).

In our text, Joshua urges the people to serve only the true God. The people promise to do so. Joshua renews the covenant and reminds the people of their decision, saying, "Ye are witnesses concerning yourselves." In like manner, other men of God, such as prophets and apostles, not only appealed to heaven and earth but also to men, and rightly so, since men have a conscience and thus are conscious of their own acts.

In verses preceding our text, the people chose the Lord. This is what Joshua now reminds them of, saying, "Ye have chosen...the Lord to serve Him." The God who had led them forth from Egypt — the God of Abram, Isaac and Jacob who had solemnly made a covenant with them and offered Himself to them as their God — Him they had chosen.

Two parties are involved in a covenant transaction. The first is the Lord God, the all-sufficient one, who enters into covenant with man, who is destitute of all things. God promises goodness ("The LORD is good unto them that wait for him, to the soul that seeketh him," Lam. 3:25). He promises to be almighty ("I am the Almighty God," Gen. 17:1), faithful ("Which keepeth truth for ever," Ps. 146:6), true, and unchangeable, ("I am the LORD, I change not; therefore ye sons of Jacob are not consumed," Mal. 3:6).

The second party in the covenant are the elect, who are miserable, condemned, and helpless (Ezek. 16). The two participants are truly unequal, yet how wonderfully they enter into covenant with each other. God makes the demand, the offer, and the promise, saying, "Thou shalt be to me a people; serve me only; observe my ways, commandments, statutes, ordinances, and I will be a God to thee." The sinner offers assent and surrender. He receives God as his God and highest good. He chooses Him, engages himself with Him, and yields himself to Him.

It is as if the Lord says, "Seek ye my face," and the believer enters the covenant by responding, "Thy face, LORD, will I seek" (Ps. 27:8), thereby solemnly declaring that he belongs to the Lord and pledging himself to Him (Isa. 42), saying, "Behold, here are we, we come unto Thee, for thou art the Lord our God." As Deuteronomy 26:17 says, "Thou hast avouched the LORD this day to be thy God, and to walk in his ways, and to keep his statutes, and his commandments, and his judgments, and to hearken unto his voice." Verse 18 adds, "The LORD hath avouched thee this day to be his peculiar people." The believer chooses God as his portion and the Lord Jesus as his Prophet, Priest, and King. This mutual agreement is the essence of the covenant.

The purpose for entering into covenant with God is to serve Him. Such service belongs only to God. To serve one sometimes means doing something for someone who cannot do it himself. That does not apply here, for God who made the world and all things in it, who is Lord of heaven and earth, does not need the work of men's hands. He does not need anything, since He gives to all life, breath, and every good thing (Acts 17:24-25). In this sense, we cannot serve God. As Eliphaz earnestly asks, "Can a man be profitable unto God?" (Job 22:2).

Sometimes serving God means doing what is acceptable to Him as well as doing what we owe Him and are obligated to do. This is what is meant here by covenant service. The believer must serve God by honestly striving to do all that is pleasing to Him. Therefore man, as a rational creature who enters into a covenant relationship with God, is powerfully bound to obey the Lord God and keep His commandments. We thus read of serving the Lord, obeying His voice, and not rebelling against His commandment (1 Sam. 12:14).

By assenting to the covenant, the children of Israel promised to serve the true God, to do His will, and to prefer His worship. Joshua reminds them of this, asking for their response.

Israel's Assent

The people answer by saying, "We are witnesses"— we have chosen the Lord; we will never forsake Him.

Doubtless many in Israel feigned this answer, promised it only outwardly (see Psalm 78:36-37), or depended too much on their own strength. Joshua warns the people about the nature of service that God requires, saying, "Ye cannot serve the LORD: for he is an holy God; he is a jealous God" (24:19).

The words of our text could be used to point out those who are strangers to the covenant, to pronounce divine threatenings upon them, and to inspire them with terror. But I would rather take this opportunity to invite and secure you, following the example of the Scottish divine who preached upon the words, "Choose ye this day whom ye will serve," then was overwhelmed by tears. He told his listeners he could not leave the place until they obeyed the divine requirement. Although I do not have the zeal of that worthy man, I do wish to follow his example, if not with equal steps, then certainly at a distance.

Listen then, readers, while I set before you "life and death, blessing and cursing: therefore choose life, that both thou and thy seed may live" (Deut. 30:19). Here are two masters; which one will you serve? Many of you might answer, "I will choose some day," while a few might say, "I will do it right now." There are two masters in the world; you cannot serve both. Each one has his kingdom, but they are mortal enemies. The one master is the Lord Christ, the other the devil. There is no other ruler. You, whoever you are, must make a choice. Whose servant will you be? Whom will you receive as master and ruler?

Will you choose Satan, the god of this world, so you may do his will and live in your lusts? Then enjoy your choice to the full. As Scripture says, "Rejoice...in thy youth; and let thy heart cheer thee in the days of thy youth, and walk in the ways of thine heart, and in the sight of thine eyes." Love the world and everything in it: "the lust of the flesh, the lust of the eyes, and the pride of life." Don't be ashamed to admit your choice, however; acknowledge and profess the devil as your lord and master. You may protest, saying that is too uncouth. Besides, it is not permitted, you say. Christ is our Lord and King, even though we live to ourselves, do the will of Satan, and live a wicked, carnal life. The devil is not our king; Christ is our King.

I tell you, Christ is not your king. As the apostle Paul says, "Know ye not, that to whom ye yield yourselves servants to obey, his servants ye are to whom ye obey; whether of sin unto death, or of obedience unto righteousness?" If you do not want Satan to be your master and king, thereby earning you a place in outer darkness, where there will be weeping and gnashing of teeth, renounce your allegiance to Satan. Forsake his kingdom, abandon his service, and enter into the kingdom of the Lord Jesus. Choose God as your Master. Promise to serve Him, receiving the Lord Jesus as your sovereign King.

You must enter into covenant with Him explicitly, formally, and devoutly. That's what the Word of God teaches. For example, Nehemiah 9:38 says, "And because of all this we make a sure covenant, and write it; and our princes, Levites, and priests, seal unto it." Isaiah 44:5 says, "One shall say, I am the LORD's; and another shall call himself by the name of Jacob; and another shall subscribe with his hand unto the LORD, and surname himself by the name of Israel."

The Church of Scotland endorses the making of such personal covenants. In addition to the national covenant, which nobles, common people, ministers, and hearers solemnly pledge to observe, church members also enter into personal covenants. For example, they can assent to *The Christian's Great Interest* by William Guthrie, particularly with respect to observing the Lord's Supper. The covenant says:

> I am here, O Lord, this day, to engage in a highly important transaction, for which I have of myself no sufficiency. I therefore beseech Thy help. The business in which I would engage is to enter into a covenant with Thee; and I pray Thee, O Lord, kindly to be a party in the engagement. Say not to me as in Psalm 50:16, "But unto the wicked God saith, What hast thou to do to declare my statutes, or that thou shouldest take my covenant in thy mouth?" But although Thou shouldst, Thou art righteous; but I plead Thine own Word, "Come unto me, all ye that labour and are heavy laden, and I will give you rest" (Matt. 11:28). O Lord, naught so afflicts me as Thine absence, and knowing naught but sin that can restrain Thee from entering into covenant with me, I desire with one of old to say, "That which I see not teach thou me: if I have done iniquity, I will do no more" (Job 34:32). O Lord, I have Thy promise, and come in Thy mercy, and pray that my sins may be blotted out for Christ's sake, and let me approach to Thy sacred table to obtain the fulfillment of my strong desires. I call heaven and earth to witness that I prefer Thee to all the riches of the world. Help me this day in my preparation to enter into covenant with Thee; for of myself I am insufficient for this great undertaking. Thou hast said in Thy Word that Thou wilt receive all that are willing to come unto Thee. Now, O Lord, I pray Thee that in

Thy kindness Thou wilt be gracious to me, and let not this fast-day be observed in vain; but take to Thyself the honor, and be not angry that I make this record, since it is intended to manifest my willingness to enter into covenant. O Lord, I beseech Thee not to come unto me at Thy table in anger, but in Thy mercy manifest unto me Thy favor. But rather than Thou shouldst be absent, come unto me with chastisements, if but it be not in Thy hot displeasure. I cannot express my insufficiency for an approach to Thy table; but like Queen Esther, when about to go into the presence of the king, I cast myself upon Thy mercy, and say, "So will I go...and if I perish, I perish" at Thy feet (Esther 4:16).

Communicants, have you ever entered into such a covenant with God? Today I call upon heaven and earth to witness that I have tried to persuade you. You and the holy angels are witnesses. The pious here are witnesses. This book, the New Testament, this pulpit in which I stand, this house in which we are assembled are all witnesses. Do not think it strange that I appeal to inanimate objects, for we know that Joshua did the same. As verses 26 and 27 say, he took a great stone and set it up under an oak. Then he said to all the people, "Behold, this stone shall be a witness unto us; for it hath heard all the words of the LORD which he spake unto us: it shall be therefore a witness unto you, lest ye deny your God."

Thus I also say, this book, this pulpit, this edifice, and this house of God shall be witnesses. But if none of this does any good, then, to my grief, I will be compelled at the Judgment Day to witness against you.

As for you, true believers who fear the Lord and have so often chosen the Lord for your God, you now have the privilege of renewing your covenant with Him. Let this remind you to trample underfoot and forsake the world. As 1 John 2:15 says, "Love not the world, neither the things that are in the world. If any man love the world, the love of the Father is not in him." This is included in the covenant into which you have entered and which this day has been sealed to you. Let your motto become: "God all my delight, my rest, my joy, my fear, the object of my service." Seek henceforth to more zealously serve the Lord and in all things to live acceptably to Him. "Serve the LORD with fear, and rejoice with trembling," as Psalm 2 says. For this reason you have been delivered out of the hands of your enemies: that you should fearlessly serve Him in holiness and righteousness all the days of your life. Let your service become more spiritual, more fervent, and more upright. "I beseech you...brethren, by the mercies of God, that ye present your bodies a living sacrifice, holy, acceptable unto God" (Rom. 12:1).

May the partaking of the Lord's Supper lead you to say with genuine piety: "I have now partaken of the sacrament and decided to be the Lord's. O Lord, make me a faithful servant. Do not let Satan entice me into sin, for Thou art my God, and I am Thy servant. I am solemnly consecrated to Thee. Make me faithful. Help me to do all things in the strength of the Lord Jesus, for without Him I can do nothing. Amen.

THIRD COLLECTION

––––––––

A SUMMONS TO REPENTANCE

TO THE

INHABITANTS OF THAT PORTION OF AMERICA DENOMINATED
NEW NETHERLANDS, NOW NEW YORK AND NEW JERSEY,
ON THE OCCASION OF AN EARTHQUAKE
WHICH OCCURRED ON THE
7TH OF DECEMBER, 1773
ABOUT 11 O'CLOCK AT NIGHT

IN TWO SERMONS,

THE FIRST UPON REVELATION 16:18;
THE SECOND UPON JOB 9:6

Explained, Applied, and Pronounced by
THEODORUS JACOBUS FRELINGHUYSEN

PRINTED AT UTRECHT BY JOHN GROENINGEN,
OPPOSITE THE STATE-HOUSE

PREFACE TO THE PIOUS READER

It is the duty, especially of Zion's watchmen, to sow beside all waters (Isa. 32:20), which includes availing themselves of suitable times and places (especially where there is an open door), and of improving all opportunities. I therefore hope that no one will take it ill of me that I have taken occasion from the earthquake which occurred here and elsewhere, as in Pennsylvania and New England, to move my hearers to godliness and stir them up to repentance.

I am now 46 years old, and already in the twentieth year of my ministry, having been ordained to my office in 1717 at Emden, in East Friesland;[1] but have never, to my knowledge, previously felt an earthquake. By this I was awakened out of sleep, which was a source of gratification rather than of regret to me, inasmuch as it afforded me occasion for varied meditation, leading me to think of the duty of watching, that I might not be reckoned among those shepherds of whom the Lord complains, "His watchmen are blind: they are all ignorant, they are all dumb dogs, they cannot bark; sleeping, lying down, loving to slumber" (Isa. 56:10); and of crying aloud, lifting up my voice like a trumpet, as Isaiah 58:1 commands, "Show my people their transgression, and the house of Jacob their sins."

I also anticipated judgments, and was led to consider what subject would now be suitable for the congregation. On this occasion these two sermons were preached, and are now published for general edification.

It is true, and we acknowledge with thankfulness, the

---

[1] By Johannes Brunius

church is provided with an abundance of stirring discourses by pious divines, and could readily dispense with ours; but should they increase the number of them they will do no injury, for I depart not from the rule of faith. No orthodox person will here detect heresy. In addition to this, there are no personal allusions here. As for cavillers, we give ourselves no trouble respecting them, since through the help of the Lord we have been a considerable time in His service, and therefore expect, with all humility, to take the same liberty as other ministers.

Dear reader, peruse these sermons with regard to the injunction of the Word of God: "Prove all things; hold fast that which is good" (1 Thes. 5:21).

It will, I hope, prove irksome to no one that there is some similarity in matter and expression in the two discourses. They were delivered in two different churches. This is also the consequence of similarity in the subject. As Paul says, "To write the same things to you, to me indeed is not grievous, but for you it is safe" (Phil. 3:1).

The God of grace favor us with the grace properly to observe His ways, to the end that thereby we may be stirred up to "serve the LORD with fear, and rejoice with trembling" (Ps. 2:11).

I am your servant and real well-wisher in the work of the gospel.

T. J. Frelinghuysen

Raritan, New Jersey, February 20, 1738

— 16 —

The Great Earthquake: Emblem of
Judgment Upon Enemies of the Church

> *"And there were voices, and thunders, and lightnings;
> and there was a great earthquake, such as was not
> since men were upon the earth, so mighty an earth-
> quake, and so great."*
>
> — Revelation 16:18

Trumpets were blown for various reasons in Israel. They were blown to assemble the people for the joyful observance of appointed feasts (Ps. 98:5-6; Joel 2:15-16). In Psalm 81:3 we read, "Blow up the trumpet in the new moon, in the time appointed, on our solemn feast day (Ps. 81:3). Matthew 24:31, 1 Corinthians 15:52, and Revelation 18:22 mention similar significant reasons for blowing trumpets.

Trumpets also were blown to assemble armies and to urge them to march forward into war. The instruments incited the warriors to fight. They signaled alarm and destruction, as we read in the book of Judges. When trumpets were blown by Gideon and his men, the Midianites took flight and were slaughtered. Joel 2:1 says, "Blow ye the trumpet...let all the inhabitants of the land tremble."

Trumpets were sounded, too, to signal danger. Watchmen upon the walls and towers of cities were instructed to blow trumpets to warn the people of impending danger and approaching enemies (Ezek. 33:3-6). Ministers also serve as watchmen upon the walls of Zion. When the Lord

God shows His anger by sending plagues and judgments from the high heavens because carelessness and corruption prevail, preachers are called to open their mouths, crying aloud, sparing not, and lifting up their voices like a trumpet (Isa. 58:1). Or as 2 Timothy 4:2 says, "Preach the word; be instant in season, out of season."

Since God, who is a righteous Judge, recently showed His anger by warning us with an earthquake, we shall deviate from our normal progression through Scripture and address the text that we have just read.

Revelation 16 describes the pouring out of vials, cups, or bottles to inflict heavy judgments and plagues. The first vial was poured out onto the earth, the second into the sea, the third into the rivers and fountains of waters (which prompted songs of praise extolling the righteousness of God), the fourth onto the sun, the fifth upon the throne of the beast (at which men repented not), the sixth into the great river Euphrates, and the seventh into the air (vv. 17-21).

Verse 17 describes what happened when the angel poured the seventh or last vial into the air: "There came a great voice out of the temple of heaven, from the throne, saying, It is done." The air, which is the portion of creation that is closest to the earth and encompasses the sea and rivers, had so far remained untouched by the vials of judgment. Air is in and around everything; it is what every living thing needs to breathe; it supports all of life. The air referred to here must not be taken literally but figuratively. It signifies the completeness of divine judgment and its extension to every foe of God and His cause, wherever they may be. Such foes will not escape judgment wherever they go, and this punishment will be visible to the entire world. The seventh vial brings all things to consummation. It is poured into the air since air is essential to life, and Satan (with divine permission) rules in this medium (Eph. 2:2).

This final judgment is confirmed by the following:

1. An audible voice. Verse 1 says, "And there came a great

voice out of the temple of heaven." The great, very important voice came out of God's heavenly habitation. It came from His throne, His glorious seat in that celestial temple, which was seen and described by John. It is the voice of God, the Judge of all, and it indicates something true and holy that was previously kept secret.

John hears the voice say, "It is done." Everything that the Word of God said would take place in the world has been completed. All the judgments and plagues have been poured out by the vials upon the enemies of God, even the last, which was especially directed against the enemies of the church. "It is done." The plagues upon the Antichrist and the enemies of the church have come to an end. The last plague, which will destroy all the enemies of the church, stands at the door. "And he said unto me, It is done" (Rev. 21:6), echoing these words of Christ: "It is finished" (John 19:30).

2. It is confirmed by results. Our text goes on to say that the judgments were followed by thunders and lightnings and a great earthquake. Such words are especially frightening for today, since for a long time there were wondrous appearances in the sky, but now we have also experienced a great earthquake. Oh how our hearts were shaken by that event. How we came trembling to the Lord, begging for His goodness. The signs that our text mentions include signs in the air (voices, thunders, and lightnings) and signs on the earth (a great earthquake).

Signs in the Air

The apostle warns of terrible exhibitions of voices, thunders, and lightnings. This brings to mind passages such as Revelation 4:5; 8:5; 10:3; and 11:19, as well as Exodus 19:16, which tells how the giving of the law was accompanied by thunders, lightnings, the sound of a great trumpet, and an earthquake. Some points to consider:

• The "voices" in our text indicate an audible sound. We

read of various voices in Revelation: of a voice as loud as a trumpet (1:10); of one as loud as the sound of many waters (v. 15); and the voices in our text, which appear to be tokens and emblems of God's almighty power, majesty, and inevitable wrath upon His enemies.

• Concerning "thunders" in our text, we shall not speculate, for thunder is better learned from experience than from any account of it. It is the sound that precedes lightning as it bursts and tears out of the clouds. It crackles, rumbles, and reverberates, in some, then many successions of sound. "Thunders" is thus spoken of in the plural sense.

• Thunders proceed from "lightnings," those dazzling flashes that drop with a loud report from the clouds. Psalm 18:13 refers to such flashes as coals of fire. The Word of God describes thunders and lightnings in various ways. It says they proceed from heaven (1 Sam. 2:10), coming, as it were, from the throne of God (Matt. 24:27); that they are formed in dense or heavy clouds (Ps. 77:17-18); and they include fire (Ps. 97:3-4). The author of thunders and lightnings is the almighty God, for the light of the Lord is seen in them (Job 37:3). They are God's lightnings (Ps. 97:4), His thunder (Job 37:4), and His voice that is heard upon the waters. "The God of glory thundereth"; He is powerful and full of majesty (Ps. 29:3-4). He roars and thunders marvelously with the voice of His excellency (Job 37:4-5), for who can truly understand the greatness and awfulness of His power (Job 26:14)?

Thunders and lightnings light the world, purify the air, terrify, astonish, discompose, and perturb the inhabitants of earth, causing them to shake and quake. These awesome works of nature fell towers, trees, and habitations, cause great damage, and destroy beasts and men.

In Revelation, thunders and lightnings are used figuratively and symbolically. The opening of the first seal is accompanied by a voice of thunder (Rev. 6:1) to get attention and to produce reverence. The sound symbolizes the manner in which the sound of the gospel will proceed from the mouths of the sons of thunder to incite terror in people throughout the length and breadth of the world (Mark 3:17). Such sounds are used to preach, teach, threaten, argue with, and announce judgments upon men. The voice of great thunder in Revelation 14:2 and 19:6 also represents the collective sound of rejoicing believers.

Voices, thunders, and lightnings, together with an earthquake, occur when the angel casts the fire of the altar upon the earth (Rev. 8:5). As thunders and lightnings fill men with fear, so these signs indicate the fearful judgments that will come upon the enemies of God and His church. Seven thunders utter their voices. John does not tell us what they say, but he does seal what they utter (Rev. 10:3-4), indicating that what they mention are exceedingly great and heavy judgments that should stir the pious to a greater exercise of faith, hope, and patience, and the ungodly to hardening of heart.

Our text says these voices, thunders, and lightnings are "heard and seen" in the air when the seventh angel pours his vial into the air. These sounds are neither the violent cries of murder or the preaching of the gospel (or the glorious results of the same). Rather, this fearful commotion in the heavens represents God's heaviest and most dreadful wrath upon the Babylon of Antichrist and all enemies of the church. It is a sign of the judgments that will occur when God gloriously reveals Himself at the last day.

The Dutch annotations say that these voices, thunders, and lightnings refer to the signs that will precede the last judgment, as declared in Matthew 24, Mark 13, Luke 21, and 2 Peter 3:10.

Signs on the Earth

The air will be affected, but so will the earth, for the earth will be torn apart by an earthquake. The earthquake in our text refers to a shaking or commotion in the earth. It is terrible in nature and has great power to affect the consciences of men, for it topples houses and destroys human beings as well as entire cities. That is frequently the case in Italy and Eastern lands, such as Smyrna, which was swallowed up by an earthquake. Likewise, the greater part of Jamaica was destroyed by earthquakes, as some of you may remember. At various times we have had slight earthquakes in our country that did not cause any injuries. But this past Wednesday, we experienced a great earthquake that shook our doors, windows, beds, and houses and rattled our china.

The Old and New Testament contain several accounts of earthquakes. When the law was given on Mount Sinai, the earth quaked (Ex. 19). In Hebrews 12:26, Paul refers to an earthquake, and in Psalm 68:8, David says, "The earth shook." When Christ died, the earth quaked (Matt. 27). When He arose from the dead, there was another earthquake (Mark 16), which was foretold in Psalm 18:7. This earthquake was proof of the Godhead of Christ as well as the wrath of God against the Jews. It caused the dissolution of their state, the destruction of their city and temple, the abolition of their ceremonial system, and the establishment, in their place, of an unchangeable mode of worship.

After Christ ascended to heaven, the place where the apostles were gathered to pray was shaken (Acts 4:31). When Paul and Silas sang praises in prison, an earthquake also rattled the place. Finally, we are told that before and during the Last Judgment, there will be famines, pestilences, and earthquakes (Matt. 24:7).

An earthquake is especially terrifying. Matthew 27 tells us that watchmen fled in fear after a great earthquake. So in our text the earthquake is a symbol of God's terrible wrath, for through His indignation the earth trembles. The nations who cannot endure His displeasure will be so terrified that they will weep, howl, and mourn (Matt. 24). The world and earth will then pass away on the last day.

The earthquake in our text is further described as "a great" one. Its shaking is so dreadful that it is called "great." It is so great that words can scarcely describe it. Such an earthquake has not occurred since men were upon the earth, either from the time of creation or within man's memory. It is like the earthquake described in Daniel 12:1, which says, "And at that time...there shall be a time of trouble, such as never was since there was a nation."

The voices, thunders, lightnings, and great earthquake suggest the most serious troubles and heaviest judgments. They evoke the greatest terror, amazement, trembling, and confusion that will accompany the entire destruction and annihilation of Antichrist as well as all the enemies of the church both before and at the Last Judgment, including the grievous punishment of hell.

Revelation tells us there will be many judgments inflicted upon Antichrist. Some of these have already occurred, but the last, which consists of the entire annihilation and full execution of the threatened judgment, is still in the future. The words of our text, therefore, well suit the purpose of John, which was to declare the execution of the seven last plagues. These plagues will cause the utter ruin of the enemies of the church, especially Babylon, which will be overthrown and brought to hell to forever drink the cup of the wrath of God. As verses 19 and 20 say, "And the great city was divided into three parts, and the cities of the nations fell: and great Babylon came in remembrance before God, to give unto her the cup of the wine of the fierceness of his wrath. And every island fled away, and the mountains were not found."

Frightful tokens and evils will precede the Last Judgment, Revelation says. That could be inferred from the words of Christ Himself, for although the Lord kept secret the precise time of that judgment, He offered in His Word various signs that will precede the coming of Christ. Many of those signs have already occurred, such as the power of delusion through heretics and false prophets causing a falling away; bloody wars; thunders, earthquakes, floods, and famines; dreadful persecutions; general carelessness and ungodliness; the preaching of the gospel over the whole earth; and the revelation of Antichrist.

The Day of Judgment will be a fearful day; that is apparent from its name and description (it is the great and terrible day) as well as the terrible signs that will precede and accompany it. For when the Lord Himself shall descend from heaven with a shout, with the voice of the archangel, and with the trump of God, there will be dreadful amazement in heaven and upon earth. Jesus the Judge will appear in great glory with thousands of angels, in the clouds, before the eyes of all (Rev. 1:7). The dead will be raised with the living, and all will be called before the judgment seat.

The Judge Himself teaches this (Matt. 24:29-31). He will separate His sheep from those who are not His sheep, setting the righteous on His right hand and the wicked on His left (Matt. 25). After this He will conduct an exceedingly detailed investigation by means of a certain book (Rev. 20:12). He will then deliver a verdict in the most delightful words to the righteous, "Come, ye blessed of my Father, inherit the kingdom prepared for you from the foundation of the world." But He will deliver these words in wrath to the wicked on His left hand: "Depart from me, ye cursed, into everlasting fire, prepared for the devil and his angels." Their execution will immediately follow. "And these shall go away into everlasting punishment: but the righteous into life eternal."

Your Response to Awful Signs

Come here, you careless ones at ease in sin; you carnal and earthly-minded ones; you unchaste whoremongers and adulterers; you proud, haughty men and women; you seekers after pleasure; you drunkards, gamblers, disobedient and wicked rejecters of the gospel; you hypocrites and dissemblers. How do you think the Lord will deal with you?

That great and terrible day will be a fearful day for you. What anguish and distress you will experience when your sins of thought, word, and deed are brought to light, and you are judged. "For...the day cometh, that shall burn as an oven; and (then shall) all the proud...and all that do wickedly, be (as) stubble; and the day that cometh shall burn them up" (Mal. 4:1). You will experience what Isaiah 33:14 says, "The sinners in Zion are afraid; fearfulness hath surprised the hypocrites." Who among us shall dwell with the devouring fire? Who can live with everlasting burnings?

Consider also what 2 Peter 3 says, and tell me, I beseech you, when the elements shall melt and pass away, when the earth and everything in it will be burned up, when everything will be wrapped in fire and flame, where will you be? The period of grace will end. All earthly satisfaction will cease. Your agony and pain in soul and body will have no end, for you will be cast into the lake of fire and brimstone, where there is weeping and gnashing of teeth. The smoke of its torment lasts forever; your worm will not die and your fire will not be quenched. You will cry out to the mountains and rocks, "Fall on us," and to the hills, "Cover us and hide us from the face of him that sitteth on the throne. Hide us from the wrath of the Lamb, for the great day of his wrath is come" (Rev. 6:16-17; Luke 23:30).

Does thunder and lightning make you shake? Did the earthquake make you tremble? How then will you respond on the last day? Will you be like Belshazzar in Daniel 5:6, which says, "Then the king's countenance was changed, and his thoughts troubled him, so that the joints of his loins were loosed, and his knees smote one against another"?

I greatly wonder how you can be so careless about such a day that even when the immovable earth, set fast by the divine hand, quakes, you remain unmoved. The devils themselves tremble in such a day. Felix, too, was filled with great fear. Who among us is not moved to exercise faith when we consider the terror of the Lord? It is surely an evil sign when one lives in sin and does not tremble at the thought of that great judgment, no matter how much he is warned by terrible signs in the heavens or upon the earth. "Awake thou that sleepest, and arise from the dead, and Christ shall give thee light" (Eph. 5:14).

Where are you going? Awake, stand up, Jerusalem, lest you drink deep from the hand of the Lord the cup of His fury (Isa. 51:17). "Awake, ye drunkards, and weep; and howl, all ye drinkers of wine" (Joel 1:5). If you remain unconverted, what else can you expect but to drink fire and brimstone? "Woe unto them that rise up early in the morning, that they may follow strong drink; that continue until night, till wine inflame them!" (Isa. 5:11).

Tremble, you who curse and swear. Someday you will not have a drop of cold water to cool your accursed tongues. You will be in flames and in such pain that you will gnaw on your tongues.

Be filled with terror, you impure swine, adulterers, and whoremongers. Without true repentance you will live with the impure devils. All who burn in their vile lusts will be cast into a fire that is hotter than that of Sodom and Gomorrah. Anything that defiles, produces abominations, or lies will not be allowed to set foot in the New Jerusalem. Only those who are written in the Lamb's book of life may enter (Rev. 21:27).

Wake up, you miserly wretches and unmerciful Nabals. Read what James 5:1-6 says: "Go to now, ye rich men, weep and howl for your miseries that shall come upon you. Your riches are corrupted, and your garments are moth eaten. Your gold and silver is cankered; and the rust of them shall be a witness against you, and shall eat your flesh as it were fire. Ye have heaped treasure together for the last days. Behold, the hire of the labourers who have reaped down your fields, which is of you kept back by fraud, crieth: and the cries of them which have reaped are entered into the ears of the Lord of sabaoth. Ye have lived in pleasure on the earth, and been wanton; ye have nourished your hearts, as in a day of slaughter. Ye have condemned and killed the just; and he doth not resist you." You who are unrighteous and covetous and idolaters will not inherit the kingdom of God.

Wake up, too, you civil ones who engage in religious performances to be seen of men. You formal, almost-Christians imitate the pious in their speech. You want to be considered pious so you creep in among them. You look like them, but you are strangers to the true power of godliness. "Be not deceived; God is not mocked: for whatsoever a man soweth, that shall he also reap." Hear these words of Christ: "For I say unto you, That except your righteousness shall exceed the righteousness of the scribes and Pharisees, ye shall in no case enter into the kingdom of heaven" (Matt. 5:20).

Wake up, you who are unconverted and without Christ. You should be ashamed and astonished that even when the earth trembles, you remain careless and unmoved. This is why the earth trembles:

1. Because our hearts do not tremble. We do not flee in terror to the Lord and His goodness.

2. The hard, fixed earth that trembles shows us how insensible we are. Our hearts are harder than rocks that are ripped apart by earthquakes.

3. The trembling earth reminds us of our earthly-mindedness. We are so obsessed with earthly things that our judgment will be written in the earth.

As Jeremiah 17:13 says, "O LORD, the hope of Israel, all that forsake thee shall be ashamed, and they that depart from me shall be written in the earth." Apostate and unconverted men will be found wanting and condemned. Learned commentators say this passage means that Christ writes the names of His disciples in heaven, whereas the

names of the apostate will be written in the earth. While
the apostate are on the earth, they are among the people of
God, the seed of Abraham according to the flesh. In general, they are numbered among the members of the
church, sometimes making up the greater portion of them.
Yet they are not members of the elect and will have no
place in heaven. They are a part of those whose inheritance
is only upon earth. Their memory will perish from the
earth as readily as anything written on earth will be erased.

4. The trembling earth opens its mouth and threatens to
consume us, like it did with Korah, Dathan, and Abiram, unless we repent. Whole cities, villages, and houses with their
inhabitants have been swallowed up by the earth. We remember especially how that happened in Italy and Turkey.

Will you not then fear the Lord and tremble at His presence? As Jeremiah 5:22 warns, true conversion and the
Christian life require holy trembling. Philippians 2:12
teaches, "Work out your own salvation with fear and trembling." We see trembling in those who were truly penitent,
such as the jailor in Acts 16:29; Paul, in Acts 9:6; the penitent
Jews in Hosea 3:5 and 11:11; and even in the established
children of God. Daniel trembled in holy awe before the
Lord. And Job says, "At this also my heart trembleth" (37:1).

Wake up you sinners, men and women; be moved.
Throw yourselves down before the Lord; tremble before
His dreadful majesty, tremble at His Word. Upon such will
the Lord look. As Isaiah 66:2 says, "But to this man will I
look, even to him that is poor and of a contrite spirit, and
trembleth at my word."

Tremble also at His judgments. As Psalm 119:120 says,
"My flesh trembleth for fear of thee; and I am afraid of thy
judgments." Come to the Lord and bow down, trembling
with penitent Israel and saying, "Wherewith shall I come
before the LORD, and bow myself before the high God?"
(Micah 6:6). Come, fearing and trembling like the woman
who touched the Lord Jesus, knowing how He had healed

her. She "came and fell down before him, and told him all
the truth" (Mark 5:33).

Tremble at your insignificance and unworthiness. A man
can be so proud that he knows nothing of his nothingness.
Think, oh proud man, what are you but dust and ashes? As
Scripture says, "The nations are as a drop of a bucket, and
are counted as the small dust of the balance" (Isa. 40:15).
Spiritually, you are a child of wrath. Is that not enough reason to tremble before the Lord and exclaim with Abraham,
"Behold...I have taken upon me to speak unto the Lord,
which am but dust and ashes" (Gen. 18:27)?

Tremble at your guilt. If you could only see your sins! Like
the servant who owed ten thousand talents and fell down
before his lord (Matt. 18:21-26), you too must tremble and
fall before the Lord, exclaiming, "My God, I am ashamed
and blush to lift up my face to thee, my God: for our iniquities are increased over our head, and our trespass is grown
up unto the heavens" (Ezra 9:6). Such guilt so dismayed
the poor publican that he stood afar off and would not lift
up his eyes to heaven. Instead, he smote upon his breast,
sobbing, "God be merciful to me a sinner" (Luke 18:13).

Turn from your evil ways. Do so while the Lord shows
by signs in heaven above and in the earth beneath that He
is angry with us and that we are living in the last days. If
Peter, in his day, could say, "The end of all things is at
hand," how much more may that be said now? The Judge
stands at the door. Every day the end is closer. As death
leaves man, judgment finds him.

Therefore today, while ye hear God's voice, do not
harden your hearts. If you refuse to turn to the Lord,
heaven and earth will witness against you. The wonders of
heaven and tokens upon earth will condemn you. "I call
heaven and earth to record this day against you, that I
have set before you life and death, blessing and cursing:
therefore choose life, that both thou and thy seed may live"
(Deut. 30:19).

Let the truly pious teach, acknowledging that they too live at too great a distance from the Lord: "Come, and let us return unto the LORD: for he hath torn, and he will heal us; he hath smitten, and he will bind us up" (Hos. 6:1).

I conclude with the words of Psalm 2:11-12: "Serve the LORD with fear, and rejoice with trembling. Kiss the Son, lest he be angry, and ye perish from the way, when his wrath is kindled but a little. Blessed are all they that put their trust in him." Amen.

— 17 —

The Great Earthquake:
A Declaration of God's Power

"Which shaketh the earth out of her place, and the pillars thereof tremble."

— Job 9:6

In 2 Timothy 4:2, Paul says to his beloved son Timothy, "Preach the word; be instant in season, out of season; reprove, rebuke, exhort with all longsuffering and doctrine." Preaching is very important. A preacher is a messenger of God who speaks in God's name to a congregation through the help of the Holy Ghost.

Timothy is told here to preach the Word, as given by inspiration from God, for it is profitable for doctrine, reproof, and correction. It is quick and powerful, sharper than a two-edged sword, and is the power of God unto salvation. The way he should preach is to be "instant in season, and out of season"; to urge, indeed, to "compel them to come in" (Luke 14:23). He must make use of all suitable occasions; for "a word fitly spoken is like apples of gold in pictures of silver" (Prov. 25:11).

The apostle also impresses upon Timothy the duty of constantly and zealously persevering in his work, without neglecting any occasion or opportunity, even if it is not convenient for him to preach or his hearers to listen. Paul himself once spoke until midnight, as we read in Acts 20:7.

Because a servant of Jesus Christ must avail himself of

every opportunity, we will take note of the recent earthquake and use the occasion to concentrate on suitable texts, as we did last Sunday in another church. We do so now, lifting our hearts to the Lord and asking for His help in understanding Job 9:6.

Upright Job acknowledges the righteousness of God (v. 2) in his response to Bildad's speech, saying that arguing with God benefits no one. "How should man be just with God?" he asks, as if to say that no one is free from guilt and its punishment (Ps. 143:2; 130:3). "If he will contend with him, he cannot answer him one of a thousand," he adds (v. 3). Or, as Romans 3:19 says, if God should enter into judgment with man, man would be found guilty and condemned (see also Prov. 24:16).

Job then offers proofs of the wisdom and power of God. God is wise in heart and mighty in strength, Job says. But he who hardens himself against the Lord must expect wrath and displeasure instead of peace. The first proof of the power of God is that He removes mountains. The second, in the words of our text, is that He "shaketh the earth out of her place, and the pillars thereof tremble." Let us examine the two parts of this second proof.

He Shakes the Earth

The one who shakes the earth is the same God who is described in the preceding verse 4 as wise in heart and mighty in strength. *El Gibbor,* the mighty God, has power to accomplish all things. He does what seems good to Him. Nothing is impossible with Him; nothing is too wonderful for Him. Everything that pleases Him, He irresistibly executes. Our God is in the heavens; His hand is stretched out, and no one shall turn it back. Since the earth is set fast (Ps. 65:6), no one can shake it but the Almighty.

God shakes the earth, meaning the dry land inhabited by man. As Scripture says, "The heavens...are the Lord's: but the earth hath he given to the children of men." The seven continents of the world yield many things, as is shown at length in Psalm 104. The earth teaches the providence of God, for it is full of God's goodness. "How manifold are thy works! in wisdom hast thou made them all: the earth is full of thy riches."

The earth is suspended in space and sustained by nothing but the great power of God. It was created for the children of men for them to live on as part of the great plan that God's name would be excellent in all the earth (Ps. 8:1) and that He would form a people to show forth His praise. It therefore contains everything necessary to support man and beast. As Psalm 36:6 says, "O LORD, thou preservest man and beast." It is fixed in space. As Psalm 93:1 says, "The world also is established, that it cannot be moved." It is so firmly affixed to its foundations that it will not be removed as long as time shall last (Ps. 104:5). It will continue according to God's decree (Ps. 119:90-91). Yet it may occasionally shake and quake through the almighty power of God.

Our text speaks of a shaking of the earth. This refers to an earthquake or disturbance of the earth that is calculated to fill with terror especially those who disobey God. Earthquakes destroy people and sometimes entire towns. These remarkable evidences of the power of God, which have occured at various times in many parts of the world, are what Job is describing here.

Earthquakes include natural as well as supernatural events. Natural earthquakes proceed from natural causes. The earth is full of combustible matter, including wood, turf, and coal, but it also contains brimstone and sulfur. We see this in volcanic mountains such as Vesuvius in Italy, Etna in Sicily, Hekla in Iceland, and others. When this oily, sulfurous matter within the earth becomes ignited, it seeks an opening, which may lead to a volcano or earthquake.

Supernatural earthquakes occur when God does not use natural means to shake the earth. That is what happened when the law was given on Mount Sinai (Ex. 19; Ps. 68), when the Savior died (Matt. 27:50-51), and when He rose from the dead (Matt. 28:2). Patient Job seems to speak of an earthquake in our text. Since the country in which we live is rocky, the earthquake that we recently experienced also seems to have been supernatural. As such, it signifies that the wrath of God is revealed from high heaven against the ungodliness and unrighteousness of men (Rom. 1:18), and that plagues and judgments are about to come upon us and the inhabitants of this land because of our wickedness (Ps. 107:34).

The Pillars of the Earth Tremble

A great earthquake causes violent agitation. Our inspired speaker portrays the earth as having pillars, which are supports, columns, or substrata foundations upon which the earth is established (Ps. 104:5). Commentators understand these pillars to mean the waters on which the earth is founded. This implies the steadfastness of the earth; "For he hath founded it upon the seas, and established it upon the floods" (Ps. 24:2). When the Lord produces an earthquake, it affects this steadfastness of the earth.

When the pillars of the earth tremble, they are moved to such an extent that houses are buried or whole cities swallowed up. The Word of God frequently mentions earthquakes, both in the Old and New Testament. For example, the earth trembled and shook when Israel passed through the Red Sea (Ps. 77:18). Psalm 114:4, 7 says, "The mountains skipped like rams, and the little hills like lambs....Tremble, thou earth, at the presence of the Lord." The earth quaked before the Lord revealed Himself to Elijah (1 Kings 19:11) and again in the days of Uzziah, king of Judah (Amos 1:1; Zech. 14:5). In the New Testament, the earth shook when the apostles prayed (Acts 4) and when Paul and Silas sang praises (Acts 16:25-26).

We're told that fearful signs, such as earthquakes, will precede the final judgment (Matt. 24:7). Revelation mentions earthquakes as symbols of fearful signs and judgments that will come upon the enemies of God and His church. Both sacred and secular history frequently mention earthquakes. For example, some of the cities of Asia that John addressed in Revelation perished in earthquakes. Colosse, which forsook the holy truths delivered to it by Paul, listened to vile seducers immediately after Paul's death. During the reign of the emperor Nero, Colosse as well as Laodicea and Hierapolis were overthrown by an earthquake. God thus righteously swallowed up those who refused to enter or continue in the way of heaven, which had been so faithfully pointed out to them.

Secular history also mentions earthquakes. Take a look at the table of contents of the histories of S. de Vries, for example. Turkey has experienced much devastation from earthquakes. Only recently, a large portion of Smyrna was destroyed by earthquakes. Likewise Mount Vesuvius, which is situated near Naples, Italy, was shaken by a great earthquake, in which many people miserably perished. On that occasion the Roman Catholics formed many processions. In the West Indies, as many of you doubtless remember, most of the island of Jamaica perished in an earthquake.

In 1727, the province of New England was affected by an earthquake. After it happened, the distinguished Cotton Mather published a small essay titled "The Terror of the Lord." It was an edifying and godly work on the meaning of earthquakes. Small earthquakes have also occured in this land, although they have, so far, caused few injuries. On December 7, however, a bigger earthquake set doors, windows, chairs, and houses into commotion. People noticed it throughout the land.

An earthquake is an unusual effect of the power of God. It thus inspires men with terror. We see that in the watchmen at the tomb of Jesus (Matt. 28), who fled and became as dead men. Earthquakes are symbolic of the wrath of God. As Psalm 18:7 says, "Then the earth shook and trembled; the foundations also of the hills moved and were shaken, because he was wroth." We find this also in Joel 3:16: "The LORD...shall roar out of Zion...and the heavens and the earth shall shake."

The effect an earthquake should have upon us is to lead us to repentance, to make us fear the Almighty, and to glorify Him. That is how people responded in Revelation 11:13, which says, "And the same hour was there a great earthquake, and the tenth part of the city fell, and in the earthquake were slain of men seven thousand: and the remnant were affrighted, and gave glory to the God of heaven" (compare this with Luke 24:5, 37). The extraordinary operations of God, specifically the righteous displays of His wrath, can soften the hardest hearts, although there are many who, like Pharaoh, harden their hearts in response to many wonders and plagues. Revelation 11:13 thus adds that the remnant "gave glory to the God of heaven," who had caused His mighty voice to be heard that He might be distinguished from all earthly gods. Some only outwardly acknowledged His hand in these things, while others truly humbled themselves and turned to Him, honoring and glorifying Him.

Pious Job offered tokens of the power of God to prove that the Almighty is wise in heart and mighty in strength, and that no one who hardens himself against Him will prosper. God is able to move mountains and shake the earth, which surely proves His almighty power, for who can shake the earth but its Maker? Let this be enough to explain the opening words of our text. Let us now go deeper into their meaning.

The almighty power of the One who removes mountains and shakes the earth so its pillars tremble should fill you with terror, you openly ungodly people, adulterers, whoremongers, drunkards, misers, dishonest persons; in short, everyone that Paul names in Galatians 5:19-21 who indulges in works of the flesh. If you remain unconverted, you will be cast into the lake of fire and brimstone (Rev. 21:8).

You ignorant people who have no knowledge of divine truths that must be known, believed, and confessed, you are without grace. Your ignorance is clear proof of that. A soul without knowledge is not good; therefore it is evil. If you persist in your ignorance, you will perish, for the Lord will come in flaming fire to take vengeance upon those who do not know God and who do not obey the gospel of our Lord Jesus Christ. You will be punished "with everlasting destruction from the presence of the Lord, and from the glory of his power" (2 Thes. 1:8-9).

You careless ones who live in ease, as if there were no death, resurrection, heaven, or hell — you too have no grounds to assure yourselves of heaven. As Amos 6:1 says, "Woe to them that are at ease in Zion, and trust in the mountain of Samaria." When you think you are in peace and safety, sudden destruction will come upon you as painfully as a woman in travail (1 Thes. 5:3).

Woe unto you, also, who are earthly minded, walking according to your carnal desires and setting your hope upon the things of this life. Woe to you who provide for nothing but momentary gratification (Rom. 13;14), for you will only have this world. You may be given your portion with the rich man in this life, but eventually all those good things will pass away. Like him, you will go to hell when you die. There you will be stripped of all things. You will suffer pain and anguish under the intolerable wrath of the Almighty "whose end is destruction" (Phil. 3:19).

No less should the almighty power of God fill you with terror, you obstinate and obdurate ones who pay no attention to warnings or judgments but recklessly persist in your sins. Your faces are harder than stone. The servants of Christ do not cease to rebuke you; they threaten you with the wrath of God; they movingly describe the terror of the Lord in more than one way and with tears in their eyes.

They cater to you to woo you. They weep before you. But you remain insensible and do not weep. Woe unto you. He who hardens his heart shall fall into mischief. As Job 9:4 asks, "He is wise in heart, and mighty in strength: who hath hardened himself against him, and hath prospered?"

You civil and outwardly religious persons, you also have reason to fear. You live morally and correctly so that nothing can be said against your outward conduct. You offer the appearance of piety. But you make this your Christ by resting on it and basing your expectations of heaven upon it. Oh, poor souls, you deceive yourselves. Hear these words of Christ: "Except your righteousness shall exceed the righteousness of the scribes and Pharisees, ye shall in no case enter into the kingdom of heaven" (Matt. 5:20). "Not every one that saith...Lord, Lord, shall enter in...but he that doeth the will of my Father which is in heaven."

But the omnipotence of Jehovah should trouble most of all you hypocrites and dissemblers who assume the appearance of godliness. You sigh and lament. You associate with the pious but only to obtain honor and esteem and to promote your worldly interests. All the while you are deceiving men. You know that what you are before men is not what you are before God, for your outward behavior does not match what is in your heart. You have more regard for the appearance than the essence and power of godliness.

You have many masters. You despise and judge the faults in others, but you flatter and overlook your own faults. As Scripture says, you see the mote in another's eye but are blind to the beam in your own. You constantly complain about the corruption and degeneracy of the church, and you presume to tell ministers how and what they should preach. You have something to say about every preacher and sermon (see Wilhelmus à Brakel, *The Christian's Reasonable Service*, 2:127-29). You who creep among the people of God as chaff upon the threshing floor and tares among the wheat, woe, woe, woe, unto you, for you are nothing but hypocrites. No greater monster exists than a hypocrite, and no hotter hell exists for anyone more than a hypocrite. He is earning a place for himself where "there shall be weeping and gnashing of teeth" (Matt. 24:51).

The almighty power of God should also alarm you who are only generally convinced of sin. You live under the conviction of an awakened conscience. You listen to the preaching of the Word of God and are convinced by the common operations of the Spirit that you cannot enter heaven as you are. Yet you remain destitute of renewing grace. How often have you been told by ministers and godly people, especially the elders and their helpers, that conviction is not conversion. But if you quench the Spirit by allowing your convictions to pass away as a morning cloud, if you become more careless and hardened, if you return with the dog and the washed sow, it would be better if you had never known the way of righteousness. For, having known it, you choose to turn away from the holy commandment (2 Pet. 2:21). All your convictions, like coals of juniper, will make intolerable the worm of your conscience.

Tremble also, you who have turned aside from the good way and have discontinued religious practices. You came for the truth and seemingly were so moved that you began acting religiously. We were encouraged to hope for better things in you. But woe to you now, for he that turns aside is an abomination to the Lord.

The almighty power of God, our *El Gibbor*, should alarm you almost-Christians who are not far from the kingdom of God, who walk with Christians and seek after Christians, but not in a right manner. As Luke 13:24 says, "Many...will seek to enter in, and shall not be able." In short, the almighty power of God should fill with terror those who remain without grace despite living with all the means of grace, all the blessings of heaven, all plagues and judgments, and all signs and wonders in heaven and upon earth. Like the old man who is without spirit and life, they remain unchanged. The fear of God is not before their eyes, "and the way of peace have they not known" (Rom. 3:17).

Fear and tremble, you ungodly, natural men, for the almighty God is your enemy. You cannot hold out against Him. There is no hiding place or refuge that will protect you or deliver you out of His hand. It is a fearful thing to fall into the hands of the living God.

You may be living here in ease and quiet. You may be unconcerned about the old man, as if you had made a covenant with death and were in agreement with hell. You may sport with the messengers of God who warn you. You may put off the evil day and try to rid your heart of fearing the judgment of God. When the trumpet of a mighty voice sounds, however, it will not fail to awaken you. How terrified you will be then! How you will shake and tremble! For the Lord Himself will descend from heaven like a dreadful storm. The voice of the archangel and the trumpet of God will sound. Everything in heaven and on earth will be in turmoil. There will be voices, thunders, and earthquakes. Then the last trumpet will sound.

You who are dead in sin will come to judgment. You will be summoned in fear and trembling before the judgment seat of Christ (Adam, where are you?), where your sins will be brought to light, even the secret ones that you would blush for shame about if you thought others knew about them. The great Judge will then pierce you through with His all-seeing eyes and say to you in His wrath, "Depart from me, ye cursed, into everlasting fire, prepared for the devil and his angels" (Matt. 25:41).

Therefore, listen to what Scripture says. "Awake thou that sleepest, and arise from the dead, and Christ shall give thee light" (Eph. 5:14). "Howl ye; for the day of the LORD is at hand; it shall come as a destruction from the Almighty" (Isa. 13:6). "Rise up, ye women that are at ease; hear my voice, ye careless daughters; give ear unto my speech....Tremble, ye women that are at ease; be troubled, ye careless ones" (Isa. 32:9,11). You must be troubled by such warnings. For the earth quakes in order that we might be moved in terror to flee to the Lord and His goodness.

We could tremble in a natural way or in an affected way. We could tremble like the Friends, who are also called Quakers; or tremble in slavish fear like Felix. But what we have in mind for you is the holy trembling that is found in the truly converted (see Haggai 2:6-7).

Come then, sinful men and women. Wake up and be troubled. Stand up, oh Jerusalem (Isa. 51:17). Here is what the Lord calls you to do:

1. Consider your insignificance. Let the godly mourn and sigh on account of their pride, which so often shows itself.

2. Know how guilty you are.

3. Acknowledge the majesty and almighty power of God. We children of men are especially at fault here. We do not comprehend the exalted sovereignty, the most perfect purity, and the most pure righteousness of the great God, for the sinner will not behold the majesty of the Lord (Isa. 26:10). As Elihu says, "Behold, God is great, and we know him not" (Job 36:26). He who recognizes the greatness of God must tremble. Laying his hand upon his mouth, he must confess, "Behold, I am vile" (Job 40:4). With Jeremiah he must exclaim, "Who would not fear thee...?" (Jer. 10:7).

4. Pray to the Father of lights for enlightened eyes of understanding.

5. Consider how horrible our insensitivity is to so many benefits and to so many warnings, reproofs, and supplications. We are not only guilty of the sin of unfaithfulness and unthankfulness but also of immovable obstinacy in it. We act like second Ahabs who are sold to do evil. How long has the Lord faithfully warned us through His servants, who rise up early, trying in more than one way and with a variety of gifts to tell us that our destruction is at hand and our way is not good? Yet how blissfully we move

forward with hearts hardened against all teaching and upon which nothing can make an impression.

How often have we heard: "Oh, that they were wise! They would understand this, they would consider their latter end." How often has the Lord Jesus, with tearful eyes and heart-breaking sighs, wept over us, as He once did over Jerusalem. How often has the Lord cried to us, "Oh that you would understand today the things that belong to your peace!" How horrible it is that we give the dear Savior reason to lament. We are indeed a "foolish people" (Jer. 5:21). God has followed us for so long, crying, "Oh that my people had hearkened unto me, and...had walked in my ways!" (Ps. 81:13). As Isaiah 42:23 says, "Who among you will give ear to this?"

We harden ourselves against verbal warnings, and we harden ourselves against the judgments of God. Is this not astonishing? Our wickedness corrects us; we see how evil and bitter it is to forsake the Lord. Yet we go heedlessly forward. Shame on us. If the hammer of God's Word does not break the rocky heart, then plagues and judgments must do it. As Jeremiah 5:3 says, "Thou hast stricken them, but they have not grieved." Therefore, "be thou instructed, O Jerusalem, lest my soul depart from thee; lest I make thee desolate, a land not inhabited" (Jer. 6:8).

Who then may comfort himself with the power of God and express the confident trust of the psalmist, who says, "Therefore will not we fear, though the earth be removed" (Ps. 46:2)? Who may long for the coming of Christ? Only children of God who know and fear the Lord may do that. At this time, we will not state the marks by which they may be known, but mention only what flows from our text. In light of verse 4, these marks are the opposite of hardening ourselves. They include:

• A broken and a contrite heart. As Isaiah 66:2 says, "But to this man will I look...to him [who] trembleth at my word. Matthew 5:4 adds, "Blessed are they that mourn: for they shall be comforted."

- Self-loathing because of one's corrupt nature and sins (see Ezekiel 36:31). In view of their universal misery of soul, these believers have fled to the Son of God as Surety and Mediator, with a sincere desire to be found in Him (Phil. 3). Paul describes this mark in Hebrews 6:11 and Romans 5:1.
- Ruled by fear of God. They are supremely anxious to do nothing that is displeasing to God. They want to do all that is pleasing in His sight.

Examine and prove yourselves by such marks, beloved. We live in such an evil time, in such a time of corruption and departure from God that the Lord Himself warns, "Awake, stand up, turn and do your first works; and all the more, since the Lord still so sweetly calls, Return, return, O Shunammite; turn ye, backsliding children" (see Jer. 3:14). Be prepared to answer, "Here are we. We come unto thee, for thou art the Lord our God." Like the prodigal, we must say, "I will arise and go to my father" (Luke 15). Pray as well for the salvation of the people in our country. Come before the Lord, begging Him, "Spare Thy people, O Lord, and give them not to reproach; we will not depart from thee; let us live. Help us, O God of our salvation" (Ps. 79:9).

I conclude with the words of that greatly beloved man, Daniel, to Nebuchadnezzar: "Wherefore, O king, let my counsel be acceptable unto thee, and break off thy sins by righteousness, and thine iniquities by showing mercy to the poor; if it may be a lengthening of thy tranquillity" (Dan. 4:27). Amen.

FOURTH COLLECTION

SELECT DISCOURSES
MOSTLY PREACHED
ON SPECIAL OCCASIONS

BY

THEODORUS JACOBUS FRELINGHUYSEN

MINISTER OF THE HOLY GOSPEL IN THE REFORMED
DUTCH CHURCH AT RARITAN, NEW BRUNSWICK,
IN NEW JERSEY, FORMERLY NEW NETHERLANDS

PRINTED AT PHILADELPHIA, BY W. BRADFORD

PREFACE TO THE PIOUS READER
Partaker of the Unction from the Holy One

Since the holy evangelist, Luke, dedicated his book denominated the Acts of the Apostles to Theophilus (Acts 1:1), dedications of treatises and books have become so common as to be regarded almost absolutely necessary. There are various kinds of dedications: The pious Wilhelmus à Brakel dedicates his *The Christian's Reasonable Service* to the churches of the Netherlands. We in our dedication shall follow the example of the reverend and departed Johannes Verschuir, during his life minister of the divine Word at Zeeryp, a bright star among the ministers of Groningen. His valuable work, *The Truth Triumphant*, is dedicated to the Lord Jesus in these words: "Dedication to the King of kings, the precious Lord Jesus, whose is the glory to all eternity."

My reasons for copying the example of this distinguished man are various — the language of Canaan which he employs shows that he has held communion with the Lord; his name is blessed among us; his works praise him in the gates; his prayers and edifying books bear much fruit in our American Zion. *The Truth Triumphant* seems to have been composed for our aid and vindication. The reverend author insists in it, that a minister should examine members by inquiring of them: What is the state of your souls? He also stresses that professors of Christianity are bound to give a reason of the hope that is in them; and that parents who present their children for baptism should be examined.

These and similar duties have here been faithfully performed by us in our ministry, and with much fruit and blessing, for which the Lord be praised. But this was done amid much opposition and contradiction, even from such as pretended to be great rabbis, who branded these pastoral acts, having reference to a knowledge of the state of the flock, as dangerous innovations, or even as a new and false doctrine. Similarly, some Elymas-like ministers have also spoken against us in this manner, even from their pulpits — improper places for pouring forth the vials of their fury — as in their libelous writings, denominated "complaints."

These have been completely refuted by the Rev. Van-Sandvoort. That departed man of God agrees with us in the smallest particulars, also maintaining that Judas did not partake of the Lord's Supper. Although this is but a problematical question, I had stated it in three of my sermons, in agreement with numerous eminent divines with whom I do not regard myself worthy to be mentioned. This was seized upon by the secretary of the lying spirit, in the so-called "complaints," as one of my heresies, as our honored defender has learnedly shown in the dialogue he wrote in reply. The second book of our dear brother, entitled *Experimental Divinity*, is also of much use here to stop the mouths of those of whom gowned personages are the chief, who represent the work of the Holy Spirit in the pious as fanaticism and enthusiasm. Our new Erastians, that is, ministers who have arisen in the Reformed churches teaching that unconverted persons have a right to the Lord's Supper, are likewise refuted in this book.

Our opponents were brought to silence; but upon Long Island a Goliath has arisen, who, in his recklessness, seeks to infuse into everyone the idea so agreeable to the flesh, that it is the duty of the unconverted to partake of the Lord's Supper as a means of grace. This Diotrephes prates against us with many malicious words, denouncing Rev. Goetchins and myself, in his mad zeal, as cursed heretics. Like Balaam, he is yearly hired by the disaffected to intrude for filthy lucre's sake to strengthen the hands of the disobedient and continually belies and slanders us. He intends to be too wise and bold for everyone. Like Ishmael, he sets his hand against every man, including Long Island orthodox men, lovers of old established truths. Since he is disposed to blame everyone and does not hesitate, even from the pulpit, to mention persons by name, whether members or not, and to denominate them liars and brutal persons, without being made an object of appropriate discipline (but what does this zealot care about discipline?), he has already fallen into the hands of the authorities and drawn the costs of a civil suit upon himself and those associated with him. If this minister did not steel himself against all the warning he has received even from Holland, he might perceive that the measure with which he meted to others has been meted to himself, and that while he pursues others, he is rushing on to his own destruction. But this man, who thus rides over everyone's head, is to be pitied; and that they may know how great is the power of God towards us also and our churches, we beseech the pious brethren upon Long Island to watch, stand fast, and contend earnestly for the faith, persevering, making much use of the illustrious writings of Verschuir. This digression will be tedious to no one acquainted with the trying situation of our church.

— T.J. Frelinghuysen

DEDICATION TO THE LORD JESUS
BY HIS OLD AND UNWORTHY SOLDIER

My Lord and God, King of kings and Lord of lords, let it not displease Thee that I lay down at Thy feet these few and imperfect lines, and that, for these two reasons: First and especially, because Thou art worthy that all things should be dedicated to Thee, and that in all things we should acknowledge our dependence upon Thee; for Thou art Alpha and Omega, having obtained all power in heaven and upon earth, being beyond measure exalted, having obtained a name that is above every name, that to Thy name every knee should bow, and all tongues confess that Thou Jesus art Lord, to the glory of the Father, holding the stars in Thy right hand.

Secondly, on account of all the benefits which I have so richly received from Thee, oh good Shepherd (although I am chief of sinners, and the least of Thy servants), inasmuch as it has not only pleased Thee to thrust me, insignificant son of man into the harvest, but also to be with me (since through Thy grace I am what I am); but especially because Thou hast been with me in so many distresses in this strange land, continually delivering me. Truly the deliverances of Thy countenance are too multiplied and Thy blessings upon my weak ministrations, person, and family are too numerous to be reckoned up in order. All the favors Thou hast shown me, even in the time of trouble, lie as so many bonds of obligation upon my soul, so that I am compelled to exclaim, "What shall I render unto Thee for all Thy benefits? Lord, I am Thy servant, and will, by Thy assistance, be faithful unto death, going in the strength of the Lord, fighting the good fight of faith, gladly suffering and enduring, saying and recording, having frequently, with the congregation, expressly sworn in our solemn covenanting, "I am the Lord's."

Enjoy, Frelinghuysen, immortal fame; bear abundantly the fruits of righteousness; let thy pious instructions distill as the dew, and compose the disorderly elements of humanity around. Such is the affectionate, filial language of,

John Frelinghuysen,
Student of Divinity

Numerous and fearful are the vicissitudes to be expected by the children of God. For comfort's sake, this is added by,

David Marinus,
Student of Divinity

— 18 —

The First Ebenezer, or Memorial of Divine Assistance

"Then Samuel took a stone, and set it between Mizpeh and Shen, and called the name of it Ebenezer, saying, Hitherto hath the LORD helped us."

— 1 Samuel 7:12

When Jesus entered Jerusalem as King, He said, "I tell you that, if these should hold their peace, the stones would immediately cry out" (Luke 19:40). The disciples were so thrilled with those words that they said, "Blessed be the King that cometh in the name of the Lord" (v. 38).

The Pharisees were offended, saying, "Master, rebuke thy disciples." Jesus answered, "I tell you that, if these should hold their peace, the stones would immediately cry out." He was echoing the words of Habakkuk 2:11: "For the stone shall cry out of the wall, and the beam out of the timber shall answer it."

This was a figurative way of reproving the Jews for their inexcusable wickedness and unbelief. It was as if the Lord Jesus was saying, "It is so evident that I am the Son of God, the King of Israel, and the Christ, that it cannot be concealed. In one way or another it will be made known in spite of all your efforts to prevent it." This prediction came true when "the veil of the temple was rent...the earth quaked...the rocks rent...the graves were opened" (Matt. 27:51-52).

Although stones cannot speak, they may be used as memorials of events and as public declarations of gratitude. According to our text, "Samuel took a stone, and set it between Mizpeh and Shen, and called the name of it Ebenezer, saying, Hitherto hath the LORD helped us." Israel had received a special benefit from God; He had scattered their enemies before their eyes. This obligated Samuel to offer a public expression of thanks, not only for himself and his people at that time, but also for generations to come. He thus set up a stone as a memorial and as an everlasting remembrance of what the Lord had done for Israel.

In the verses that precede our text, we learn that the ark was moved and placed at Kirjathjearim. Samuel asked the people to turn to the Lord and put away their strange gods. The Israelites obeyed him and observed a day of fasting and prayer. The Philistines then prepared to attack the Israelites. The Israelites were afraid, so Samuel prayed for Israel. The Lord heard the prayer and afflicted the Philistines with such terrible thunder that they scattered. Samuel now raises a memorial at Mizpeh as a symbol of God's wonderful deliverance. We will consider two points in our text:

• The setting aside of a stone
• The meaning of the stone

The Stone Set Aside

Samuel came from a pious family in Ramah. His father's name was Elkanah and his mother was Hannah, who was barren before the birth of Samuel. In her great distress she "prayed unto the LORD, and wept sore" (1 Sam. 1:10). God heard her prayer and gave her a son, whom she called Samuel (in Hebrew, *Shemuel*), which means "one received from God in answer to prayer." God heard the prayer of this pious mother (v. 20). Therefore Samuel was a son of natural birth as well as of the heart and lips. For while Hannah prayed, she promised that if the Lord gave her a son, she would give him to the Lord all the days of his life. (vv. 11, 24, 28). So Samuel served the Lord from when he was very young under the leadership of Eli the priest. Samuel was a Nazarite, consecrated by vow to God, and a Levite who wore a linen ephod (2:18).

As Samuel grew, he grew in favor with God and men. The Lord called him twice, but Samuel did not yet know the Lord. He was not acquainted with how Jehovah revealed Himself to His prophets. He therefore went to Eli, who told him how to respond to God. God then told Samuel what He would do through him. Samuel was thus established as a prophet (3:19-21). After Eli died, Samuel was appointed judge over Israel to rule over and deliver the people. Scripture records many of his virtues and deeds:

1. He was much loved as a prophet and teacher. He was clear in his teachings, solemn in his reproofs, convincing in his preaching, and compassionate in giving comfort. He reproved everyone without bias, making no distinction between king and commoner. He zealously promoted all that was good, and faithfully supported the pure worship of God (1 Sam. 7:3; 12:14, 15, 20, 25).

2. He was sincere and mighty in prayer. He persevered in praying for his people, as we read in 1 Samuel 12:18-19. He is therefore eminent among those who called upon the name of God. Psalm 99:6 identifies him with Moses and Aaron, saying that like them, Samuel called upon God's name. When God threatened Israel with extreme punishment, He said, "Though Moses and Samuel stood before me, yet my mind could not be toward this people" (Jer. 15:1).

3. Samuel was extremely faithful in his ministry. He persevered in performing his duty to the people and sought their welfare even when he was old (1 Sam. 12:23). His upright appeal to the people in 1 Samuel 12:3, 5 is proof of a clear conscience. He has the honor of being placed with Paul and Daniel and other prophets in the list of those who were righteous (Heb. 11:32-33).

4. He enjoyed the favor of God and of the people. He was pious from his youth, and he increased in knowledge

and in gifts (1 Sam. 2:26). God favored Samuel by hearing his prayers and blessing his work. The people showed their love for him with their high regard for him and his services. If they had problems or questions, they went to Samuel with them. They obeyed his commands and testified of his faithfulness. When he died, all of Israel came together to mourn for him. They buried him in his own house at Ramah. Samuel died at a good old age, which is a special blessing. This blessing was also promised to Abram (Gen. 15:15) and fulfilled (Gen. 25:8). Samuel's death was precious in the sight of the Lord (Ps. 116:15). He served in two offices: ruler and judge in the state and prophet in the church. As representatives of two offices, he showed his thankfulness when he "took a stone, and set it between Mizpeh and Shen, and called the name of it Ebenezer."

He took a stone, possibly a large and attractive one, and set it up, not to worship it (knowing that was forbidden), but as a monument to the victory gained by Israel over the Philistines and as a proper token of thankfulness. Since ancient times, men have raised memorials of conquest. We find that men of God adopted the same practice to remember God's benefits. This was the case with Jacob. After his brilliant vision, he "took the stone that he had used for a pillow and set it up as a pillar, pouring oil on top of it" (Gen. 28:18).

Heathen people also set up stones, anointing them and worshiping them. In our country there are great heaps of stone in the forests, which the Indians add to when they pass by them. Joshua, the servant of the Lord, also set up stones (Josh. 4:8-9). Moses built an altar he called "Jehovah is my banner" (Ex. 17:15). The sign thus received a name which stood for a special event. Likewise, Samuel called the stone which he raised "Ebenezer," which means stone of help.

The Meaning of the Stone

Our text says the stone means "Hitherto hath the Lord helped us." The Lord is Jehovah, who reveals Himself in the Old Testament as "I AM THAT I AM" (Exod. 3:14); and in the New Testament as "which is, and which was, and which is to come" (Rev. 1:4). He is unchangeable in essence and faithful to His promises. As Malachi 3:6 says, "I am the LORD, I change not." Samuel does not say the stone helped Israel; he says Jehovah did that. Israel did not win the victory over an enemy because of the strength of its horses or chariots or weapons but because of the Lord. This was clear to everyone, for the Lord had thundered with a great thunder, and that is a work that only God can do. He alone has power over thunder. As Psalm 29:3 says, "The God of glory thundereth." The Almighty fought for Israel with His thunder. He often uses the thunder of His power to destroy His enemies and help His people. The victory was thus the Lord's.

Samuel also says the Lord "helped." Because the Israelites could not overcome their enemies, they were graciously helped. The verses prior to our text tell us that this help was the Lord's answer to Samuel's prayer. The Lord sent such fearful thunder upon the Philistines as they were preparing for battle that they fled in terror. Fear of thunder won the battle for the Israelites. It eliminated the battle that they had feared and brought them victory over their enemies. The pious confess and acknowledge that victory comes from God. Asa acknowledged that in his war with Zerah the Ethiopian. That is also what King Uzziah learned when God helped him against the Philistines.

Samuel says "hitherto" has the Lord helped, referring also, perhaps, to the place where the stone was set up. He might be saying, "Here is where the Lord thundered, where His help was evident." The stone would help people remember that event forever, for in that place and at that time God sent thunder. Then the thunder ceased, which was also from the Lord.

"Hitherto" could also express admiration for such a great deliverance. Samuel might be saying, "Who could have expected so large and important a victory, indeed, the entire destruction of the enemy?" Or "hitherto" might imply that the children of Israel realized they were a great people because the Lord had thus far blessed them.

"Hitherto" may also suggest that Israel had not yet experienced full deliverance. The people had been delivered "hitherto" and for some time from the Philistines. Although the power of the Philistines was greatly weakened, it was not yet entirely crushed. And although the Israelites would not always remain free of their enemies, they were free of them at present. For this they were thankful. "Hitherto" had the Lord helped them.

Finally, "hitherto" might express their hope that the Lord would help them further; that what He had begun He would also complete. "Hitherto" everything was done in such a way that they could hope for the future. Likewise David hoped because of what had been done for him, saying, "The LORD that delivered me out of the paw of the lion, and out of the paw of the bear, will deliver me out of the hand of this Philistine" (1 Sam. 17:37). "Hitherto" they had been delivered, and what the Lord had done was marvelous in their eyes.

The response to such deliverance is to "Offer unto God thanksgiving; and pay thy vows unto the most High." Great benefits demand great acknowledgments. Throughout the ages, upright Israelites have performed this duty. Godly leaders, magistrates, and ministers publicly acknowledge God's benefits, but the godly also do so privately so that the memory of divine benefits may live on forever. The church in every age must not only preserve those memories but pass on the knowledge of them to future generations (see Psalm 78:1, 6 and 105:6).

"Forget not all his benefits," says Psalm 103:2. The church teaches God's benefits to its children (Ps. 44:1) by establishing memorials and observing days of thanksgiving. One example is the feast of Purim, which the Jews observe in remembrance of Israel's deliverance from evil Haman, who tried to destroy them. Read about that in the book of Esther. The Netherlands observes days that commemorate its deliverance from French and Spanish tyranny. It has issued medals in honor of special events, such as the destruction of the mighty Spanish fleet in the year 1588, which was struck by a terrible storm near the coast of Ireland. Medals that recall this event bear on one side the inscription "Soli Deo Gloria" (to God alone be the glory), and on the other an image of ships with these words: *Classis Hispania* (Spanish Fleet), with the words "Come; Gone;" written around the ships.

Another medal shows on one side a wrecked ship in flight, and on the other the figures of four men in supplication and thanksgiving, encircled by the words, "*Homo proponit; Deus disponit*" (Man proposes; God disposes). Still another medal was issued in memory of Prince Maurice, who captured ten cities and three castles in a three-month campaign in 1597. On one side the medal says in Latin, "This is the Lord's doing, and it is wonderful in our eyes." The other side says, "*Venit, Vidit, Deus vicit*" (He came, He saw, God conquered). Thus have others followed the example of our text: "Hitherto hath the Lord helped us."

Note, then, how Samuel acknowledges Jehovah's great deliverance of Israel. He says, "Hitherto hath the Lord helped us." The church that is assembled here may likewise say with thanks, "Hitherto hath the Lord helped us." For the Lord has helped us in remarkable ways.

The dangerous circumstances in which we have been helped are too numerous to list. We will mention some of the most remarkable, however, for if we keep silent, the stones might cry out. The pulpit and beams of our church would chastise us for our unthankfulness. The forests and trees of the woods, the streams and rivers that we pass as we travel to places where we preach, might testify against us; for they have seen our trouble and have heard our sighs.

Therefore let this little flock, this American Zion, this young vine of the Israel of God, say, "Hitherto, hath the Lord helped us" in these ways:

1. The Lord helped us through persecution. As Psalm 124:2-4 says, "If it had not been the LORD who was on our side, when men rose up against us: Then they had swallowed us up quick, when their wrath was kindled against us: Then the waters had overwhelmed us, the stream had gone over our soul." In storms and waves, the Lord of hosts was with us (Ps. 46:7).

2. The Lord helped us against our enemies. These enemies showed what spirit was motivating them when they shut our churches and drove us to preach in barns in the year 1725, yet, "Hitherto hath the Lord helped us." We may now assemble without disruption in houses of worship, fulfilling the words of Psalm 122:1, "I was glad when they said unto me, Let us go into the house of the LORD."

3. The Lord upheld our honor. In 1725, our enemies wrote a book against us that was full of lies and false accusations (revealed by the replies of two pastors); but the Lord used the occasion to extend His truth. How appropriate, then, are Job's words: "Oh...that mine adversary had written a book. Surely, I would take it upon my shoulder, and bind it as a crown to me" (31:35-36).

4. The Lord granted us favor with the government. Although our enemies sought help from the English government and tried to turn the governor and other officers against us, our King Jesus, in whose hands are the hearts of kings, moved their hearts so that they were for us instead of against us. So the enemies' plan was frustrated. "Hitherto hath the Lord helped us."

5. The Lord saved us from wicked schemes. Almost everyone here knows how many assemblies and councils were held against us. Both learned and unlearned people made it their daily business to devise schemes against our small flock. But "hitherto hath the Lord helped us." Therefore,

"Take counsel together, and it shall come to nought"; for "no weapon that is formed against thee shall prosper" (Isa. 8:10; 54:17).

6. The Lord upheld our cause. Uneducated wealthy country people as well as learned and acute divines (principally Dutch) opposed us, but we were not silenced; for we had a good cause, a good conscience, and the Mighty One of Jacob on our side. Thus, "Hitherto hath the Lord helped us." However, we are persuaded that the majority of the ministers were misled by evil rumors and did not regard the ancient admonition to give us an impartial hearing (*Audi et alteram Partem*).

7. The Lord defended us. Although our enemies spent a great deal of money to prosecute us, and the saying of Solomon that "Money answereth all things" is true, yet "Hitherto hath the Lord helped us."

8. The Lord won our case before classis. Although many complaints were made against us at the Classis of Amsterdam, the Lord so remarkably helped us in our defense that we were pronounced orthodox. Our enemies were urged to seek peace with us and to return us to the church.

9. The Lord protects us from false teachers. From time to time, unauthorized teachers and helpers paid by our opponents have come among us to stir up strife and afflict us. In spite of the bustle and noise, "Hitherto hath the Lord helped us."

10. The Lord protects us from nonbelievers. Some have crept in among us who speak and act like Christians and who pretend to be of one mind with us. But they are tares in our field and chaff on the threshing floor of the church. Secretly they are opposed to us and try to harm us. "Hitherto hath the Lord helped us."

11. The Lord delivers us from affliction. In this new land we have often been severely afflicted and chastened by the hand of God in bodily sickness as well as spiritual desertion. We frequently had to exclaim, "Thy hand was heavy

upon me: my moisture was turned into the drought of summer" (Ps. 32:4). We were compelled to preach on the words, "I am the man that hath seen affliction by the rod of his wrath" (Lam. 3:1); and, "I am as a wonder unto many; but thou art my strong refuge" (Ps. 71:7).

Yet we have been delivered from death by Him who "bringeth down to the grave, and bringeth up" (1 Sam. 2:6). Who knows how often our enemies rejoiced over our affliction, saying "Aha, aha!" We could then reply, "Rejoice not...O mine enemy: when I fall, I shall arise; when I sit in darkness, the LORD shall be a light unto me." Surely, if the Lord had not helped us, we would have perished in our affliction. Therefore (although with humble mind) I say with Paul, "Having...obtained help of God, I continue unto this day, witnessing both to small and great, saying none other things than those which the prophets and Moses did say" (Acts 26:22).

Have we earned God's help because of our goodness? No, our "goodness extendeth not to thee" (Ps. 16:2). "Not unto us, O LORD, not unto us, but unto thy name give glory" (Ps. 115:1). We are completely unworthy. The great Benefactor has loaded us with benefits. He has fed us with the finest wheat and satisfied us with honey out of the rock (Ps. 81:16). He has prepared a table before us in the presence of our enemies; our cup runneth over (Ps. 23:5). He richly gives all things for our enjoyment. We are the people of God in covenant with Him. We are His vineyard, for which He spared no pains and no cost; we are planted upon a fruitful hill, richly watered with the dews of heaven (for the means of grace are here in all their fullness); and He has wonderfully preserved and helped us to this day.

But oh, how unthankful and unfaithful we are! Like Israel (for the stern words "Do ye thus requite the LORD, O foolish people and unwise?" said to them also apply to us), we have forsaken the God who made us. We have lightly esteemed the Rock of our salvation (Deut. 32:15). Is this how we thank Him for His help? Is this how we reward Him for His goodness, long-suffering, and forbearance (failing to recognize that His goodness leads us to repentance)? Who acknowledges the help of the Lord as he should? Who appreciates it? Who responds with thankfulness? In want and distress, we promise to change our lives and serve the Lord more diligently, but who obeys those promises? It is common to verbally acknowledge the help and the good hand of God, but not as common to respond to His favors by walking in holiness. Oh what unbecoming, inexcusable conduct! Even more abominable, though, is how people credit the help, prosperity, and other blessings that they have received from God to their own wisdom, understanding, and diligence.

But you who love the truth and are children of Zion, come. Let us not only raise a mere outward memorial with Samuel, but let us offer substantial evidence of our thankful remembrance of the Lord's help shown to our congregation. "Hitherto hath the Lord helped us." We must credit the help given to us only to Jehovah and only give glory to Him. As Psalm 118:23 says, "This is the LORD'S doing; it is marvellous in our eyes." Let us say with the church, "For they got not the land in possession by their own sword, neither did their own arm save them: but thy right hand, and thine arm, and the light of thy countenance" (Ps. 44:3). God alone is our help and our deliverer (Ps. 70:5).

We must also acknowledge that we have received help from good men, however, such as:

1. Two ministers, Freeman and VanSantvoort, who defended our cause in print. They would not condemn us without hearing us. Then they took an interest in our affairs. In their warm and brotherly letters, they frequently refreshed and strengthened us.

2. Faithful and godly people in this country, who showed their compassion by praying for us in our afflic-

tion. Among these, the English Presbyterian believers were
especially helpful.

3. Godly people in Holland and East Friesland who remembered us in their prayers and public religious services.
Their spiritual and edifying letters frequently encouraged
us when we were discouraged.

Such are the means that Jehovah used to help us. We
must not look to men, though, for the creature must step
aside. As Psalm 60:11 says, "Give us help from trouble: for
vain is the help of man." Like Israel, we must trust only in
the Lord (Ps. 115:9). We must acknowledge the help of the
Lord, thank Him for it, and openly praise Him. The godly
have always done so in thanksgivings and songs of praise,
such as "Bless the LORD, O my soul: and all that is within
me, bless his holy name. Bless the LORD, O my soul, and
forget not all his benefits" (Ps. 103:1-2).

Above all, we must show gratitude by living godly lives.
If only we were truly thankful. If only we would sincerely
turn to God and live uprightly, yielding ourselves to be instruments of righteousness, wholly consecrated with soul
and body to God and His service because of His benefits.
As Romans 12:1 says, "I beseech you therefore, brethren, by
the mercies of God, that ye present your bodies a living
sacrifice, holy, acceptable unto God, which is your reasonable service."

Finally, we must remember that "hitherto" we are
helped; for we cannot yet say that we have finished our
race, fought the fight, and overcome the enemy. The devil
still goes about "as a roaring lion" (1 Pet. 5:8). The words of
Revelation 12:12 also apply to our church: "For the devil is
come down unto you, having great wrath, because he
knoweth that he hath but a short time." As Ephesians 6:12
says, "For we wrestle not against flesh and blood, but
against principalities, against powers, against the rulers of
the darkness of this world, against spiritual wickedness in
high places." Our enemies are never at rest; there is a "re-

mainder of wrath" (Ps. 76:10). There are still false teachers among us. As 2 Peter 2:1 warns, "There were false prophets also among the people, even as there shall be false teachers among you." We still receive yearly visits from a person who, like Diotrephes, talks against us and in his zeal without knowledge reviles us as accursed heretics.

Do not charge him with such, however. Our church is as a "lily among thorns"; we dwell among thorns, scorpions, and evil persons. But we "have not yet resisted unto blood, striving against sin." We must still "contend for the faith...once delivered unto the saints" (Jude 3). As Ephesians 6:13 reminds us, "Wherefore take unto you the whole armour of God, that ye may be able to withstand in the evil day." We must continue to pray for help against our many enemies, humbly acknowledging our helplessness. Like the godly king Jehoshaphat we must pray, "O our God...we have no might against this great company...but our eyes are upon thee." With the psalmist we must pray, "I will lift up mine eyes unto the hills, from whence cometh my help. My help cometh from the LORD, which made heaven and earth" (Ps. 121:1-2). We will do this with the help of God, for prayers and tears are the weapons of the church.

In closing, children of God, commit yourselves to the Lord, especially on the days we set apart for special religious services and in prayer meetings (which hereafter will be held in public). I urge you to be faithful to Him with the assurance that Jehovah, who has helped us "hitherto," will help us further. "Who delivered us from so great a death, and doth deliver: in whom we trust that he will yet deliver us" (2 Cor. 1:10). To Him alone be the honor and thanksgiving.

"Now unto the King eternal, immortal, invisible, the only wise God, be honour and glory for ever and ever. Amen" (1 Tim. 1:17).

— 19 —

Duties of Watchmen on
the Walls of Zion

Preached at the ordination of
Rev. John Henry Goetschius, minister at Jamaica

"Son of man, I have made thee a watchman unto the
house of Israel: therefore hear the word at my mouth,
and give them warning from me. When I say unto the
wicked, Thou shalt surely die; and thou givest him not
warning, nor speakest to warn the wicked from his
wicked way, to save his life; the same wicked man shall
die in his iniquity; but his blood will I require at thine
hand. Yet if thou warn the wicked, and he turn not
from his wickedness, nor from his wicked way, he shall
die in his iniquity; but thou hast delivered thy soul."
— Ezekiel 3:17-19

Faithfulness is one of the most important qualities required
in a church leader. As 1 Corinthians 4:1-2 says, "Let a man
so account of us, as of the ministers of Christ, and stewards
of the mysteries of God. Moreover it is required in stewards, that a man be found faithful."

The original word for faithful is *pistos*. When applied to
the ministry, as it does here, it means to conduct oneself in
obedience to the design and expectation of the person who
calls one to it. Scripture is consistent in using the word in
this context. Hebrews 3:5, for example, says, "And Moses
verily was faithful in all his house."

A servant of the Lord is faithful when he is upright; when he discharges his ministerial duties actually as the person he seems to be (1 Tim. 1:12). He is faithful when he performs all the responsibilities assigned to him by the Lord without avoiding any; when he takes care of the difficult as well as the easy, the private as well as the public, endeavoring to perform the one as well as the other as required by the high and wise God. He obeys the words of Luke 16:10: "He that is faithful in that which is least is faithful also in much."

He is faithful when he does his work out of pure motivation, not seeking to gratify himself or to acquire vain applause but to please and glorify God in ministering to souls. This is how Paul describes faithfulness in his epistles to Timothy.

He is faithful when he perseveres in the zealous performance of his duties without being alarmed by difficulties and opposition but remains "faithful unto death" (Rev. 2:10). In such a way, Antipas was a faithful martyr of the Lord (Rev. 2:13).

He is faithful because he can look forward to the glorious and gracious reward of hearing the Lord say to him, "Well done, good and faithful servant." He is also faithful to the prescribed method by which he is to discharge his ministerial duties. He may not exceed appropriate bounds, acting capriciously or discriminating against others. Rather, as a watchman appointed by God, he must strictly regard his commission to bear God's Word at His mouth and pass on God's warnings. This is the charge presented in our text.

The verses prior to our text tell how the prophet Ezekiel is commanded by God to eat a roll. God then charges, instructs, and strengthens the prophet against the stubbornness of the people (v. 4). In our text, God gives Ezekiel the necessary information about being a faithful prophet and watchman, thereby strengthening him in his calling. These words are suitable today for inducting a new minister of the gospel into office. We will consider three points in our text:

- The prophet's appointment to the office of watchman
- The watchman's charge and commission
- The consequences of obeying or disobeying the charge

The Prophet's Appointment to the Office of Watchman

In verse 17, God addresses Ezekiel as "son of man," which in Hebrew is *Ben Adam,* which means "a son of Adam." This name reminds the prophet of his humble condition as a descendant of Adam. He is a man of like passions with all men who are called children of Adam, or children of men, meaning they are guilty and depraved by nature. We might wonder why this prophet is so frequently called the son of man while others are called men of God, holy men, servants of the Lord, or, like Daniel, greatly beloved. God does that so that Ezekiel will not become proud because of the incredible excellence of the holy and heavenly vision that He favors the prophet with. He will be kept humble by remembering his human frailty. In His humility, Christ often called Himself the Son of man.

Ezekiel is appointed to a new office. God says, "I have made thee a watchman." Watchmen guard and care for certain things, persons, or places. During the time of Ezekiel, watchmen were stationed on walls and towers to guard against danger and commotion. They would be like today's policemen or soldiers. The Holy Scriptures refer to teachers and rulers of the church as watchmen. Isaiah 21:11 asks, "Watchman, what of the night?" And in Isaiah 62:6, God says, "I have set watchmen upon thy walls, O Jerusalem." The idea here is that watchmen of the church are to its believers' spiritual condition what watchmen of the state are to the physical condition of people entrusted to their care. There are more similarities:

1. Watchmen are entrusted with a certain condition, people, or post. Ministers are committed to care for the city of

God, of which highly "glorious things are spoken" (Ps. 87:3). That consists of the church, the people of God, who are often referred to as Jerusalem, or the house of Israel.

2. Watchmen must be aware of everything that goes on, both far and near (1 Sam. 14; 2 Kings 9). The original word implies observing as well as exploring. It also means to lie in wait. Ministers must observe everything — things that are a great distance away as well as those that are close by — in order to spot approaching danger, evil design, or pernicious behavior. Therefore they are also called *episkopoi*, or overseers.

3. Ministers may be called watchmen, because they are entrusted with the solemn oversight and care of the souls of men. They are to watch over themselves as well as the flock in caring for souls (Heb. 13:17; Acts 20:28).

4. Watchmen should be cheerful and courageous in the greatest dangers. They must follow the example of Paul, who says: "But none of these things move me, neither count I my life dear unto myself" (Acts 20:24).

5. Watchmen should carefully watch every thing that happens, from the least to the most important. It was shameful to neglect such a duty in Israel. Isaiah 56:10 says, "His watchmen are blind...loving to slumber." Timothy is charged as an overseer to "Watch thou in all things" (2 Tim. 4:5), for "A bishop...must be...vigilant" (1 Tim. 3:2).

6. Watchmen must be well armed, continually having their swords ready. Ministers must likewise be practiced in spiritual warfare, knowing how to meet the enemy. In 2 Timothy 2:3, Paul says Timothy must "endure hardness as a good soldier of Jesus Christ." He must have his weapon, the sword of the Lord's Word, ready at all times. The Song of Solomon 3:7-8 speaks of the valiant men around the bed of Solomon, all of whom bear swords.

7. Watchmen are under the authority of those who have appointed them to office. This is also true of spiritual watchmen. "I have set watchmen upon thy walls," says Isaiah 62:6. The one who appoints overseers in the church

is God (Heb. 3:2); particularly the Father (Gal. 1:15), the Son (Eph. 4:11), and the Holy Spirit (Acts 13:2). The charge flows out of divine power and is an attribute of the divine essence common to the three persons of the Trinity.

The Lord appoints a man when He chooses, calls, and qualifies for the purpose. Paul therefore says, "Let a man so account of us, as of the ministers of Christ" (1 Cor. 4:1). The prophets were holy men of the tribes of Israel, who were called by God in an extraordinary manner and infallibly guided by His Spirit.

8. As a watchman is appointed over a certain city, place, or people, so Ezekiel was appointed over the house of Israel, that is, the church (Ps. 147:2; Rom. 9:4).

9. Watchmen must sound an alarm in case of danger, arousing those who are sleeping, and calling out when the enemy approaches. Likewise, ministers must awaken those who are securely drowsy and make them understand that the enemy of their souls is near. Ministers must sound the alarm about the spiritual conflict and warn their listeners of destruction. Jehovah Himself urges this duty upon watchmen in Ezekiel 33:6, saying that if they see the sword approaching, they must blow the trumpet. Ezekiel was severely tasked to give such warning.

The Watchman's Charge and Commission

In the last part of verse 17, God issues this command to his newly appointed watchman: "Therefore hear the word at my mouth, and give them warning from me." Although the Lord our God is pure spirit, human characteristics are sometimes ascribed to Him. The mouth is what men use to outwardly express and communicate their thoughts. So the Lord is said to have a mouth here to communicate the thoughts and purposes of His heart as well as His will and commands.

The mouth of the Lord refers to His instructions and commands. When Jehovah says, "Thou shalt hear the word at my mouth," He is saying, "You ask for my advice and will receive the following instruction." This is followed by the words, "and give them warning from me," which means, according to the original Hebrew, "in my name and at my command." The word for warn means to glitter, shine, or signal. Thus to teach or give warning means to offer others teaching in light and clearness of mind that will benefit them. Overseers of the church are thus appointed as watchmen to warn the people in the name of God.

Verse 8 of our text clarifies the results of Ezekiel's commission. He responds to the Lord by saying, "When I say unto the wicked" (compare Ezekiel 33:8). What he means by "the wicked" here is:

1. Someone who is restless and disturbed (Job 34:25). Wicked signifies a person with a disturbed mind, one who has a restless spirit, who disturbs good order, and whose passions constantly tend toward evil. As Scripture says, "There the wicked cease from troubling" (Job 3:17); "The wicked are like the troubled sea, when it cannot rest" (Isa. 57:20); and "Raging waves of the sea" (Jude 13).

2. Someone who cannot stand in the divine judgment. He is condemned. Someone who cannot defend his cause when summoned before a judge is, with good reason, disquieted. Job says, "Let mine enemy be as the wicked" (Job 27:7), that is, as a criminal who is condemned (Ps. 109:7). A wicked person has no righteousness; he is the antithesis of a righteous person.

All men are wicked by nature; all are destitute. The wicked, however, vary in kind and degree. There are the openly profane who are endlessly and intolerably wicked (1 Cor. 6:10) as well as the externally and morally correct wicked, like the Pharisees (Luke 18), who justify themselves (Matt. 9:13) and are outwardly religious, but only appear to be pious.

We must not just think of the wicked as those who live openly in abominations and sins. Those who are civil and virtuous in outward behavior are also wicked as long as they lack the righteousness of Christ and are unrenewed. As Isaiah 57 says, "There is no peace, saith my God, to the wicked." Such wicked ones are outside and inside the church. As Jeremiah 5:26 says, "Among my people are found wicked men."

The watchman must warn such wicked ones. He must tell them that God does not only say to the wicked, "What hast thou to do to declare my statutes?" (Ps. 50:16), but also, "The soul that sinneth...shall die," and "The wages of sin is death." When the Lord says, "Thou shalt die," He means temporal as well as eternal death. The wicked will perish and be lost forever.

This is what the watchmen must proclaim. This is also clearly taught by our Catechism, which says that it is declared and testified to all unbelievers and to those who do not turn to God that as long as they do not turn, they are subject to the wrath of God and eternal condemnation (Q. 84). If the watchmen do not fulfil this charge, what is the consequence?

The Consequences of Obeying or Disobeying the Charge

Verse 18 includes the phrase "If he give him not warning, nor speak to warn the wicked from his wicked way." The watchman's goal is to help the wicked change and live, to deliver him from the evil way (Prov. 2:12), and to save his life. He cannot do this as God, the great first cause, does by His own power. But he can do this as God's instrument through the ministry of the Word, which is called the power of God (1 Cor. 1:18). The ministers of God justify many (Dan. 12:3) by becoming fishers of men (Matt. 4:19) and light and salvation to the heathen (Acts 13:44) to open the eyes of men (Acts 26:18), to save themselves and those that hear them, and to hide a multitude of sins (James 5:20).

But if the wicked are not warned, "The same wicked man shall die in his iniquity." This is the miserable state of those who are lost. Like Saul, they die in their sins. The

Lord Jesus warned the Jews about their unhappy condition in the life to come when He said, "Ye shall die in your sins." Likewise, Ezekiel 18:24 says, "In his trespass that he hath trespassed, and in his sin that he hath sinned, in them shall he die." The wicked perish in their sins because they do not turn to God.

Yet their destruction will be a mark against the watchman, for "His blood will I require at thy hands" (see also Genesis 42:22). Blood is another word for guilt, so the watchman will be charged with guilt. He has helped cause the destruction and misery that comes upon the wicked because he has not warned them or tried to pull them out of the fire (Jude 23).

If the watchman does his duty, however, the text says, "Yet if thou warn the wicked, and he turn not from...wickedness...he shall die in his iniquity, but thou hast delivered thy soul" from my wrath and punishment, which would otherwise come upon thee. Paul thus could say, "I am pure from the blood of all men" (Acts 20:26), that is, I am not the cause of the destruction and misery that may come upon any of you because I have surely warned you.

We will not elaborate on how well these words suit God's purpose here, which is to fortify Ezekiel against the stubbornness of His people. Time also prevents us from dwelling on the weighty responsibility of the ministerial office. No wonder that holy men such as prophets and apostles were so reluctant to take on the work that it was necessary to send them out. For if a sinner goes unwarned to hell, his blood is on the minister's account. As Scripture says, "His blood will I require at thy hand." Oh what an intolerable burden lies upon the soul of the poor watchman! "Who is sufficient for these things?" (2 Cor. 2:16).

In the exalted Mediator's great goodness, providence, and love to man, He gave to His church first prophets, apostles, and evangelists, and later pastors and teachers (Eph. 4). In the sinful American wilderness in which we live, Jehovah has set watchmen upon the walls of Zion. Meantime, He has taken them away from many other places. As the candlestick is removed, one can hear the bitter complaint: "We see not our signs" (Ps. 74:9). Or, "My sheep wandered through all the mountains, and upon every high hill" (Ezek. 34:5-6).

God's patience allows watchmen to remain among us. Although the number of those who publish good tidings among us is not great, there are some who, in every language and with every kind of talent, warn sinners in God's name. If one watchman is transferred or taken away by death, he is succeeded by another, as we see today. How we wish that all of our overseers obeyed the Lord to be godly and faithful watchmen!

But alas, the Word of God and sad experience teach us the contrary. The lamentations of the prophet Isaiah can be applied to our times: "His watchmen are blind: they are all ignorant, they are all dumb dogs they cannot bark; sleeping, lying down, loving to slumber" (Isa. 56:10). Godly divines have written volumes on this subject. We read about evil, unfaithful watchmen in Song of Solomon 5:7. Those who are destitute of grace do not know the bride, the true people of Jesus. Therefore they cannot be true guides who feed the Lord's people with knowledge and understanding (Jer. 3:15). They are "the leaders of this people [who] cause them to err" (Isa. 9:16). As Jeremiah 23:11 says, "For both prophet and priest are profane."

The ones who are unfaithful include:

- Those who are enemies of true godliness.
- Those who speak ill of the godly in their public discourse or in slanderous writings, giving them scurrilous labels such as hypocrites, Pharisees, Puritans, Pietists, Quakers, schismatics, new-lights, or whatever other labels they can think up. They make the godly look like a body of pretenders whose religion consists of continuous bowing down. Such lies grieve the righteous. The

distinguished Professor Van Driessen says there has always been and always will be conflict between the seed of the woman and the seed of the serpent. This enmity is most evident in unsanctified ministers, as their ministry reveals.

- Those who mistreat the godly by giving them poor advice and by failing to comfort those who need comfort. Such are worthless, foolish pastors. Woe unto you, unfaithful watchmen!

Reverend Brother, let us remind ourselves that it is our duty to examine ourselves; for to be a watchman in name only is not enough. There are evil and unfaithful watchmen. Paul thus asks, "Thou...which teachest another, teachest thou not thyself?" (Rom. 2). We teach our people that they should examine themselves; shall we then fail to do this ourselves? Or shall we persuade ourselves along with the ignorant masses that all ministers are true believers, really good, and shall certainly be saved? We know better from the case of Judas, Demas, and those who shall say at the last day, "Have we not prophesied in thy name?" Thorough literary training, an ecclesiastical license, and a lawful call are not enough to make us faithful watchmen. Let us judge ourselves to see whether we bear the marks of the faithful.

I shall not ask you my own questions but some proposed by well-known divines, who in learning and piety shine as stars in the firmament of the church of Christ, and at whose feet I would gladly sit. They would have you ask:

- Have I been sent and appointed of God, or have I run into this on my own?
- Was I aware of the seriousness of the office?
- Have I experienced conviction, regeneration, the love and leading of the Spirit of God, and the various conditions of the pious soul so that I may from this good treasure of my heart and my experience bring forth new and old things and offer to each what he needs?

- Do I have a special desire to preach Christ, to convert souls, to build up the church?
- Do I experience continual desires to undertake the work?
- Do I have a desire to know whether the Lord appointed and sent me? Have I prayed to know it?
- Have I hesitated in the work because it is so great and I am so unfit? Were the sinful motives that arose in my mind an affliction to me? Do I feel a readiness to part with goods, honor, and life for the Lord Jesus? Or have I sought honor, respect, and ease, using the office to make a living and get through the world without difficulty?
- What is the character of my ministry? Do I look to God for direction, hearing the word at His mouth? Have I ever carefully considered what it means to watch for souls and to warn sinners, that their blood may not be upon me and they would not cry for vengeance upon me?
- Is it my goal to reveal men to themselves to separate the precious from the vile? Is it my chief care to comfort the sorrowful?
- In relation to the external call, how have I obtained my present position? Have I indulged in flattery to the consistory or any members of the congregation?
- What motivates me to move from one place to another? Is it the summons "Come over and help us"?

Leaders who do not approve of such inquiries may be assured that a time of reckoning will surely come, and that things will be far different than what they imagine. Oh how miserable they will be when God casts them away as wicked and slothful servants (Matt. 25:26)! If anyone here is convinced that he has not been appointed to this weighty office but has entered it with wrong motives and means, let him humble himself before God and seek reconciliation through the blood of Jesus Christ. Let him also seek after a proper calling. If he is not called, it would be better for him to stop preaching, no matter how poor he would become, for a wicked preacher is the most abominable person in the world. The terrible judgment of God is suspended over him. "His blood will I require of thy hands."

But happy is he who, after careful investigation, finds that he has been appointed and called of the Lord. He is like the pious à Brakel who was assured by God in an extraordinary manner by the words, "I have called thee; I have called thee."

I must now remind you, as well as myself, of some of the duties that belong to a minister's office apart from the general ones of prayer, catechizing, administering the sacraments, and exercising discipline. We must be reasonably acquainted with our duties, yet it is sometimes necessary that we hear about them in a different light. Some of the duties that flow out of our text include:

1. Seeking Christ's glory, not our own. We are children of men, meaning we are flesh of flesh and men of like passions with others. Therefore we should not be proud, exalting ourselves by treating others haughtily or seeking our own glory. He who is puffed up with pride falls under the power of the devil. He preaches himself and not Christ. Paul complains of this in Philippians 2:21 when he says, they all seek their own. This can yield the most bitter fruits. For example, an eminent preacher who was endowed with extraordinary gifts, fell into the depths of despair because, as he later expressed it, he had "preached himself."

When ministers are converted in the course of their ministry (as sometimes happens), they grieve about the selfish motives that brought them into the work. Old and new ministers alike should guard themselves against such motives.

2. Recognizing God's call. Watchmen are appointed by God. They are a gift of the ascended Lord. Therefore they must not run before they are sent by Him to constantly seek new places (Jer. 23:21). If we seek a new position that God has not given us, we incur His anger and may be taken away in His wrath.

3. Preaching what God tells us. We must hear the Word at His mouth, looking to Him for instruction and following His directions. We should not preach our own ideas, much less our hearts' deceptions, doubtful conjectures, incoherent allegories, ridiculous predictions, or impertinent illustrations. Rather, we should offer sound words and substantial truths by which the soul lives (Isa. 30:24). It is therefore necessary that we be much in prayer and look up unto God.

4. Warning the wicked. If we are appointed watchmen, we must faithfully give warning. We serve in a city where many people are confidently hastening to destruction. Let us be careful to save souls, faithfully proclaiming God's warning. As Isaiah 58:1 says, "Cry aloud, spare not, lift up thy voice like a trumpet," that their blood be not required at our hands.

5. Warning our people. The salvation or destruction of precious and noble souls depends upon the discharge of our ministry. Every person in our congregation has an immortal soul. By nature they all pursue the broad way. The only means of deliverance they have is our preaching God's word of reconciliation. If we give them no warning, they will perish forever. Who would not want to rescue them? We must do all we can to save the body. When someone falls into the fire or water, will not we, as appointed watchmen, try to pluck sinners out of the fire? How the Lord Jesus was moved by the sight of the multitude! Paul, likewise, was affected by the state of his brethren according to the flesh (Rom. 9:3).

6. Making judicious applications. Though I would not prescribe a method of preaching to anyone, yet I believe that the application should be discriminating, adapted to the various conditions of the hearers (Jude 20-21; Jer. 15). The church includes all kinds of people: wicked and unconverted persons, moral persons, and Christians in appearance and profession. This last group is the largest, for "many are called, but few are chosen."

There are also converted people in the church. These include babes in grace as well as those who are more advanced. Each has desires and needs. Each must therefore be preached to and dealt with according to his condition, as Jeremiah 15:19 says. Many zealous divines have shown how dangerous general applications can be (Ezek. 13:19-20).

7. Remaining faithful. Like watchmen, we must give account to God of the souls entrusted to us. If we are unfaithful, woe unto us. If we are faithful, it will be well with us. Indeed, we will appear before the Lord in judgment, and He will say to us, "Give account of thy office."

How have you answered your calling and mission? How have you used your talents and used your opportunities? How have you dealt with souls? Have any perished because of you? Have you strengthened the hands of the ungodly and made sad the hearts of the righteous? Have you allowed the dying to die? Have you exercised special care over my lambs, or have you carelessly grieved them? Where are the souls that you have comforted, converted, and built up through your ministry?

Oh how sad a time that inquisition will be for many overseers! How dreadful a sentence. They will wish they had never been born, much less been overseers or watchmen. To perish for their own sins while bearing the burden of so many other souls — how dreadful! How awful to see others rise up against you on the Last Day, saying, "You soul-murderer, you knew that I was ignorant, that I lived in sin, that I neglected the worship of God in my household. If you had proper regard for me, if you had warned me, I would have been converted and saved. But now I perish, you unfaithful minister. God will require my blood at your hand and will deal with you as unfaithful."

Some people invoke divine vengeance even in this life. I read about a distinguished, rich man who lived as his heart pleased. He became sick and fell into depression, seeing nothing before him but eternal misery. A minister who was a good friend of his, visited the rich man. The rich man was busy, so the minister asked if the rich man was busy trying to dispose of his property. The rich man exclaimed, with a most distressing, piercing, and bitter cry, "Yes, I am! But first, I bequeath your soul to the devil, because you have not warned me."

What a fearful legacy! Although the rich man did not have the soul of the minister at his disposal, yet his distress reveals that he was one whose blood would cry out against the minister, demanding vengeance because of his unfaithfulness.

Dear listeners, here is the watchman whom you have called. I have told you how to give an account. According to the rules of our church: "The election shall take place after previous fasting and prayer, as in the times of the apostles."

Since the office of the ministry is a divine institution, it must by no means be regarded as a human device contrived to keep the public under restraint, as impious atheists slanderously say. Nor is it to be seen as superfluous and unnecessary, as enthusiasts maintain. No, the ascended Son of God has appointed some as apostles, some as prophets, some as evangelists, and some as pastors and teachers (Eph. 4:11). The office of the ministry is evidence of the Lord's compassion. We are by nature blind and perverse. We are born into the broad way of destruction. We wander as lost sheep. We thus need instruction and warning from the mouth of God Himself.

If Jehovah called us with His majestic voice from heaven, we would be so overcome that we would cry out as Israel did in Exodus 20:19, "Let not God speak with us, lest we die"; for "so terrible was the sight, that Moses said, I exceedingly fear and quake" (Heb. 12:21). If He commissioned angels to speak to us, their glory and luster would so frighten us that we would, like the watchmen and women in the Bible, become as dead men. Therefore God in His compassion adapts Himself to our human weakness. He sends His Son in the form and essence of a man so that the fullness of the Godhead in Him may be concealed and not overpower us with terror. When Christ ascended to heaven, He also made His will known to us, using as His mouth men with like passions as ourselves, whose feet are beautiful but whose presence does not terrify us. We may freely ask such men about things that we do not understand, seeking the law at their mouth, for they are messengers of the Lord of hosts (Mal. 2:7).

These messengers also struggle with infirmity so that they may comfort others with the comfort that they themselves receive from God (2 Cor. 1:4). That is a special favor, for as Amos 2:11 says, "I raised up of your sons for prophets, and of your young men for Nazarites." Oh what wonderful compassion God shows by adapting Himself to our weakness and declaring His will to us through men!

Since it is easy for listeners to incorrectly judge their teachers, listen to this advice from Mr. Campe:

We must distinguish between ministers. Those who conduct themselves offensively and unworthily in their office and reveal themselves as enemies of the truth and godliness are worthy of no honor. Their office cannot protect them; it but attaches to them a more indelible stigma. They should be dealt with in the severest manner; and although this is not done, a true believer can not regard them but as slaves of a base self-love, until by true conversion they change their unedifying mode of life.

As for those who exhibit only external decency and propriety, although we can cherish no firm assurance of their gracious state, we must say nothing. An unregenerate minister can be a source of edification by his capacity for presenting divine truth, so long as his walk does not disagree with his words. Impressive examples of this are the apostle Judas as well as carnal men in the primitive Church who were endowed with miraculous gifts of the Spirit, although Jesus had never known them.

Those whose fruits indicate inward saving grace must be embraced wholeheartedly, with love for them as persons and obedience to the pure Word, which they teach. These are the teachings of 1 Thessalonians 5:12-13.

To those words I add those of Hebrews 13:17: "Obey them that have the rule over you, and submit yourselves: for they watch for your souls, as they that must give account, that they may do it with joy, and not with grief: for that is unprofitable for you."

I conclude with the words of Isaiah 3:10-11: "Say ye to the righteous, that it shall be well with him: for they shall eat the fruit of their doings. Woe unto the wicked! it shall be ill with him: for the reward of his hands shall be given him." Amen.

Preached in Bucks County, in Pennsylvania.

— 20 —

Christ's Bitter Lamentation Over the Inhabitants of Jerusalem

"O Jerusalem, Jerusalem, thou that killest the prophets, and stonest them which are sent unto thee, how often would I have gathered thy children together, even as a hen gathereth her chickens under her wings, and ye would not!"

— Matthew 23:37

Isaiah 49:4 speaks of the Messiah when it says, "Then I said, I have laboured in vain, I have spent my strength for nought, and in vain." The Messiah is complaining that He had worked in vain and spent His strength for nothing. Strength here refers to His physical energy, which must have been far more vigorous in the Lord Jesus than in ordinary men, considering His many journeys. But we must also understand strength here to mean the powers of His mind. This includes Jesus' ability for teaching with much wisdom and for performing His mighty and wonderful works.

The work of His prophetical office included preaching and miracles. He displayed zeal of no ordinary kind in that work. As Psalm 69:9 tells us: "The zeal of thine house hath eaten me up." With strength the Messiah had labored. When He says all of this was in vain and to no purpose, we must understand that He means that His work yielded little or no fruit compared with what it should have yielded. There were some for whom He did not labor in vain, but they were few. His labors were in vain in relation to the greater part in Israel. As Isaiah 49:5 states, "Though Israel be not gathered," that is, the greater part of Israel refuses to be gathered.

So it was, for neither His discourses or miracles were accepted by the majority of the Jews. The chief priests and scribes remained hardened, bitter enemies of the Lord Jesus. As John 1:11 says, "He came unto his own, and his own received him not."

The end result of this is stated in our text, Matthew 23:37, which begins, "O Jerusalem, Jerusalem, thou that killest the prophets."

Prior to that verse, the Lord Jesus pronounces eight woes upon the Pharisees and scribes because of their sins, which include:

• Hindering the gospel (v. 13)
• Covetousness (v. 14)
• Blind zeal (vv. 15-16)
• Erroneous teachings (vv. 17-22)
• Zeal regarding the fine points of the law, while neglecting its weightier duties (vv. 23-24)
• Pretense of great holiness in using food (vv. 25-26)
• Deceiving people with the mere appearance of righteousness (vv. 27-28)
• Pretense of high regard for departed saints, while persecuting the living.

They were ready to stone Christ Himself (vv. 29-32). For these sins Jesus severely reproves the rulers of Israel. He then sharply criticizes them in the words of our text, which mourns the obstinacy and unbelief of the inhabitants of Jerusalem, then predicts the city's destruction. These words are suitable for our present evil days, which may make us cry out in distress.

But oh how we should also mourn over our own condition and seek to know in our day the things that belong to our peace.

We will examine our text in two parts:

• The Savior's lament over Jerusalem
• Jerusalem is reproached for its unwillingness

The Savior's Lament Over Jerusalem

Jesus speaks here to the city of Jerusalem, capital of the whole Jewish land, seat and court of the Jewish state, beautiful city of the great King. Jerusalem was the joy of the whole earth. It was where the thrones of judgment and the tribes of Israel were assembled. It was the holy city where people met to worship (Matt. 4:5) in the holy temple, the place of God's fire and heat (Isa. 31:9). Jerusalem was the city of God; it was called Jehovah Shammah, the place favored with His special presence.

But here "Jerusalem" stands for the Jewish people, the inhabitants of Jerusalem. The repetition of the word emphasizes its importance. This kind of repetition occurs elsewhere in the Scriptures. Words are repeated three times in verses such as Jeremiah 22:29: "O earth, earth, earth, hear the word of the LORD", and Revelation 8:13: "Woe, woe, woe…!" Words are repeated twice in verses such as Ezekiel 21:6: "Sigh…sigh," and John 3:3: "Verily, verily."

Our text says "Jerusalem, Jerusalem" to stress the earnestness, zeal, and emotion of the Lord Jesus. It also indicates the importance of the subject; the awfulness of its unbelief and the certainty of its destruction and desolation. Jerusalem is severely reproved with Jesus' accusation: "Thou that killest the prophets." Prophets were holy men raised up from the tribes and families of Israel. They were endowed with extraordinary gifts and infallibly moved by the Spirit of God to teach the people of God. They foretold future events and confirmed their words with godly living. The Lord Himself had sent prophets to Jerusalem, as is stated in the text: "Which are sent unto thee." These prophets surely were sent to be of great benefit; for "Where there is no vision, the people perish" (Prov. 29:18). What base ingratitude Jerusalem then exhibited when it killed and stoned the prophets whom the Lord had sent to them.

Stoning was one method the Jews used for capital punishment, and Jerusalem was the usual place where prophets were killed (Luke 13:33). By making itself guilty of such tyrannical acts, Jerusalem had become a den of thieves instead of the house of God. Thus we read, "How is the faithful city become an harlot! it was full of judgment; righteousness lodged in it; but now murderers" (Isa. 1:21); and, "Also in thy skirts is found the blood of the souls of the poor innocents" (Jer. 2:34). In Matthew 21:35-39, the chief priests and elders of the people are described as husbandmen who beat, killed, and stoned servants whom the Lord of the vineyard sent to them.

The Lord Jesus adds, "How often would I have gathered thy children together." Here the city is represented as a mother, and the Jews who came there from all parts of the land of Canaan are called her children.

Jesus says he "would gather" these children. That is, He would diligently use every means possible to convert them, to form them into a new people, and to bless them in His kingdom. He used the means of grace that God granted them: He taught and preached among them, proclaiming the gospel of the kingdom ("Repent...and believe the gospel"). He did all kinds of wonders, working miracles and healing their sick. And He traveled throughout their land doing good. For this purpose He also chose His disciples whose business was to gather the Jews, inviting them into the kingdom, saying, "Come; for all things are... ready" (Luke 14).

Furthermore, He would gather them "as a hen gathereth her chickens." A hen makes a peculiar sound when she sees birds of prey hovering, by which she calls her young together. At the same time she raises her feathers and spreads out her wings, forming a place of refuge for the chicks. Such wings are ascribed to God in passages such as Psalm 17:8; 36:7; 63:7; and Deuteronomy 32:11, and to the Lord Jesus in Malachi 4:2.

The Lord Jesus, then, compares Himself to a hen who extends her wings over her chickens. Like that hen, He lifts his wings to attract and gather sinners to Himself. He is not only a lion, roaring over His prey to keep it, but he is a bird that will defend Jerusalem (Isa. 31:4-5), covering the righteous with His wings. The psalmist also describes God as a shadow. So the way in which the sun defends the inhabitants of the world against wind and cold is how the shadow of God's wings protects sinners who find shelter under them. These wings of Christ offer two great benefits:

1. Defense and protection. The sinner finds these by faith in Christ against the deserved wrath of God, the power of temptation, and the attacks of Satan. The Lord Jesus is a hiding place from the wind (Isa. 32:2). This is the benefit that God promises to His Church (Isa. 4:5-6; Ps. 91:4).

2. Refreshment and consolation. The godly find this with God in Christ, in whom many have found refuge. They are consoled as one who flees from a storm to a hiding place, or revived as one who finds refreshing shade from the burning rays of the sun in the shadow of a great rock. So says the bride in Song of Solomon 2:3, "I sat down under his shadow with great delight"; and Malachi 4:2, "With healing in his wings."

The great Prophet and compassionate High Priest Jesus knows the dangers to which men will be exposed, including the hellish aim of Satan. He thus extensively and frequently calls men through the voice of the gospel, asking them to shelter themselves under the protecting wings of His grace. During the entire time of His public ministry, He stretched out His hands to them, but they were a contentious people; an evil, hardened, and unbelieving generation.

Jerusalem Reproached for Its Unwillingness

"And ye would not," our text says, as if the Savior was saying, "You have constantly opposed my designs." The unceasing goal of the Pharisees and scribes was to do whatever they could to hinder the progress of the gospel. They would not come to Jesus themselves, they tried to prevent others from being gathered in, and furthermore, up to that moment they had also tried to remove the Prince of life in Israel from among His people.

Their unwillingness to allow Jesus to gather the children of Jerusalem was not enough to make His work ineffective, however. Many whom Jesus called were gathered, and others who were prevented at first by malicious opposers were later brought to Jesus through the ministry of the apostles; at least "as many as were ordained to eternal life" (Acts 13:48).

Advocates of free will cite this text to support their erroneous belief, as if man had power in his own will to obey the divine call. That is a faulty interpretation, since this text speaks of the divine call by which Christ is offered for justification. We admit that men who are not elected resist that divine call, for the carnal mind is at enmity with God. The natural man hates the Father and the Son (John 15:24) as well as all true holiness. In their natural helplessness, men cannot come to God (John 6:44), but they may slight the outward means. They do this willingly and with an evil desire not to permit themselves to be gathered. It is their pleasure, their delight, to do so.

The Lord Jesus reproves the Jews saying, "And ye would not." We cannot infer free will from this, or the ability in the natural man to believe without supernatural grace and effectual calling, as do the Pelagians, Arminians, and all devotees of free will. It is not legitimate to say that since men can choose not to will, therefore they can also choose to come and believe. The logic does not follow, for the sinful by nature are not willing, whereas we need supernatural grace for a holy and right willingness.

Christ does not say that the Pharisees and scribes and inhabitants of Jerusalem could believe and turn; rather, He reproves them by saying, "They would not." This emphasizes their disobedience and shows their determination, obstinacy, and willfulness not to come to Christ. They would not calmly consider His person, His works, and His doctrines; but with bitter and settled prejudice persisted in their opposition to Him and willfully hardened themselves. They were so totally wicked that they would not tolerate allowing any of their children to be gathered by Him. Therefore their choice did not proceed from ignorance, but from unwillingness. The Lord Jesus reminds them of this when He says: "Ye will not come to me, that ye might have life." He compares them to people who are invited to a marriage feast, but will not come (Matt. 22:3).

The compassionate Savior's purpose here is not only to censure the scribes, but also to sharply reprimand and threaten them. For their wickedness towards Him immeasurably aggravates their guilt and hastens their destruction. Jesus cries, "O Jerusalem, Jerusalem...ye would not! Behold, your house is left unto you desolate" (vv. 37-38).

Let us remind ourselves here that the words of our text came from the mouth of He who was the best of preachers. They are full of such power, earnestness, compassion, and emotion that I have not been able to study them without emotion. Give them, I beseech you, your particular attention.

When the merciful Jesus says, "O Jerusalem, Jerusalem!" it is as if He is saying as tears run from His eyes, "Because Chorazin and Bethsaida have not made use of my mighty works by repenting, I must pronounce a woe upon them.

"The exalted Capernaum has not turned at my Word and must therefore be thrust into hell, aggravating its condemnation beyond that of Sodom. I can readily forget that my hometown of Nazareth so lightly esteems my prophets

(Matt. 11:20,24; Luke 4:23,24). That the Gergesenes preferred their swine to Me gives me little concern (Matt. 8:34), but that you, Jerusalem, Jerusalem, my vineyard planted on a fruitful hill in which I have done all that could be done; that you, Zion, should so maliciously reject my grace, breaks my heart and causes me to sigh.

"I neither can nor will easily forget you, the scene of my wonders whom I have made great among the nations and appointed prince among the provinces (Lam. 1:1), and exalted above all as my habitation and dwelling place (Ps. 132:13-14). I have revealed myself and my grace too clearly to be rejected by you. If your's was the sin of an Amorite, a Canaanite or Jebusite, I would bear with it four hundred years; were it that of the first world, I would give them one hundred and twenty years to repent; were it Sodom and Gomorrah, Admah, or Zeboim, I would spare for the sake of ten righteous men (Gen. 18:32; Deut. 28:23); but because it is you, Jerusalem, who shall find an excuse for you? Who shall have compassion on you?

"You have forsaken me (Jer. 15:5-6) and for what reason? If you only knew how evil and bitter it is that you have forsaken me (Jer. 2:15)! If you only knew the things that belong to your peace but now are hidden from you! You would not come to me that you might have life. Though year after year I have stretched out my hands to you and would gather you as a hen gathers her chickens under her wings; though I have sent my servants and prophets to you, who have risen early and spoken in my name (Jer. 7:13), yet you would not!"

You would have to be strangers to our American Jerusalem not to see how such words apply to ourselves and our consistory. Raritan, Raritan! how often would I have gathered you, but you would not. It is true that God has not sent us prophets, in the strict sense of that term, who foretell future events. These people were peculiar to the old dispensation and the beginning of the new. God has, however, given us pastors and teachers — ministers of the New Testament — who are also prophets.

It is also true that leaders are not being stoned and killed at the present time. But how many resist them today? If these opposers had the power, who knows if they would not even be killing us? How many evil and rude persons in every way molest faithful ministers, so that they can do their work only with much difficulty? How many are disobedient, remaining ignorant and unconverted, and of whom we must say, "I have labored in vain"? To how many must we say, "How often would the Lord have gathered you by His Word and servants, but ye would not?" The church swarms with such evil ones who will not. Thousands are to be found throughout Christendom. Even among ourselves, the greater part would prompt Jesus to say, "Ye would not come to me."

Let me clarify two things before going on. First, the Lord Jesus has long sought to gather you, as a hen does her chickens. And second, that all who remain unconverted thus far, "would not."

As long as you read and listen to the Word of God, as long as you enjoy the preaching of the Word, the Lord is engaged in gathering you. How often have you heard the divine sigh: "O that they were wise, that they understood this, that they would consider their latter end!" (Deut. 32:29); "Oh that my people had hearkened unto me" (Ps. 81:13); "O that thou hadst hearkened to my commandments!" (Isa. 48:18); oh that "thou hadst known, even thou, at least in this thy day, the things which belong unto thy peace!" (Luke 19:42).

How often have you heard the invitations of the gospel? Surely these are intended for everyone who hears them. For Isaiah 45:22 says, "Look unto me, and be ye saved, all the ends of the earth." Revelation 22:17 adds: "And let him that is athirst come. And whosoever will, let him take the water of life freely"; and Revelation 3:18, "I counsel thee to

buy of me gold tried in the fire, that thou mayest be rich."
How long has the Lord Jesus warned and invited you
through the servants He has sent to you, piping and
mourning? How often has the Lord Jesus, with weeping
eyes and cheeks covered with tears, mourned over you as
He did over Jerusalem?

Certainly, the Lord Jesus weeps when His servants express grief, for it is in His name that they come. It is His
Word that they utter the words: "He that heareth you
heareth me" (Matt. 10). They are ambassadors for Christ,
and they pray "in Christ's stead" (2 Cor. 5:20). How appropriate, then, are the words of the text, "How oft would I
have gathered you" but how sad that we must also say to
you, "and ye would not!"

This is true of the following:

• The wicked who persist in their sins
• The unconverted who live without true holiness
• Those who have not fled for refuge to Jesus
• Those who are still strangers to Christ, having never
  seen Him
• Those who have never been convinced that they need
  Jesus to be saved
• Those who have not realized the preciousness of Jesus,
  and
• Those who have never been in covenant with the Lord
  Jesus.

How many years have you been invited to come to Jesus? What has prevented you from heeding the divine call?
Is it your own unwillingness, or do you imagine the divine
decree to be at fault? (Heedless men accuse God of injustice, as if He were the cause of their unregeneracy and
destruction.) The decree of God neither compels nor prevents you. His revealed will governs what you should do
and not do. You have not remained unbelieving and un-

converted because you imagined that God prevented you, but because you felt no desire.

Will you shift the blame, saying that God has never worked the will in you and that He has never drawn you? That would be wrong, for how can you say that the Lord is obligated to perform those acts towards you? Have you ever, with real earnestness, asked Him to draw you?

If you tried to come, have others prevented you? They may have tried, but others also urged you to flee destruction. They preceded you in coming to Christ, encouraging you with their word as well as their example.

Will you blame your own inability? Those who are secure in unbelief use their inability as an excuse. But you know that the fault is your own. Inability does not excuse you, for you have really not done all that you should. "I have done my utmost," you say. But if you did, you would make use of all the means of grace; you would not neglect church attendance, catechism, or other public religious exercises. You would search the Word of God, be more diligent in prayer, and bow before the Lord Jesus.

Have you remained unconverted because you felt you could not be saved? Your difficulty is a "will not" rather than a "can not." For all your evasions, your attempts to cover yourselves with fig leaves, I must say with the Lord Jesus, "Ye would not!" He has given you His Word and servants, the means and time for repentance, and even the Spirit to convict and exercise your conscience. But you resist the Spirit; therefore the obstacle is your will. You will not come to Christ. You are unwilling because:

1. You do not sufficiently see the need of coming to the Lord Jesus. Your alienation from God and lost state are not a burden to you.

2. You cannot properly come to Jesus without denying yourself, forsaking all your vain pleasures, honor, and esteem. Like the young man in the gospels, you have too

much worldly good. You are still too much attached to the world and your sins.

3. You imagine that you are saved because of what you do. You attend church and go to the Lord's Table, repeat some forms of prayer, perform some moral deeds, and do good works and other kinds of self-righteous performances.

4. You think you can come when you will. You put it off, thinking there is always time for repentance. You procrastinate, saying, "I'll do it later."

5. You reject the way. You say you will come to Christ and you want to go to heaven. But who would not want to go to heaven? Who would not gladly be saved? But you take no pleasure in the method, in the way of salvation. The way is too narrow for you. The holiness of it is not congenial to your feelings. If the way to Jesus and heaven were a broad and sinful way, oh how many would come. You would serve God and mammon; you would willingly keep your sins. You take no pleasure in the consequences of the narrow way — the cross, reproach, derision, persecution. Through much tribulation we must enter into the kingdom of God (Acts 14:22).

6. You imagine that you are already believers and regenerated persons because you were born of Christian parents and presume that you cannot fall short of heaven. This is false ground and a soul-destroying imagination by which thousands deceive themselves under the gospel. This is a way that seems right to a man, but which Satan uses to keep millions away from God. See how it is with natural men.

These are the reasons for your unwillingness. Oh how unhappy and miserable is your state, for you are still alienated from the Lord Jesus, who will gather His people as a hen does her chickens. It is a fearful thing to reject the revealed way of salvation, for it is an awful insult to the Father; it shows contempt for the Son of God, the fountain and Rock of salvation; and it shows reckless disregard for the day of grace.

How this increases your guilt, how it aggravates your condemnation, that the Lord would gather you! He was patient with you and so often would have taken you under His wings, but "ye would not." He invited and you refused, He stretched out His hands, but you opposed His counsel. You were not willing that He should be King over you (Prov. 1). If anything will make the worm of conscience tormenting and intolerable, it is knowing that the dear Savior would have gathered you, "and ye would not." Oh miserable sinners, if only you were wise and willing! How long will the Lord bear with you, you unbelieving and perverse generation? How long will you refuse?

I beg you, allow yourselves to be gathered. There is still time for repentance. The Lord Jesus stands with outstretched arms to gather you. He still waits for you. Nowhere else can you find such protection. It is absolutely necessary that you put your trust under the shadow of His wings, for otherwise you will not see life. The wrath of God will abide on you (John 3:36).

All that Jesus promises can be enjoyed under His wings. That place is so inviting and so refreshing. How I wish that you would experience it! As the bride says, "I sat down under his shadow with great delight, and his fruit was sweet to my taste" (Song of Sol. 2:3). Oh sinner, how can you refuse any longer? If you come to Him, you will not be cast out.

Consider this. Will the kindness and love of the great God and good Savior move you? He would gather you to defend you from the wrath that you deserve. He will be your Rock and refreshment. Will you come? Do you have pleasure in these things? Then how can you resist Him? Is the kindness of God important to you? It is so great that David exclaims, "How excellent is thy lovingkindness... therefore the children of men put their trust under the shadow of thy wings." Should you not then forsake the pleasures of sin and the joys of this world and come to Christ? Or will you violate your own soul? Do you not contradict your own judgment when you despise Jesus and sin against Him (Prov. 8:36)?

Where will you flee to on the day when heaven and earth go up in flames? What wings will cover you from the face of God and the wrath of the Lamb? There will be no place of refuge offered to you then; only a fearful expectation of the fiery wrath that will destroy all of God's enemies (Heb. 10).

I therefore beg you to arise and come to Jesus. Realize the danger that is all around you and threatens you. Acknowledge the necessity of coming to Jesus so you may have life. For He says, "Whoso findeth me findeth life" (Prov. 8).

I pray that you will have such a lively impression of your inability and unwillingness that in holy fear you will look for the drawing that the Lord Jesus promised when He said, "I, if I be lifted up from the earth, will draw all men unto me" (John 12). Therefore pray with the spouse, "Draw me, we will run after thee" (Song of Sol. 1:4).

We conclude with Hebrews 12:25: "See that ye refuse not him that speaketh." Amen.

Preached at New Brunswick, 1745

The Christian's Encouragement in Spiritual Conflict

"And the Lord said, Simon, Simon, behold, Satan hath desired to have you, that he may sift you as wheat: But I have prayed for thee, that thy faith fail not: and when thou art converted, strengthen thy brethren."
— Luke 22:31-32

David's words in Psalm 37:24 are full of consolation for the children of God. He says, "Though he [the righteous] fall, he shall not be utterly cast down: for the LORD upholdeth him with his hand."

A righteous or just person is not perfect, for such a one is not found among the children of Adam. Perfection is the prerogative only of the second Adam. No, a righteous person is one who has fled for refuge to the grace of God and is justified by faith in Christ. All men sin, even the righteous. As James says, "We all offend in many things." Likewise, Solomon says in Proverbs 24:16: "A just man falleth seven times," that is, frequently. He falls into miseries and difficulties, or (as the pious also do) into sins and imperfections. "Let him that thinketh he standeth take heed lest he fall" (1 Cor. 10:12).

When a righteous man falls into misery or sin, however, he is not utterly cast down. He "riseth up again," Solomon says. By new repentance he is raised up and helped out of his situation, "for the Lord upholdeth...his hand." God raises him up and strengthens him inwardly so that he may fall but does not fall away. We have many examples of this, such as David, who fell and was not cast away but rose up (Ps. 51); and of Peter, who fell grievously but was not cast away, for the Lord upheld him, or prayed for him, as is taught in the words of our text.

In the verses that precede our text, Jesus reproves the ambition of the disciples, then adds a wonderful promise in verses 24-30. After that, Jesus predicts Peter's fall, which is our text. We note three points in this verse:

• Jesus predicts Peter's fall
• Jesus prays that Peter's faith will not fail
• Jesus gives Peter work to do

Jesus Predicts Peter's Fall

The person who speaks in our text is the Son of God, the Lord Jesus who is both Lord God and Lord Mediator as well as Lord and proprietor of His people. This is explained more at length in Lord's Day 13, Question 34, of our Catechism. The person who is spoken to here is Peter, whom Jesus addresses as "Simon, Simon." Christ speaks to all of His disciples in the name of Peter here, even as Peter often spoke to Christ in the name of the other apostles (Matt. 16).

The name of Simon is frequently found in Scripture. We read of Simon the leper, Simon the Pharisee, Simon of Cyrene, and Simon Peter. The first time the name appears in Scripture is in Genesis 29:33, where we read that Leah, having brought forth her second child, says, "Because the LORD hath heard that I was hated...and she called his name Simeon [Simon]." Simon means hearer, which may be said of Peter, for when Christ called him, Peter heard the Savior and immediately followed Him (Matt. 4:18, 20).

Simon's other name is Peter, which means rock. Christ promised to give this name to Simon when he was called to be an apostle. That was confirmed after the disciple made his wonderful confession of Christ. Jesus responded by saying,

"Thou art Peter, and upon this rock I will build my church" (Matt. 16:18). Elsewhere Peter is also called Cephas, which is the Hebrew name for Peter (John 1:42). Peter's father was Jonas, which is why the disciple was also called Simon Barjonas, that is, the son of Jonas (Matt. 16:17; John 21:15).

This disciple was in an extremely humble condition before he was called, for he was a fisherman by trade (Matt. 4). Afterwards, when he followed Jesus, he displayed numerous and great imperfections. Through ignorance and misguided compassion, he even tried to dissuade Christ from His sufferings. Jesus responded by telling Peter, "Get thee behind me, Satan." He also made himself chargeable with dissimulation (Gal. 2:12-14). Yet this same Peter was honored with the privilege of being an eyewitness of Christ's glory upon earth (Matt. 26).

Christ addresses Peter emphatically, which is indicated by His repetition of the name, "Simon, Simon." The prophets and apostles frequently indulged in similar repetition. Ezekiel 21:6 says, "Sigh...sigh," and Jeremiah 22:29, "O earth, earth, earth, hear the word of the LORD." Revelation 8:13 says, "Woe, woe, woe, to the inhabiters of the earth." Christ also duplicated words for emphasis, saying, "Verily, verily" (John 3); "Jerusalem, Jerusalem!" (Matt. 23:37); and now, "Simon, Simon." In doing this, Christ expresses His love and compassion for His disciples. It is as if He is saying, "Simon, you are not aware of the danger you are in, for if you were, you would not be so cheerful. You would not depend upon your own strength. Therefore, listen and take notice of what I say."

This warning foretells a sad event that Peter knows nothing about. Christ adds, "Satan hath desired to have you, that he may sift you as wheat." Scripture clearly tells that many angels have fallen and become devils. They are called by various names, one of which is Satan, which means adversary, antagonist, hater (Ps. 8), enemy, and revengeful one (1 Pet. 5:8); for he opposes God and His glory.

He opposes the salvation of men; their faith, holy exercises, obedience, prayers, righteousness, outward zeal, and eternal salvation (Mal. 3:13; Gen. 3; Matt. 4; John 8:44). Paul calls Satan Belial. He is also called the enemy and the tempter of Christ as well as of believers (1 Cor. 7). He is called Beelzebub, the god of filth or of flies, because he is so contemptible, impure, and abominable in the sight of God and His saints. He is further called the strong man who is armed (2 Cor. 4:4) to rule this world with God's permission over the children of disobedience. He is used by God to execute His vengeance upon the disobedient in the air and upon the world, and to cause many commotions and disturbances and events that are strange and incomprehensible to us (Job 1:12; Rev. 9:12; 13:6).

Satan has a variety of operations that affect the following:

1. God. Satan is the enemy of God. He slanders God (Gen. 3), perverts His Word (Matt. 4), hinders the proclamation of His Word, and opposes it (1 Cor. 16:9).

2. Christ. Satan resists Christ's work of saving men. We see that in the vision of Joshua the high priest (Zech. 3:1; Jude 9; Rev. 12), whom Satan tempted (Matt. 4) and betrayed through Judas (John 18:2). Satan opposes Christ with all his might and violence (John 14:30; Luke 22:53), bruising His heel (Gen. 3), and seeking to destroy His kingdom (Rev. 12: Matt. 12).

3. Man. Satan tries in every way to use man, to lead him astray, and, as far as he can, to keep him under his control. He threatens, accuses, and seeks to injure him and to destroy him. He uses all his devious ways, lies, and excuses to draw man away from the right ways of the Lord, taking from him what is good (Matt. 13:12). As Scripture testifies, Satan works powerfully in the children of disobedience.

4. Believers. The pious are not free from Satan's temptations. Christ therefore teaches His disciples to pray: "Lead us not into temptation" (Matt. 6). Satan tempts believers to do

evil, leading them into sin. He did that with King David. He likewise opposes or pollutes what is good in believers.

The Spirit of God refers to this as buffetings. Paul complained of being given a messenger from Satan, a thorn in the flesh to buffet him (2 Cor. 12:7). These fiery darts of the adversary (Eph. 6:16) are the evil thoughts that Satan continually injects into true believers, causing them great distress. He does this in an exceedingly wily manner, concealing his efforts, which are referred to as "wiles of the devil."

His methods are so diverse that it is impossible to number them. The Word of God thus speaks of the depths of Satan. He lies in ambush against believers; he persecutes, terrifies, and injures them in soul and body, as we see in the case of Job. How much that righteous man had to suffer at the hands of Satan! He was plagued by terrors; everything that he had was in Satan's hand except for his very life. With God's permission, Satan produced a storm that deprived Job of all his children, robbed him of all of his possessions, and afflicted him with boils all over his body. Satan hates the children of God; their knowledge, illumination, faith, hope, love, prayers, good conscience, patience, steadfastness in holiness, and works of righteousness.

This sifting can be seen as two kinds: external sifting through perplexity, vexation, and assaults of the adversary; and internal sifting, which leads to unbelief, desperation, absolute despair, and self-destruction. This is the kind of sifting the Savior warns Peter and the other apostles about when He says: "Satan hath desired to have you (all my apostles), that he may sift you as wheat."

Wheat refers to the best grain that grew in Canaan, which is the best kind of food. Scripture speaks glowingly of the "fatness" of wheat (Ps. 81:16). On various occasions, such as in Matthew 13:24, Christ uses wheat as a symbol. Paul does the same in 1 Corinthians 15:37. You know how wheat is treated. It is sowed, and when it is ripe is cut and gathered into the barn (Matt. 3:12). It is then threshed, fanned, and sifted — which is the word the Savior uses in our text when He says the disciples will be "sifted as wheat." This means:

1. Wheat is tossed hither and thither and kept in constant motion when it is sifted. Likewise, Satan will sift the believer, tossing him to and fro with difficulties so that he may, if possible, seduce him from the faith. Satan gives the believer no rest but assaults him with temptation upon temptation.

2. Wheat is sifted to separate from it all chaff, impurities, and spurious grain. Likewise, temptation serves to promote the welfare of believers, for even though they fall into temptation, they will rise again and become more humble and cautious. For all things work together for good to them (Rom. 8:28). God keeps His children by His power through faith unto salvation; not one of Christ's children will perish.

Jesus Prays That Peter's Faith Will Not Fail

In the second part of our text, Christ says, "But I have prayed for thee, that thy faith fail not." He prays especially for Peter, knowing that temptation will be directed with the greatest force against Peter and that he will be in great danger of being overcome.

Christ prayed for His people while He was still on earth (John 17:19-20), presenting Himself to His Father as their Surety. He would pay for all their sins and reveal His will to them. He deeply desired that they might experience the power and fruit of His sacrifice.

Christ also prays for His children from heaven (Rom. 8). We explained how He does this when we preached from the Catechism about the priestly office of Christ. But our text says that Christ prays "that thy faith fail not." Faith cannot fail completely in principle and habit, but it can become weak and impaired in how it is exercised. So when Christ says, "I have prayed for thee, that thy faith fail not," His intent is that Peter's faith will not be entirely extinguished by the temptation of Satan that would come upon him. Truly, this shows great love to Peter, which in turn prompts love from the disciple.

Jesus Gives Peter Work to Do

Christ now says to Peter, "And when thou art converted, strengthen thy brethren." Peter had already experienced the first conversion, for when he was called, he followed Christ, forsaking all. But now we see what the Reformed divines refer to as the second conversion, meaning the occasion when a believer arises after a grievous fall and by repentance returns to the Lord. After Peter has recovered from temptation and falling, the Savior gives him the duty, "Strengthen thy brethren."

"Brethren," in Scripture, has many meanings. It can mean those who are literally brothers and are born of the same parents. It can mean those who are closely related to each other, or are whom the Hebrews calls cousins. It can refer to people who are related by profession, or to people who are members of the same church, even if some are unconverted (1 Cor. 5:11). But in the true sense of the word, brethren are believers because they have one God for their Father, one Jesus for their Savior, and one church for their mother. Christ thus says, "I ascend to my Father, and your Father" (John 20:17). This is why the early Christians began calling one another brethren (James 1:2).

The brethren that Christ talks about in our text are believers that Peter is asked to strengthen, confirm, and comfort. It is as if the Lord is saying, "When you have recovered from your trial, do your best to strengthen other believers. Pray for them as I have prayed for you, and encourage them that they may not fail as you have. Seek to influence them by your example." For this Peter would then be more qualified; for he who has endured danger and temptation can better caution others against it. He who has been delivered from falling can better comfort others with that comfort with which he himself has been comforted.

Peter did comfort his brethren after his repentance, becoming exceedingly bold and zealous in doing so. He not only was used to convert thousands of people (Acts 2), but he also strengthened many brethren, as we read in his two epistles which were addressed to converted Jews. Read those books and you will see how faithfully he discharged his duty. See especially 1 Peter 5:10. In the end, Peter died as a martyr (John 21:18-19). He alludes to that in 2 Peter 1:14.

The Book of Martyrs (which some of you own) tells us that Peter died by crucifixion, and upside down at his own request, because he did not consider himself worthy to die like his Lord and Master. Oh Peter, what wondrous ways the Lord Jesus pursued with you! What did you say to the Lord when you went to Him in heaven? As the aged and pious à Brakel said with dying lips upon his deathbed: "Oh how much shall I have to tell my Lord, when I arrive at my home above!" How much can you say to Him about your own temptations? How much about how you were delivered from them? How relieved were you when you were delivered out of the sieve of Satan?

Poor Peter, when you were so tossed to and fro in the sieve of Satan that you denied your Lord and Master, what bitter mourning did that cause you! How many tears you shed! But how happy you became when you were delivered from that! You are now free from Satan's temptations and persecutions. How great was your joy when you came into the presence of your Lord, who wiped your tears from your eyes! Who would not be glad if like you, through the power of God and the prayers of Christ, he would also overcome and could say, "I have fought the good fight!"

Oh favored Peter, in this you could glorify your Lord by your death, which was so precious in the eyes of the Lord!

From this explanation of the words of our text, we learn that Satan's temptations and assaults are very real, and that he works not only in the children of disobedience, but also in the pious, afflicting them with great suffering. He sets himself in direct opposition to the Word of God. What is said of him or his evil angels cannot be attributed to evil men, sinful emotions, disordered conditions, perverted imagination, disease, frenzy, or the like. For we can do Satan no more agreeable service than by denying his work and seeking to rid the fear of it from the minds of men. The Reformed Church clearly teaches that there are assaults and temptation of Satan (see the sixth petition of Lord's Day 52). The truth of this is confirmed by saints of the Old Testament, such as Job and David, and in the New Testament by Peter, Paul (2 Cor. 12), and others in later times.

Those who have written of such experiences mention not only their convictions, comforts, and sweet manifestations, but also their struggles, conflicts, attacks of Satan, and deliverances. For example, the great Reformer Martin Luther experienced such siftings of Satan that on one occasion he went to bed so ill that he despaired of life. He even made out a will, which said: "Lord God, I thank Thee that it has been Thy will that I should be poor in this world. I have no landed estate nor money to leave behind me. Thou hast given me wife and children, whom I return to Thee. Feed them, teach them, and keep them, as Thou hast done me hitherto, oh Father of the fatherless and Judge of the widow!"

The next day Luther said to Justas Jonas: "Yesterday I shall never forget. I was under the schoolmaster, and suffered what is not easy to express." He frequently talked to his friends of such temptations, calling them, like Paul, "buffetings of Satan." Luther said three things were necessary attributes of a minister: meditation, prayer, and temptation.

Is it true that all the saints are subject to temptation in this vale of tears and place of conflict? How is it then, that some of you have no awareness of danger, have experienced no siftings, are acquainted with no temptations, and, like the people of Lais, are quiet and secure in the midst of sinful enticements? Why do you have no fear?

Perhaps you think you can protect yourselves against danger. If someone said to you, "You may yet fall into this or that sin," you would not be pleased. You might even respond that you would not fail to take care of that. Let me say, there is no clearer proof that you are still in your natural sin and under the dominion of the devil than that; for those whom Satan still has in his power he keeps quiet and at ease in the sleep of security. Christ Himself says so in Luke 11:21-22.

When you pray or repeat the sixth petition of the Lord's Prayer, are you sincere even as you willfully rush into temptation? Do you want to be delivered from temptation or evil as you eagerly pursue vanities? For, no matter who argues with you, you will not be kept from attending horse races or other vain amusements. No matter what the danger, you want to be there. By doing such, do you not bring yourself into temptation, much like Dinah who went out to see the daughters of the land and experienced a fall? When you pursue the riches of the world, you fall into many temptations. Paul plainly teaches that in 1 Timothy 6:9. How frequently you place yourself in the sieve of Satan by entertaining the lusts of the flesh and indulging in sinful meditations. The licentious who tempt others to licentiousness do that. So do the revellers and drunkards, who say, "Come, I will fetch wine" (Isa. 56:12). Oh sinners, behold, I beg you, your misery, and awake out of the snares of the devil. He seeks to drag you to destruction, and you know it not. He goes about as a roaring lion, and you see it not. Be concerned about your condition. Call earnestly upon the Lord, asking Him to deliver you from Satan, the world, and self.

You may say, "We know that Satan roams about, but Christ has come to destroy the works of the devil. He is praying for us." Oh how happy you would be if you had Christ for your Intercessor! I wish you that blessedness. But let me be faithful to you by warning you and reminding you that the intercession of Christ is a privilege granted only to the people of God who have been reconciled by a true faith with God in Christ. They have become His property; He calls them His. He does not pray for the world, but only for His own (John 17:9). As Romans 7:5 says, the heart by nature is altogether filled with and enslaved to earthly things. Or 1 John 4:5: "They are of the world: therefore speak they of the world, and the world heareth them." Oh that we would all be roused to resist Satan so that he might flee from us! Would that we might put on the whole armor of God so we might fight him, quenching his fiery darts and not yielding to his temptations or following his seductions. Would that we were always sober and in unceasing prayer to God, striving earnestly to give no place to the devil (Eph. 4).

You upright ones who know by experience what it means to be tempted and cast into the sieve of Satan, this is what you should do:

1. Look for conflict rather than ease. As your Lord says, "Strive to enter in" (Luke 13:24).

2. Fight the good fight (1 Tim. 6:12). Your tempters cannot accept the fact that you have forsaken their service. They will try everything to get you back in their power. So remember that the Lord called you by grace. Fight temptation.

3. Know who your enemies are. Give them no place in your heart. Otherwise you will be no match for the siftings of Satan. To know his devices is to be half-delivered from them.

4. Stay active in God's service so you are not unexpectedly overcome. "Be sober, be vigilant" (1 Pet. 5:8).

5. Guard against pride. Do not imagine that you can preserve yourself from temptations or sins, for this is the quickest way to fail. Peter's sad fall should remind you of that. As Romans 11:20 says, "Be not highminded, but fear." Like all the the saints, pray, "Keep back thy servant...from presumptuous sins; let them not have dominion over me:

then shall I be upright, and I shall be innocent from the great transgression" (Ps. 19:13).

You may say, "Satan is great and powerful, and I am weak. I therefore fear that I shall yet fall into the hands of Saul." Be of good courage; your foes will be conquered. Trust not in your own strength, however, but remain at the side of your Captain, Jesus. Hide in Him; go forward in His strength. He prays for you. Rest upon Him so that through Him you will overcome. The Lord, who is faithful, will strengthen you and preserve you from evil, so that the gates of hell (their cunning, power, or violence) will not overcome you (Matt. 16). Satan and all his forces will be bruised under your feet (Rom. 6:2).

Have you already fallen? Do not remain so but, like Peter, arise. You have been endowed with grace. You have been converted. So now, through the help of your faithful Lord and Master, Jesus, strengthen your brethren. Listen to your duty as it is given from the mouth of Jesus Himself. How proper this work is, since those you are called to help are not only your brethren, but the brethren of Christ. The apostle John asks that we lay down our lives for the brethren. How much more, then, are we called to strengthen them.

When you have been honored, by the grace of God, with turning a sinner from the error of his way, you will also have saved a soul from death, as James says. And having enjoyed the honor of strengthening and comforting your brethren in the Lord, how delightful you will find their company when all of you dwell with your Lord in glory! For then you will recount the ways the Lord has pursued with you, what temptations and siftings you have experienced, and how you escaped from them.

We conclude with the words of Paul, "Now we exhort you, brethren, warn them that are unruly, comfort the feebleminded, support the weak, be patient toward all men" (1 Thes. 5:14). Amen.

APPENDIX

A MIRROR THAT DOES NOT FLATTER

A serious discourse on Proverbs 14:12 that
uncovers false grounds of salvation and
an admonition to proceed with zeal
in the narrow way of godliness

— 22 —

A Mirror That Does Not Flatter

A serious discourse on Proverbs 14:12 that uncovers false grounds of salvation and an admonition to proceed with zeal in the narrow way of godliness

> *"There is a way which seemeth right unto a man, but the end thereof are the ways of death."*
>
> — Proverbs 14:12

As remarkable and as certain as this verse from Proverbs are the words of Jeremiah 17:9: "The heart is deceitful above all things, and desperately wicked: who can know it?"

The heart here refers to the soul of man, a reasonable being who is endowed with understanding, judgment, conscience, will, and desires, all of which have been affected by the fall. As long as that heart is not renewed by the spirit of regeneration, it has become and will remain deceitful.

The original word for deceitful that is used here is the same one that the patriarch Jacob derived his name from, because when Jacob was born, he held onto his brother's heel. But the word also suggests subtlety, craft, fraud, and snares (see Josh. 8:13 and Gen. 27:36). Deceitful here thus signifies fraud, reservation, and an inclination to deceive. The heart so inclined is deadly, moving toward death, and is fastened to death. It is incurable and evil beyond measure.

So deceitful and corrupt are the hearts of men that their wickedness is revealed even when they try to deceive themselves and others in concealing their subtle wickedness. When Herod intended to murder Christ, for example, he pretended that he would worship the infant (Matt. 2:8). Likewise, Judas tried to hide his covetousness by feigning affection to the poor.

If men cannot fully conceal the evil of their sins, they try to make those sins look like less than they are. They practice hypocrisy in trying to appear better to others than what they are. But even worse is their self-deceit in trying to convince themselves that they are not as bad as they are, thinking they are in good condition. They hope to be saved when they are still miserable objects of damnation.

So it was with the church of Laodicea. The people there were rich with goods and therefore thought they were in need of nothing, but they were really poor, miserable, naked, and blind (Rev. 3:17). As the apostle Paul said, if a man thinks he is something when he is nothing, he deceives himself (Gal. 6:3). This kind of self-deceit is very common, but it is also very dangerous. For a man whose heart is deceitful is like a man who is hungry and thirsty. In his sleep, the man dreams that he is eating and drinking, but when he awakens, he finds he has been deceived. He is still hungry and thirsty (Isa. 29:8).

In such a way the deceitful heart, which believes itself within the favor of God, will become aware of its deceitfulness only after death and in the day of judgment. For then it will realize that its imaginations have only been a dream leading to an imaginary heaven, and that he will really open his eyes in hell. A man who persuades himself without any grounds that he is a believer makes himself even more wretched. It is deplorable that such deceit, which is so dangerous, is so common.

In the words of our text, Solomon says there is a way that seems right to a man, but the end of it is the way of death. Such words contain a faithful and true warning, however, that everyone who dreads self-deceit should not be deceived in those expectations and become ashamed at the coming of the Lord Jesus.

Let us study this text in two parts:

1. The proposal: "There is a way which seemeth right unto a man."

2. The definitive sentence: "but the end thereof are the ways of death.

The Way That Seems Right

A way is what a man does or how he lives to attain a certain end. For example, a traveler takes a certain path to arrive at a certain destination. In various passages Scripture mentions two ways this path can take: a broad and a narrow way; and two types of travelers who come to two different destinations. As Psalm 1:6 says, "The LORD knoweth the way of the righteous [their actions and manner of living]: but the way of the ungodly shall perish."

There is also a way, or manner of living, that seems right to a man but which leads to a miserable end. Solomon here refers to people who so deceive themselves. And as Proverbs 12:15 says, he considers such people to be fools. These people have not been enlightened; they are without the wisdom which is from above and without the fear of God. They are natural people, whom Solomon calls ungodly; they are unconverted and will come to a miserable end. They have a way, or manner of living, which will lead them to a wrong end. They seek after earthly happiness, riches, honor, and delight, inwardly thinking that their houses will continue forever (Ps. 49:11). They are so earthly minded that they make a god of their belly, says Philippians 3:19. They love pleasure more than they love God (2 Tim. 3:4).

In short, as Psalm 17:14 says, they are men of this world who have their portion in this life. When they can keep the

earth no longer, they will try to attain heaven and everlasting happiness and be delivered from hell. We can say the
following about the way that seems right to such men:

- It is the way of sin. People who go this way give in fully
  to their lusts and their corrupt evil nature. They know
  nothing of crucifying the flesh but indulge in envy,
  strife, hatred, drunkenness, revenge, lying, and backbiting (although some more than others). They willfully
  retain such sins. David describes the way of the ungodly
  by saying such a man devises mischief upon his bed, sets
  himself in a way that is not good, and does not abhor
  evil (Ps. 36:2-4). And, as Romans 6:23 says, the wages of
  sin is death.

- It is a way of deception. People who live this way can act
  quite civil and moral, either because they fear hell, damage, or shame, or because their consciences convince
  them not to engage in gross sins. They can be very diligent about practicing the external and lesser parts of the
  law and living so that nobody has anything bad to say
  about them. The rich young man in Matthew 19:19-20
  was such a person. He had kept all of God's law outwardly, but had given little heed to the internal
  condition of his heart. He did not understand the spiritual sense of the law, which condemns the smallest lust
  of one's heart.

- It is a way only of external godliness. The Jews who exercised and performed so many duties, sought God daily,
  and delighted in knowing His ways, were deceiving
  themselves because their behavior was only for show
  (Isa. 58). Inwardly, their hearts were full of sin. At the last
  day many such people who practice only external godliness will arise and beseech the Lord, saying, "Lord, have
  we not eaten and drunk in thy presence, and in thy
  name cast out devils, and in thy name done many wonderful works?" (Matt. 7:22-23; Luke 13:26-27). But the

Lord will tell them, "I never knew you: depart from me,
ye that work iniquity."

- It is a way of seeming repentance and conversion. People like Saul can appear to be convicted, moved, and
troubled. They can confess their sins and weep for them
(1 Sam. 15:24, 25). Like Agrippa in Acts 26, they can be almost persuaded. They can forsake some sins and evil
customs. Like Herod, they can listen eagerly to the Word
of God that's proclaimed and do some good things, yet
still be wicked. And some people can know enough of
Christ to escape the pollutions of the world, yet still continue in their old way of unconvertedness (2 Pet. 2:20).

- It is a way of self-righteousness. Such people do what
they do so they can feel secure about their salvation.
They do good according to their consciences, believing
that will satisfy God and supposing that heaven will in
no wise escape them. But they trust in themselves rather
than God. And of such a way the Lord says, "Thou didst
trust in thy way" (Hos. 10:13).

- It is not the way of repentance. Men choose such a way
according to their own judgment. It is a careless way
that does not involve true repentance of sin or a narrow
search of one's heart. Rather, it seeks self-honor, ease,
and profit in the world, and those who practice it show
as much religion as the world can tolerate. They do it out
of custom, for their own sake, so that others will see
them as honest men and good Christians, or to stop the
mouth of their conscience to keep from suffering regret.
They may even do it to serve God so that He will be
obliged to save them. Therefore, all of their life and actions are sin because they only live for themselves and
not for God. They do everything, not to honor and glorify God, but to suit their own purposes. They love only
themselves (2 Tim. 3:2).

How perverse and wretched such a way is! Yet people
who live this way think this way is right and good. As Solo-

mon says, this is the way that "seemeth right unto a man." According to the original text, the words for "seemeth right" here suggest that it is right before the face of man, or in his own eyes. Or, as Ecclesiastes 2:26 says, what seems good in his sight. Solomon would thus say that the unspiritual man may think that his way of life and deeds are good and acceptable unto God, and that his way is right. He does not question this way but depends upon it, for he trusts it to be true and certain. Matthew 6:7 says that the heathen think they will be heard for their much speaking, but they are mistaken, for no matter how sure they are of their way and think it to be sure, it is still only their own imagination. Like Herod, they do many good things, but only for show. Likewise Saul only sought to be honored before the people for serving and honoring the Lord (1 Sam. 15:30). The Pharisees in John 5:44 also looked for that kind of recognition.

So it goes for the unconverted sinner, for he not only thinks that his way is right, but that others should honor him as a pious man because he seems to be one. Simon the sorcerer said of himself that he was a great one (Acts 8:9). The Jews also thought that way in supposing that they were Abraham's seed. Yet they did not do his works but those of their father the devil (Matt. 3; John 8). It is the same with the nominal Christian who assumes that his way is right and that he shall be saved but in the meantime is quite out of the way.

There are various reasons why the sinner, with such false imaginations, deceives himself and thinks that his way is right. He does that even though God in His Word makes such a clear difference between the broad and the narrow way, that is, between the way of the ungodly and the way of the righteous, between a natural condition and a state of grace, and between those that fear God and those who do not so, that the state of one differs as much from the other as light and darkness, or heaven and hell. Here are some of the reasons.

1. Man is blind to the right way. By nature man is spiritually blind. He has some innate knowledge of divine things, but much of that is justly taken from him because of sin (Matt. 13:12). His foolish heart becomes more darkened, says Romans 1:21. He deceives himself, saying, "I am rich and increased with goods" (Rev. 3:17) but as 2 Thessalonians 2:10-11 says, his heart becomes hard as a stone. He is beyond feeling and becomes obstinate. Prior to this he was tender enough to weep for his sins and fear his ruin, but no longer. God is very angry with him and lets the sinner's heart grow fat. His ears close and he shuts his eyes to the thought of being converted and healed (Isa. 6:9-10). God gives such a sinner over to himself, and he becomes such a slave to sin that he falls from one sin to another (Ps. 81:11-12). The lusts of such men are set loose. They are driven by those lusts. Their minds are evil so they do things that should not be done (Rom. 1:28).

2. Satan encourages the wrong way. Satan, that revengeful and great enemy of man's happiness and salvation, keeps the poor sinner not only captive to his will (2 Tim. 2:26), but so blinds his mind that the light of the gospel (which otherwise would have shown him his wretched state) no longer shines for him (2 Cor. 4:6; Luke 8:12). Satan takes the seed (the Word of God) out of the heart, lest the sinner believe and be saved. From that point the Word of God has no power in the sinner's heart; it no longer serves as hammer and fire (Jer. 23:29), nor is it quick and powerful (Heb. 4:12). Rather, it is a dead letter (2 Cor. 3). The Word that is preached to such a sinner does not profit him, for it is not mixed with faith (Heb. 4:2). As Satan through his subtlety deceived Eve, even so he deceives and ensnares man. He persuades the sinner that he will not die, thus putting into his hands a false, presumptuous faith instead of a true, saving faith.

"Oh," Satan says, "you must believe that you shall be saved and that Jesus is your Savior and that consists of simply trusting that all your sins are pardoned. Then you can rest at ease. If a minister should tell you otherwise and cause you to doubt, do not believe him." In this way, the devil tries to get people to rest in a desire only for a civil life instead of a spiritual life, and a presumptive faith instead of an upright faith. By such is the sinner deceived.

3. Teachers fail to warn him. Deceit is encouraged by teachers who do not warn people of this dreadful sin. They do not seek to discover this deceit or reveal the subtlety of Satan and the deceitfulness of their own hearts. They do not show people the falseness of such byways and do not rightly divide the way of truth. Rather, like the Arminians, they throw around the promises for people to scramble at. Like unscrupulous physicians, they slightly treat wounds, daubing them with untempered mortar and "sew pillows to armholes" (Ezek. 13:18). They cry, "Peace, peace," when there is no peace (Jer. 8:11). Because of their failure to engage in discovering, convicting, and powerful preaching, the people continue to dream that their way is right.

4. Man's willingness to delude himself. Man's heart is deceitful, says Jeremiah 17:9. It seduces him to love himself, which is like feeding on ashes (Isa. 44:20). The false imaginations of the flesh and the faulty conclusions that proceed from the deceitful heart so blind man's judgment that he wrongly judges himself. He thinks he is something when he is nothing. In so doing, he deceives himself (Gal. 6:3) and, to his own destruction, falsely perverts God's Word (2 Pet. 3). He uses the doctrine of the imperfectness of the saints (especially the complaints of Paul in Romans 7) and the justification of sinners as a cushion for carelessness. He interprets the grace of God as wantonness (Jude 4). And, rather than seeking true, saving faith, he trusts his own imagination that Christ is his Savior and that his way is right.

5. It is the natural way. The way of self-deceit seems

right to sinners because it is the way of flesh. It is such an easy way that it seems right to them. The broad way of loose and careless living encourages all kinds of lusts that come forth from a corrupt nature. It allows men to do whatever their hearts desire, for that is what comes easiest and most naturally to them. Their understanding, will, and desires all incline that way. They find it most acceptable to satisfy their carnal desires according to their minds, for they know nothing of crucifying the flesh (Gal. 5), denying their earthly desires (Col. 3) or any part of themselves (Matt. 16) in striving to enter the kingdom (Luke 13). They will not aggressively seek the kingdom of heaven (Matt. 11), pursue holiness, or suffer any disdain or oppression for Christ's sake. They are aimless things that blow in the wind, knowing nothing of private godly exercise, conversation with the Lord, or disciplined living before God and man. Rather, they live only to fulfill the lusts of the flesh (Gal. 5:16). Because this way is so easy to them, it seems right to them.

6. The wicked prosper. This way seems right to men because so many people who walk in it receive honor, respect, riches, and other indications of outward blessings and prosperity in the world. It only seems that way, however. In answering the question of why the way of the wicked seems to prosper, passages such as Jeremiah 6:1 and Proverbs 1:32 clearly teach that the prosperity of fools will eventually destroy them.

7. So many people walk this way. A great number of people walking one way does not necessarily mean it is the right way. For as Christ said, broad is the way that leads to destruction, and many enter hell through this way (Matt. 7:13). By nature, people want to walk this way, and they encourage each other to do the same.

These are some of the reasons why unconverted people imagine that their way is right. But no matter how firm and strong their opinion is of themselves and what they are doing, and no matter how right their way seems to them, they will be proven wrong in the end. That is what Solomon teaches in the second part of the text, when he says, "But the end thereof are the ways of death."

The Ways of Death

The word *end* in our text means the final, utmost point of destination. The way that seems right to man leads to ways of destruction, the final point of which is death. It is like one who is walking along a pleasant way. The road ends in a secret pit, but the person does not know it. He quietly walks forward until he tumbles into the pit. He awakens to the danger too late.

In such a way the sinner moves through life contentedly with the vain hope and assurance that his way is the right way. He thinks that his life is good and prosperous until it ends. For eventually he will be utterly lost. The end of his way, no matter how right it seems in his eyes, is destruction and death.

Three kinds of death await him: Natural death, which begins with the miseries of this life and culminates in the separation of soul and body; spiritual death, which is living without God; and eternal death, which is separation from God's fellowship along with bearing the endless pain and punishment, both in soul and body, of being without the saving fellowship of God, the chiefest good.

When, at the end of life, the damned finally come to the realization that they lack all that is happy, light, peace, joy, rest, contentment, love, holiness (in short, all the good that God in His longsuffering love granted them to enjoy in this life) — it will be taken from them. Missing out on all of these signs of God's favor will then be intolerable to them, even though they are presently insensitive to them because they are too busy diverting themselves with the things of this world.

In 2 Thessalonians 1:9, Paul says sinners will be punished with everlasting destruction. They will be cast out of the presence of the Lord and be forever separated from the glory of His power. They will weep and gnash their teeth when they see Abraham, Isaac, and Jacob and all the prophets in the kingdom of God while they themselves are cast out (Luke 13:28). They will then weep and wail about missing God and will gnash their teeth as they envy the happiness of the children of God.

Likewise, eternal death involves the most painful experience of God's wrath in every part of the sinner: his understanding, will, and conscience. It will cause frightful despair in all the powers of the soul and body that will suffer eternal punishment in the place of torment. Revelation 16:10 describes the horror of eternal death by saying sinners will gnaw their tongues from the pain as they blaspheme God. The situation will be inconceivably dreadful. In Romans 2, Paul says that indignation, wrath, tribulation, and anguish will fall upon the soul of every person that does evil. As Mark 9:44 says, "Their worm dieth not, and the fire is not quenched."

This is eternal death, the wretched end of this way. God has no pleasure in this death, however; it is an abomination to Him, says Proverbs 15:9. He hates the ways of sin that people choose to their own judgment. Presently they suppose that their way of civility and external godliness will bring them to salvation, even though they continue to sin and give way to the flesh. They think that their way is right and that they shall be saved, but they will not. In the end what they do will fall short; it will not bring them to salvation. As Christ warned in Luke 13:24: "Many...will seek to enter in, and shall not be able."

Although this way seems right to them, it is the way of sin, of unconvertedness, and it will end in eternal damnation, for the wages of sin is death (Rom. 6:23). As Matthew 7:13 says, it is the broad way that leads to destruction. Or as David says in Psalm 1:6, the way of the ungodly shall perish. In such a way our text warns that there is a way that seems right unto a man, but the end thereof are the ways of death.

What Are We To Do?

Listen to me as I ask you, How can people be so miserably deceived and imagine that their way is right and that they will be saved, when the way they are going will end in death? What about you? Don't you likewise think that your way is right? It seems that you do, for else you would not walk along so unconcerned. We should therefore ask, What would become of you if you died? You might imagine that you will be saved, but you must realize that there is a way that may seem right to you but will end in death.

Few people, even if they are drunkards, greedy misers, liars, backbiters, ignorant, or worldly minded think anything different but that they will be saved, just like anyone else, and no wonder. For Satan, that murderer of man, and deceitful hearts blind such men through self-love so that they flatter themselves with the strong hope of being saved. But think about this: There is a way that seems right to a man, but the end thereof are the ways of death.

Christ, the mouth of truth, has taught us that the gate is straight and the way narrow that leads to life, and few there are who find it (Matt. 7). Only a few will be saved. If it were true that all who imagine they will be saved shall indeed be saved, then there would be many saved and few damned. Then, too, the narrow way would lead to hell, and the broad way to heaven.

Oh, how many are the straying souls who suppose that their way is right and who trust like fools in their own hearts (Prov. 28:26)! How many cannot give the least account of the hope that is in them and have no foundation in Christ! How many are void of spirit and life! How many are ignorant, carnal, and unregenerate and live that way even as they assume that their way is right!

My friends, do you suppose that your way is right and your condition is good? Do you hope to be saved? If you do not have the right foundation for your hope, and your life does not show it, your hope may yet deceive you and bring you to shame. Oh, know this in your heart that there is a way that seems right to a man, but, take notice of it, the end thereof are the ways of death.

Pray tell me, what is your foundation?

1. Does your way seem right because you believe that your heart is upright, that you have good intentions even if your works are sinful? Then, as Proverbs 28:26 says, "He that trusteth in his own heart is a fool." Because your works are vile, you must understand that your heart is also vile. As Matthew 12:35 says, "An evil man out of the evil treasure [of his heart] bringeth forth evil things."

2. Perhaps your foundation is that you believe and do not doubt that Christ is your Savior and that you shall be saved. You suppose that this conviction is true faith and that you are therefore a believer. You must realize that this assumption could be false. Satan, that subtle deceiver, and our own deceitful hearts may persuade us to deceive ourselves into thinking we are believers, but someone is not necessarily wise just because he thinks he is wise. More likely, he who thinks he is wise is really a fool.

Anyone who thinks he is in good condition because he believes he is saved may not be so, for the Jews themselves said they were Abraham's children and called God their father. Jesus, however, told them, "Ye are of your father the devil" (John 8). Likewise, the foolish virgins thought they would be saved when they cried out, "Lord, Lord, open to us." But the answer they received was, "I know you not" (Matt. 25). Anyone can say he is saved and persuade himself of it. The state of grace involves more than that. Not everyone who says, "Lord, Lord," will be saved.

3. Perhaps you think that your way is right and your condition good because you are free of gross public sins,

such as swearing, drunkenness, whoremongering, stealing, and the like. Don't you know that was the argument of the Pharisee, who nevertheless was deceived (Luke 18:12)? Just because you live such a virtuous, civil, and outwardly blameless life that nobody can say anything against you, you must understand this does not prove you are saved. For even Paul, who testified of himself that he was blameless before the law, became a persecutor of Christ (Phil. 3).

Think of the rich young man in Matthew 19 who came to Jesus asking, "Good Master, what good thing shall I do, that I may have eternal life?" When Jesus told the young man, "Keep the commandments," the man said he had kept all the commandments from the time he was young. "What lack I yet?" he asked Jesus. Think of how far this young man had come in keeping all the commandments (not just one or a few) and not just for a little time, but from his youth up. Think, too, of how willing he was to do even more in asking, "What lack I yet?" He was so concerned about his salvation that he asked, "Good Master, what shall I do?"

But when he heard that all that he had done and was willing to do could not help him and that what he had to do was deny himself and follow Jesus, he went away sorrowful. His unwillingness to do that was a sign that he could not enter into the kingdom of heaven.

4. Is your foundation for going the way that seems right to you that you are very religious, pray often, willingly hear and read God's Word, and give much money? These are necessary and profitable things, but they do not always prove that we are in a good way and in a good state. For if it were so, then the way of the Pharisees and scribes must have been right, or their state good, because many of them made great work of such duties. They prayed often and out of devotion fasted twice a week, and gave many alms (Luke 18). Likewise, the Savior taught that we can preach

God's Word, do miracles, and go to the Lord's Supper, yet He will say to many of us, "I never knew you" (Matt. 7).

The apostle Paul went on to say in 1 Corinthians 13 that even if he sold all of his goods to feed the poor and gave his body to be burned (meaning that he could be free from all gross sins and diligently use all religious means possible), he could still fail to be in a good state and miss the right to salvation.

5. Perhaps your foundation is that you have delight and joy in God's Word and that you have been afraid, troubled, distressed, moved, and sorrowful for your sins. Even that is not sufficient for salvation, for the Lord Jesus showed in Luke 8 that a temporary believer can receive the Word with joy, yet not be saved. Likewise, Felix trembled when Paul preached judgment to him (Acts 24), and Agrippa, who listened to Paul preach, was almost persuaded (Acts 26). And King Saul wept for his sins and confessed them (1 Sam. 15:24 and 14:17).

To be troubled, moved, touched, and thereupon concerned about one's salvation is not necessarily a sign of God's saving work in you. This restless condition can also be brought about by a disturbed conscience that goes over and over a problem until you feel like you are seasick. This can happen to the unconverted who are not upon the right way. Thus, all of these things are not sufficient to prove that your state is good and well-pleasing to God, and that salvation will follow.

6. You may be convinced that you are on the right way because, from all outward appearances, your life has reformed and changed. You have more knowledge of spiritual things, live much better, and are improving in conduct. This is a faulty foundation for believing you are saved, however. For in 1 Samuel 10:9, we read that even though God gave Saul another heart, Saul continued to operate in his old natural state.

Peter thus warns in 2 Peter 2:20 that after we have escaped the pollutions of the world through the knowledge of the Lord and Savior Jesus Christ that we might still become entangled in them and be overcome. A man may thus become externally reformed from many extravagancies and abstain from many gross sins and, like Jehu, show great zeal, yet he may not be on the narrow way that leads to heaven.

Thus you see that what you placed your hopes in are not true and sure principles whereon you may conclude that your condition is good and that you will thus be saved, for this is the way that seems right unto a man, but the end of it are the ways of death. If you are still convinced, based on principles such as these, that your way is right, then you are miserably deceiving yourself. If you have concluded from all of this that your way is right and your state good, then you are misleading your soul, and if you persist in this presumptuous imagination, you will further deceive yourself and make yourself more wretched.

Oh, how many people do not come even this far and still conclude, against all evidence to the contrary, that they are in a good state! They lie upon the brink of hell, and many will not wake up until they open their eyes in hell, when it will be too late.

Alas, you that still walk in the ways of sin and will not forsake sin. Alas, you who love sin and live in it with pleasure; you who walk in the ways of self-righteousness, trusting your heart and your good intentions; you who have come no farther than the way of civility and external godliness but know nothing of true change and are not regenerated and renewed. Here is sorrowful news, for the end of your way is death! Although your way seems right to you, the end of it are the ways of death. Think seriously about what wretchedness will come to you. Perhaps the following reminders may yet be the means for leading you to conviction and conversion:

1. Your way leads to death. The way you live will not

bring you to happiness but to a sure death, where every hope you have of being saved will perish. For when a wicked man dies, all his hopes perish (Prov. 11:7). As Job 8:13 says, the hope of hypocrites will be cut off. Oh how horrible it will be for them to witness the death of the hope they imagined for so long!

2. You will never be peaceful again. Your quiet, tranquil, and careless peace will also perish in the end. We warn you about the curse of the law, the wrath of God, and the inability of your miserable and wretched state to deliver you from that, but alas, you go on merrily, with a tranquil mind, as if you had no ailments. We cry aloud to you and lift up our voices like a trumpet, but you are not convinced. You think there is no danger.

As Luke 11:21 says, the devil keeps all things at peace within you. Your deceitful, wicked heart tells you all is peace and safety. But, as Scripture teaches, destruction may come upon you as suddenly as labor comes upon a woman with child, and you will not escape (1 Thes. 5:3). Who can imagine the remorse the wretched sinner will experience when he sees that all his peace, rest, and happiness is past and gone? He will find he has been deceived, but by then it is too late. The way of peace is gone to him forever.

3. You will never experience communion with God. No matter how good and right your way seems to you, it will never bring you to true communion with God. Instead, you will be forever barred from the presence of the Lord and from the glory of His power because your way of living will bring you to everlasting death and eternal destruction (2 Thes. 1:9). When you try to enter into God's presence, you will find that you have deceived yourself, for you will be excluded from entering it. You will then hear that dreadful sentence: "Depart from me, for I never knew you" (Matt. 7 & 25).

Oh dreadful destruction, oh miserable death! Oh the terrible thought of being abandoned by God through all eternity, of forever missing God's favor, of eternally bearing the wrath of the Almighty! Oh sorrowful condition, which is as certainly the portion of all unconverted people as God's Word is true. Think about it; the end of these ways are the ways of death.

Oh that you might thus look about you, determine to leave your erroneous way, and walk in the way of understanding. Oh that God would open your eyes that you might see that the way that seems right in your eyes leads to the ways of death. I beg you to see that you have a wicked, deceitful heart; that you carry a murderer in your own bosom; and that those who trust in their own hearts are fools, as Solomon said. Oh, Satan is so subtle, so crafty, and our hearts so deceitful that we mistake outward godliness and civility for true holiness and are so easily persuaded that we are in a good state. What can change your belief that your condition is good, when in time you will discover that you have been deceived? Can that imagination make you happy? Oh no, it will make you most unhappy. To see and feel your true misery is the first means to come to redemption.

It is true that on this way that seems right to you that you may live easily and merrily. You will walk in the ways of your heart and in the sight of your eyes and take delight in all kinds of pleasure and lust. You may be outwardly prosperous and be part of a great company of people who like to be with you and who speak and act as you want them to. But know that in all of these things God will bring you to judgment (Eccl. 11:9). And if you associate with a rich glutton in this life, you will associate likewise with him in hell.

There are two ways that you can go in this life: the broad way, in which you will have lots of company and which will offer you ease of mind, desire, and lust. It will keep you occupied with the things of this world, which you will use as you please and heap up in abundance, as most people do. You can live much the same as you now do, without praying and wrestling and flying to Jesus for reconciliation and sanctification. But know this, and depend upon it, that the end of that way is eternal death and perdition.

The other choice is the narrow way, in which you must deny yourself, your own understanding, righteousness, will, mind, worthiness, and power. Along this way you must depart from your bosom sins and from the vanities of this world and seek the kingdom of God and its righteousness above all things (Matt. 6). You must bring forth fruits worthy of repentance, live a precise and holy life, and follow the footsteps and virtues of Christ. It is a way that promises oppressions, adversities, and hardships against flesh and blood. But oh, what a happy and glorious destination this way leads to, for the end of it is eternal life, everlasting glory, everlasting joy, and eternal salvation!

Here, then, are two ways. You cannot walk in them both, for as Scripture teaches, you cannot serve two masters at the same time. You must leave the one if you would cleave to the other. You must therefore choose one of the two ways: to be entirely wicked or entirely godly. As Revelation 3:16 says, you must be either cold or hot, for God will spew those that are lukewarm out of His mouth.

I therefore set before you life and death, blessing or a curse. Oh, choose life that you may live! Sinners, abandon the way that seems so right to you. Turn away from your careless tranquility, your self-righteousness, your sins and lusts, your own thoughts, and turn to the Lord. Forsake the foolish supporters and false grounds and go in the way of true understanding.

You have lived twenty, thirty, forty, fifty years, some longer, and walked in the way that seems right in your eyes. But now you are nearer to eternity, and God is warning you not to proceed any farther in your own ways. Do not turn away from all these warnings and remain convinced that your way is right. Do not deceive your poor souls any longer. Give ear to the counsel of God. Listen to what Jeremiah 6:16 says, "Thus saith the LORD, Stand ye in the ways, and see, and ask for the old paths, where is the good way, and walk therein, and ye shall find rest for your souls."

There is a way that may seem wrong to the world, which nevertheless is the right way. That is the way of faith, of regeneration, of sanctification, of self-denial, of heavenly mindedness and love. This is that narrow way that our Savior speaks of in Matthew 7. Happy are those who have set their feet on this way, who have left the broad way of sin and are now walking the narrow way of virtue and godliness. As Psalm 119:30 says, they have chosen the way of truth. If you are already on that way, I urge you to:

1. Give God the glory for His grace in showing unto you the harm of that way you once walked in and which once seemed right to you. Thank Him for bringing you to the way that you now travel and for the loveliness of that way.

2. Travel steadfastly along the narrow way, allowing no regrets that you have chosen that way. Many people will criticize the narrow way and try to find fault with it. They will try to pervert the right way of the Lord. You must thus often renew your choice for that way so that you might be surer in traveling it. Remind yourself of the blessings of traveling it. Above all, accompany that walk with the fruits of a holy life so that even those who speak evil of this way might see those fruits and be drawn to the way. To keep going along the narrow way, pray often, as David says in Psalm 119:32, 33, 35, and 25:5.

3. Continue to go forward with high esteem for the narrow way. As Psalm 138:5 says, "They shall sing in the ways of the LORD."

4. Seek to attract others to the narrow way, for that way is not only for you but for others. We must seek company along this way to heaven. You must want to make known God's way to others and to hold forth the excellency of that way.

5. Walk with caution, liveliness, wisdom, holiness, and

tenderness of conscience in the narrow way, which is the way of life and wisdom. Be especially careful that you do nothing that is inappropriate to this way, but as He who called you is holy, so be ye holy in all manner of conversation (1 Pet. 1:15-16). Think what a difference there is between heaven and hell, and therefore how great a difference there must be between your walk on the narrow way and the walk of those on the broad way. If you rightly direct your steps on the narrow way, you will increase in strength and peace. You will become increasingly sure that your way is right and that God will lead you on it to heaven.

If you struggle with fear, concern, and doubt that your way might be the one that seems right but which will surely end in destruction, then follow David's example and wrestle earnestly with God in prayer before His throne. Ask Him to clarify your condition by asking, "Search me, O God, and know my heart: try me, and know my thoughts: and see if there be any wicked way in me, and lead me in the way everlasting" (Ps. 139:23-24). Then depend on the promise of a faithful God, who says in Jeremiah 31:9: "I will cause them to walk...in a straight way, wherein they shall not stumble."

As Psalm 37:34 says, "Wait on the LORD, and keep his way, and he shall exalt thee." He will lead you through darkness by His light, and He who has taken hold of your right hand will lead you by His counsel through the wilderness of the world, after which He will bring you to immortality, where you will be with the Lord forever. Amen.

Annotated Bibliography of English Sources

Joel R. Beeke

Primary Sources

Boel, Henricus. *Boel's Complaint Against Frelinghuysen.* Trans. and ed. Joseph Anthony Loux, Jr. Rensselaer, New York: Hamilton, 1979. Includes first full translation of *Klagte van Eenige Leeden der Nederduytse Hervormde Kerk . . .* (New York: William Bradford and J. Peter Zenger, 1725). Introductory essay by Loux is biased against Frelinghuysen.

Frelinghuysen, Theodorus Jacobus. *A Clear Demonstration of a Righteous and Ungodly Man, in Their Frame, Way and End.* Trans. Hendrick Fischer. New York: John Peter, 1731. Contains five sermons, all of which are included in this volume.

_____. *Sermons.* Ed. and trans. William Demarest. Intro. Thomas DeWitt. New York: Board of Publication of the Reformed Protestant Dutch Church, 1856. This work contains twenty-one of Frelinghuysen's twenty-two extant sermons, translated from Dutch in mid-Victorian English. Includes *Drie Predicatien* (New York: William Bradford, 1721); *Een Trouwhertig Vertoog van Een waare Rechtveerdige, in Tegenstellinge van Een Godloose Sondaar* (New York: John Peter Zenger, 1729); *Een Bundelken Leer-redenen* (Amsterdam, 1736); *Versamelinge van Eenige Keur-Texten* (Philadelphia: W. Bradford, 1748).

Hastings, Hugh. *Ecclesiastical Records of the State of New York.* 7 vols. Albany, New York: James B. Lyon, 1901-1916. Volumes III and IV contain considerable primary source material dealing with Frelinghuysen's controversial ministry; an invaluable source.

Messler, Abraham. *Forty Years at Raritan: Eight Memorial Sermons, with Notes for a History of the Reformed Dutch Churches in Somerset County, New Jersey.* New York: A. Lloyd, 1873. Written by a Reformed church historian, and a successor and defender of Frelinghuysen. Contains eight of Messler's own memorial sermons preached at five-year intervals of his forty-year ministry at Raritan, as well as 175 pages of historical notes on the Dutch Reformed churches of Somerset County, New Jersey. For valuable material on Frelinghuysen's ministry, see the second memorial sermon and pages 162-212 of the historical notes.

Roberts, Richard Owen. *Salvation in Full Color: Twenty Sermons by Great Awakening Preachers.* Wheaton, Ill.: International Awakening Press, 1994. Contains Frelinghuysen's sermon, "The Righteous Are Scarcely Saved" (pp. 77-94).

Secondary Sources

Balmer, Randall H. *A Perfect Babel of Confusion: Dutch Religion and English Culture in the Middle Colonies.* New York: Oxford University Press, 1989. Chapter 5, "Flames of Contention: The Raritan Dispute and the Spread of Pietism," disparages Frelinghuysen's ministry and motives.

_____. "The Social Roots of Dutch Pietism in the Middle Colonies." *Church History* 53 (1984):187-99. Downplays Frelinghuysen's experiential emphases and exaggerates his being motivated by social roots.

Beardslee, John W., III. "Orthodoxy and Piety: Two Styles of Faith in the Colonial Period." In *Word and World: Reformed Theology in America.* Ed. James W. Van Hoeven. Grand Rapids: Eerdmans, 1986, pages 1-14. Contrasts the styles of faith of Gisbertus Voetius and Johannes Cocceius. Confirms that Frelinghuysen was Voetian in his theology and preaching.

Brienen, Teunis. *De prediking van de Nadere Reformatie.* Amsterdam: Ton Bolland, 1974. Examines and criticizes the classification method of *Nadere Reformatie* preaching that Frelinghuysen popularized in America.

Chambers, Talbot W. *Memoir of the Life and Character of the late Hon. Theo. Frelinghuysen, LL.D.* New York: Harper & Brothers, 1863. Chapter 1 sheds light on Rev. Frelinghuysen's children and grandchildren.

Coalter, Milton, Jr. *Gilbert Tennent, Son of Thunder: A Case Study of Continental Pietism's Impact on the First Great Awakening in the Middle Colonies.* Westport, Connecticut: Greenwood Press, 1986, pages 12-25. Underscores Frelinghuysen's influence on Tennent.

DeJong, Gerald F. *The Dutch Reformed Church in the American Colonies.* Ed. Donald J. Bruggink. The Historical Series of the Reformed

Church in America, No. 5. Grand Rapids: Eerdmans, 1978. Focuses on the internal discord and controversy surrounding Frelinghuysen's ministry (pp. 170-179).

Frelinghuysen, Joseph S. "The Church in the Raritan Valley." In *Tercentenary Studies, 1928: Reformed Church in America, A Record of Beginnings*. New York: General Synod, 1928, pages 209-226. Strongly supportive of Frelinghuysen.

Frelinghuysen, Peter Hood Ballantine, Jr. *Theodorus Jacobus Frelinghuysen*. Princeton: privately printed, 1938. A 90-page, pro-Frelinghuysen work. Relies on English sources.

Hardman, K. "Theodore Jacob Frelinghuysen in the Middle Colonies." *Christian History* 8, 3, 23 (1989):10-11. Views Frelinghuysen as an important source of the Great Awakening.

Harmelink III, Herman. "Another Look at Frelinghuysen and His 'Awakening.'" *Church History* 37 (1968):423-38. Argues for disaffection rather than an awakening under Frelinghuysen's ministry.

Lodge, Martin Ellsworth. "The Great Awakening in the Middle Colonies." Ph.D. dissertation, University of California, Berkeley, 1964, chapters 8-9. Helpful, but sheds little new light.

Klunder, Jack Douglas. "The Application of Holy Things: A Study of the Covenant Preaching in the Eighteenth Century Dutch Colonial Church." Th.D. dissertation, Westminster Theological Seminary, 1984. Based on the extant sermons of four representative Dutch ministers: Theodorus Frelinghuysen, Archibald Laidlie, John H. Livingston, and William Linn. An innovative study but Klunder argues too strongly for a covenantal framework in Frelinghuysen's sermons. Excursus II examines the historical and theological context for the complaints raised against Frelinghuysen.

Luidens, John Pershing. "The Americanization of the Dutch Reformed Church." Ph.D. dissertation, University of Oklahoma, 1969. Chapter 3 contains an excellent summary of Frelinghuysen's ministry and of the subsequent development of the Coetus and Conferentie parties in the Dutch Reformed Church.

Maxson, Charles Hartshorn. *The Great Awakening in the Middle Colonies*. Chicago: University of Chicago Press, 1920, chapter 2. A condensed, supportive, and helpful chapter on Frelinghuysen; relies largely on Messler and the *Ecclesiastical Records of the State of New York.*

McFarland, George Kennedy. "Clergy, Lay Leaders, and the People: An Analysis of 'Faith and Works' in Albany and Boston, 1630-1750." Unpublished manuscript. Pages 287-93 present a helpful summary of conflicts that swirled around Frelinghuysen. Drawn from *Ecclesiastical Records of the State of New York.*

Messler, Abraham. "Theodorus Jacobus Frelinghuysen," in *Annals of the American Reformed Dutch Pulpit* by William Sprague. New York: Robert Carter & Brothers, 1869, pages 8-15. General overview; also contained in *Forty Years at Raritan.*

Osterhaven, M. Eugene. "Experiential Theology of Early Dutch Calvinism." *Reformed Review* 27 (1974):180-89. Focuses on William Ames and Frelinghuysen to get at the heart of Dutch Reformed experiential theology.

Pals, Daniel L. "Several Christologies of the Great Awakening." *Anglican Theological Review* 72 (1990):412-27. Examines christologies of Frelinghuysen, Tennent, Edwards, and Whitefield; argues that Frelinghuysen's christology balances the Reformed emphases of dogma and devotion.

Pointer, Richard W. *Protestant Pluralism and the New York Experience: A Study of Eighteenth-Century Religious Diversity.* Indianapolis: Indiana University Press, 1988. Views Frelinghuysen as a "radical Pietist," but acknowledges that the awakenings under his ministry spilled over into the Great Awakening.

Rollins, John William. "Frederick Theodore Frelinghuysen, 1817-1885: The Politics and Diplomacy of Stewardship." 2 vols. Ph.D. dissertation, University of Wisconsin, 1974. Chapter 1, "The Garden of the Dutch Church," accents the Dutch commitment of piety that Theodorus Frelinghuysen brought to America (pp. 25-59).

Schrag, F. J. "Theodorus Jacobus Frelinghuysen, the Father of American Pietism." *Church History* 14 (1945):201-216. The best over-all article on Frelinghuysen, but overplays the influence of German Pietism.

Swanson, Thomas Lee. "A Critical Analysis of the Reformed Piety of Theodore Frelinghuysen." Th.M. thesis, Dallas Theological

Seminary, 1983. Examines Frelinghuysen's doctrines of soteriology and ecclesiology, and concludes that he was a Reformed orthodox minister notwithstanding his deviations from a strict observance of church order.

Tanis, James. *Dutch Calvinistic Pietism in the Middle Colonies: A Study in the Life and Theology of Theodorus Jacobus Frelinghuysen*. The Hague: Martinus Nijhoff, 1967. The premier work on Frelinghuysen's life and theology; contains considerable fresh study. Free of hagiography and caricature.

_____. "Frelinghuysen, the Dutch Clergy, and the Great Awakening in the Middle Colonies." *Reformed Review* 28 (1985):109-118. Proves that Frelinghuysen was influenced by the *Nadere Reformatie* divines.

_____. "Reformed Pietism in Colonial America." In *Continental Pietism and Early American Christianity*, ed. F. Ernest Stoeffler. Grand Rapids: Eerdmans, 1976, pages 34-74. Examines the influence of the Huguenots, Labadism, the *Nadere Reformatie*, and German Pietism in colonial America. Frelinghuysen is set in the context of Reformed experiential divines.

Trinterud, Leonard J. *The Forming of an American Tradition: A Reexamination of Colonial Presbyterianism*. Philadelphia: Westminster Press, 1949, pages 54-56. Argues that Frelinghuysen was influenced by the Reformers and *Nadere Reformatie* divines rather than by German Pietists.

Vincent, Lorena Cole. *Readington Reformed Church, Readington, New Jersey, 1719-1969*. Somerville, N.J.: Somerville Press, 1969. A balanced treatment of Frelinghuysen (pp. 5-18).